CRIMINAL MAN

BOOKS BY THE SAME AUTHOR

NOVELS

The Eternal Forest
Why Stay We Here?
Empty Victory
Anna Berger
The Lake of Memory

BIOGRAPHY

Vancouver: A Life

MISCELLANEOUS

Cain or the Future of Crime
Columbia or the Future of Canada
Discovery
Trial of Peter Griffiths
Queen Mary College
The Land Our Larder
Our Woods In War
Peter Kuerten
The Middle Temple
The Great Mystics (3rd edition)
The Great Revivalists

PLAY

The Disciple

CRIMINAL MAN

by

GEORGE S. GODWIN

1957
GEORGE BRAZILLER, INC.
NEW YORK

First American Edition

CONTENTS

PART ONE

The Criminal: Who Is He?

PART TWO

The Criminal: Can He Be Cured?

PART THREE

Murder and Madness

v

PART FOUR

Crime: Prevention and Detection

THE CRIMINAL: WHO IS HE?

CHAPTER ONE

Lombroso: *Criminal Man*

HYPOTHESIS: That the criminal is born, not made

I

WE are in the Forensic Laboratory of the University of Turin. On the Director's table lie three photographs of a skull, the small skull of a woman, of a young woman, a skull that would be a little yellowed now by time, since life had gone from it so long ago as 1793.

These photographs have recently arrived. They have been sent by the Prince Napoleon Bonaparte as a token of the royal regard for the great Italian savant.

The two men who are engaged in examining so eagerly this royal gift have no such thoughts about the symbol of mortality before them as those that oppressed Hamlet by the grave. Meditations upon a skull or its image, that was for philosophers and poets, perhaps; but not for men of science, not for anthropometrists, for master measurers, seeking in the articulation of a human skull, of many skulls, the secrets of the criminal mind of man.

They are talking now, talking in the strange language of their science.

" Platycephalic—most certainly."

It is Professor Lombroso who speaks. He is a short, olive-complexioned man with an imperial beard. Bright brown eyes look keenly from behind pince-nez glasses. Like most Italians, he speaks very fast, and generally vehemently.

" And that, Professor, is rarer in women than in men, would you say? "

" You are right, my good Ferrero. . . . And now observe! Here! How truly remarkable the jugular apophysis, with the strongly arched brows concave below."

Ferrero is a younger man, tall and handsome. His attitude to the other suggests veneration, affection even.

Lombroso again takes the magnifying glass and peers closely through his myopic eyes.

" Yes, it is most clearly shown. One can see very easily how it is—confluent with the median line. And beyond it, too! Why, observe, Ferrero, all the sutures are open, as in a young man of twenty-four or so."

Ferrero takes the photograph and quizzes it closely.

" Also, observe, Master, that coronary suture. This is indeed a royal gift! "

Lombroso, in turn, considers this anatomical detail, as one who comes upon what has been long sought—which indeed was the case; for the famous authority on the criminal nature of man had for long been seeking for facts to fit his long-since-formed theory.

There was at that time no doubt in Lombroso's mind but that his theory was right. This skull of a young woman, it seemed to him, made it unassailable.

" Yes, this is indeed a virile skull that is portrayed. I saw it when I held the skull in my hands in Paris. Come, let us make a start on the orbital area. Why, with the naked eye one can see that it is bigger than the average. . . ."

At this point let us leave for a moment Professor Cesare Lombroso, Professor of Forensic Medicine and Psychiatry in the University of Turin, and his devoted colleague and disciple, Ferrero, as they set about the measurements of this so curious skull, and go back a little in time from that year, which was 1889.

II

Towards the end of the eighteenth century there was practising in Vienna a German physician named Joseph Gall. He was a noted anatomist and physiologist, and his studies in these sciences had led him to a curious theory—namely, that talents and character depend on the function of the brain, and that the brain, in turn, moulds the form of the skull.

Gall erected an elaborate system of empirical psychology on the unproven theory that the mental powers can be identified as a number of independent faculties, each with its own site in the brain; and, further, that the degree of the development of each faculty is reflected in the development of the appropriate part of the brain.

Finally, Gall held that the shape of the head is determined by the constituent parts of the brain, so that by the measurement of the external skull, the disposition, character, and talents of the subject can be scientifically determined and described.

Anatomically considered, Gall's theory of phrenology was about as valuable as the charts of the unexplored parts of the earth's surface made by the " closet philosophers " of the eighteenth century.

Nevertheless, Gall's theory was widely accepted, and phrenology became very popular. From 1796 to 1802 Gall lectured to crowded audiences in Vienna; and even in scientific circles his theory obtained wide acceptance.

Indeed, so flourishing did this new cult become that the Church began to look upon it, and its exponent, as dangerous to orthodoxy. For, it was reasoned, if it were to be scientifically proved that character and abilities depended on, and were conditioned by, the anatomical structure of the brain, the issue of moral responsibility, the dogma of original sin, and other theological considerations would be involved.

In 1802, at the height of his popularity, Gall was forbidden to lecture on phrenology and there was a general attack upon the " science " from the pulpits of Vienna. Gall thereupon packed up and went off to Paris. The French might be more liberal.

He was, indeed, heard with respect in Paris, and presently he was elaborating his theory by the assertion that criminality was a propensity anatomically innate, and therefore, by phrenological techniques, susceptible to detection or diagnosis by the shape of the skull.

Today, anatomists, physiologists, and psychologists are in agreement as to the worthlessness of Gall's phrenology. It survives, therefore, merely as an amusement at the level of the tented itinerant fortune-teller of the country fair.

There is no evidence that Lombroso knew of Gall and his theory of phrenology; and if Gall is mentioned here it is because he was actually the first man of science to put forward the theory that the shape of the skull and its size reveal the personality, character, and attainments of an individual.

Gall consequently has his place, though, since his was but a pseudo-science, it is not an important one, in any account of the early history of criminology, when it was taking shape as a science of measurement.

III

Lombroso, like Gall, held that the skull was a writing in the secret language of its bones, and that the anthropologist had to attack its secrets as the archæologist the enigmas of engraved stone or inscribed papyrus.

He had by the year 1862 already made a great and important contribution to the science of criminology, in that he had directed attention away from the study of crime, to the study of the criminal. Seen in retrospect, this was perhaps the greatest contribution made by this indefatigable worker in mensuration and statistics.

Convinced that the skull was the key to the riddle of criminal man, Lombroso embarked upon an investigation which became the work of a life-time.

No man can claim for his work that it is entirely *sui generis*; and though Lombroso broke new ground, he was from the start conditioned intellectually by the work of his predecessors.

Both Comte and Darwin greatly influenced Lombroso. Comte, whose positivist philosophy postulated that all mental facts arise out of biological causes, was Lombroso's scientific godfather. Darwin's thesis that species evolve by natural selection, with here and there an individual displaying vestigial anatomical evidence of earlier and more primitive life-forms, appealed at once to Lombroso's receptive and non-traditionalist mind.

Lombroso came to the conclusion that the criminal falls into one of two categories. Either he is an imperfectly developed or " evolved " being, or he is one who has regressed or gone back biologically.

The one type, as it were, has not managed the last lap upon

the hill of evolution; the other has climbed high, only to slip back to the biological level of the lower animals.

He also held that in either case the fact of criminal propensity can be diagnosed by physical, nervous, and mental anomalies. The " great criminal," Lombroso concluded, was a congenital malefactor whose physical anomalies were in part pathological and in part atavistic. In short, he claimed to have discovered *homo delinquens*—a creature foredoomed and hapless before his dark destiny.

" I formed," he wrote, " two fundamental ideas—namely, that it is not crime in the abstract, but the criminal himself that must be the subject of study. The congenital criminal is an anomaly, partly pathological, partly atavistic, a survival of the primitive savage.

" These ideas did not come to me instantaneously under the spell of a single deep impression, but of a series of impressions. The first idea came to me in 1864, when, as an army surgeon, I made studies of the Italian soldier. One thing distinguished the honest soldier from his vicious comrade: the indecent tattooing with which the latter's body was covered.

" The second impression came when my mind was directed upon psychology. I saw that one must, contrary to general practice, make the patient and not the disease the object of observation. I began to study the skull, measuring and weighing it by means of the Esthesiometer and Craniometer. This method I next applied to the study of criminals. My object was to apply the experimental method to the study of the *diversity*, rather than the anomalies between lunatics, criminals, and normal individuals."

IV

Every man has his daemon, and Lombroso's was a sort of blind faith in the infallibility of statistics based on physical measurement. Not long for this luminous Jew were the arid paths of academic German philosophy which had entranced him as a medical student in Vienna; the endless, futile debate upon the freedom of the will, the nature of ideas, and so forth. But if by the time we meet him Lombroso has turned his back upon German academic philosophy, he has retained his admiration for much in the Teutonic character. The idea of the " criminal type," when it did form itself in his mind, came to him from the early theory of Virchow, the celebrated German pathologist.

Virchow was a many-sided genius, a brilliant pathologist whose work in histology had won for him wide recognition and the eulogies of the great surgeon, Lister, of Edinburgh.

Virchow was also an anthropologist, and among his studies in this field was a survey of the school-children of Germany to determine the incidence of blondness among them. From that starting point Virchow had gone on to conduct a survey of a number of criminals. And he had found in the skulls of a number of these certain peculiarities reminiscent of the anatomical features of some of the lower animals.

Put simply, his argument ran somewhat as follows.

Man has evolved from the lower animals in an ascending evolutionary line. In the process he has discarded certain physical characteristics. If, then, we find in an individual certain organic characteristics of the lower animals, we may reason that these are evidence of regression, and that the individual may have reverted also on the moral level to the standards of the lower animals, or at least to prehistory man.

Virchow published his theory, which he named theromorphism, in 1871. Lombroso was aware of Virchow's theory. Here was a measurer after his own heart. And what a fascinating theory! Fascinating—yes. But true? That remained to be established.

Theromorphism was either a scientific chimera or it was a great scientific discovery. And there was but one way of finding out—namely, by the systematic measurement survey of a large number of criminals.

In 1871 Lombroso was appointed to the Chair of Forensic Medicine in the University of Pavia. There he began a great survey of the skulls and other anatomical features of the convict population of the large prison at Pesaro. This work he continued when, in 1876, he was appointed to the Turin Chair. This appointment carried with it that of physician to the prison of that city. Lombroso thus had the ideal opportunity he sought to examine, measure, and compare. For many years, with infinite patience and scrupulous care, he measured 200 convicts a year.

Whenever the opportunity occurred, Lombroso conducted post-mortem examinations of criminals. And he found, he has recorded, recurrent anomalies—the median occipital fossa, for example, similar to that of the monkeys—and this suggested to him a biological throwback to a time biologically remote. In the terminology of Darwin, here was an atavism.

Lombroso pursued this line of anthropometry with tremendous zest. Nothing was without significance for him. Even the facial expression of the criminal betrayed him, and he liked to cite in this connection Géricault's *Tête d'un Supplicié*— the head of an executed man.

It was one of Lombroso's pupils who made the curious observation that in a large number of recidivists there was a deep furrow down the cheek to the corner of the mouth. He noted that this facial peculiarity was seldom found in " normal " individuals. Lombroso, who grasped, perhaps too readily, at any new fact that seemed to support his general thesis, added this to his growing catalogue of the stigmata of degeneracy. He named it the *ride du vice*.

V

One cold grey November morning in the year 1876 Lombroso uncovered a body that had been brought to the Forensic Laboratory for post-mortem examination. It was, in its grim fashion, such a prize as did not very often come his way, for it provided him with precisely the type of material he needed for his purpose. It was the body of Vilella, an infamous brigand.

Vilella had lived and died a professional bandit, as a wild man seeing life through the eyes of a predatory animal.

" Vilella possessed such extraordinary agility," Lombroso wrote, " that he has been known to scale mountain heights bearing a sheep on his shoulders. His cynical effrontery was such that he openly boasted of his crimes."

If any doubts as to the correctness of his theory of criminal man remained, then the skull of Vilella should, surely, provide conclusive evidence? This skull would not be, by the criteria of anthropometry, as the skulls of normal, law-abiding humanity? No! It should exhibit, in classical perfection, the anomalies, peculiarities, and deviations from the normal characteristic of the great criminal. And all this should be demonstrable by the exact procedures and techniques of weighing and measuring.

And, sure enough, Lombroso found what he expected to find. Exactly at that place where a spine is found in a normal skull, Lombroso found a distinct depression. He gave it the name *median occipital fossa* because of its situation, precisely in the middle of the occiput, *as in the inferior animals, and in particular, as in the rodent tribe.*

That must have been for Lombroso an exciting moment of discovery, when whatever lurking doubt may have harboured itself in his mind was finally driven forth by conviction.

" It was revelation," he wrote, " and at the sight of that skull I seemed to see all of a sudden, lighted up as a vast plain under a flaming sky, the problem of the nature of the criminal—an atavistic being who reproduces in his person the ferocious instincts of primitive humanity and the lower animals.

" Thus are explained, anatomically, the enormous jaws, high cheek-bones, prominent superciliary arches, solitary lines in the palms, extreme size of the orbits, handle-shaped or sessile ears that are found in criminals, savages, and apes, with insensitivity to pain, extremely acute vision, tattooing, excessive idleness, love of orgies, and the irresistible craving for evil for its own sake."

VI

If, as you hold this book in your hand, you take the helix of your ear between thumb and finger, you will discover that it is not a flat spiral rim, but one that curves in as a partial fold.

Now, Darwin, whose theory of evolution had been received by Lombroso with acclamation, had noted certain vestigial physical characteristics which the orthodox anatomists had not observed. One of these was the little nodule on the edge of the helix of the ear. Thereafter this nodule became known as the *Tubercle of Darwin*.

The discovery, which is just possible, that you have such a nodule does not mark you off as a person exhibiting one of the anatomical anomalies by which the criminal type is to be identified. It merely means that, of a large number of such anomalies of face, features, skull, and bones, you just happen to have inherited one.

What Lombroso observed was that such characteristics occur most frequently in criminals. And he came upon similar curious anatomical reminiscences of a remote past in the large jaw of the brigand's skull, as though Nature had designed this lower jaw for the purpose of tearing raw flesh. And, again, here were long, ape-like arms, reminiscent of arboreal ape-man.

The completion of the anthropometrical examination of Vilella left Lombroso convinced of the soundness of his theory.

More evidence was to follow. It came as anatomical and also as psychological evidence: two bodies to yield up their dark secrets to the questing anthropologist.

VII

Verzeni was a sadist convicted of many crimes, including rape. The cannibalistic propensities of this man suggested strongly the man-ape of prehistory—the beast of prey.

Under examination, Verzeni exhibited the stigmata of degeneracy in a very high degree. To Lombroso, meditating upon Verzeni's curious skull, this was clearly a case of atavism, of regression; a throw-back by some inexplicable default of the genes to a past of extreme remoteness in biological time.

Finally, as a sort of keystone to the fabric of his theoretical structure, there was the final convincing phenomenon in the body of Misdea.

Misdea was a soldier, twenty-one years of age. He was neither particularly stupid nor vicious, but merely a colourless, nondescript young fellow. That was the character given him by the officers and comrades of his regiment.

B

Then one day eight officers and soldiers are found massacred in their beds.

In his quarters Misdea sleeps, peacefully as a little child.

When he is awakened, and the evidence of his guilt is made clear to him—for he is all bloody—he is distressed.

" I remember nothing," he protests—" nothing at all! "

And, strangely enough, he is speaking the truth.

" It flashed across my mind," wrote Lombroso, " that many criminal characteristics not attributable to atavism, such as facial asymmetry, cerebral sclerosis, impulsiveness, the periodicity of criminal acts, the desire for evil for its own sake, were morbid characteristics common to epilepsy, with others due to atavism."

These were clinical observations, and they came to Lombroso as further confirmation of the rightness of his theory.   He considered their significance and recorded his conclusions:

" The greatest criminals showed themselves to be epileptics; and, on the other hand, epileptics manifest the same abnormalities as criminals."

More.   He noted that epileptics often reproduced atavistic characteristics, including anatomical reminiscences of the lower animals.

VIII

In such ways, using such methods, reasoning as he did—perhaps, time has shown, rather over-confidently—Lombroso came to the conclusion that he had founded a new science, the science of criminal anthropology.   It was pre-eminently a science of measurement, a statistical science, with all the pitfalls and limitations of the statistical method.   And Lombroso was its prophet.   The criminal, by demonstration, was revealed by his physical and mental anomalies as a being apart from the race of normal mankind, differing from that race anatomically and psychologically, a creature foredoomed to a horrible destiny.

There was no doubt in the mind of this tremendously patient harvester of facts that he had achieved a synthesis.

" That synthesis," he wrote, " which mighty geniuses have

often succeeded in creating by one inspiration, but at the risk of error, was deduced by me gradually from various sources—the study of the normal individual, the lunatic, the criminal, the savage and, finally, the child."

Had Lombroso escaped the snare of over-confidence? Not entirely.

So far as his theory is of the criminal as a constitutional inferior, a throw-back, revealing in his person his atavistic characteristics, modern psychology has no quarrel with him. There is general agreement here. But Lombroso himself, and those associated with him in the movement, in those great anthropometrical surveys, went further in the sweeping conclusions they drew than modern psychologists or anatomists would go.

The late Dr Hamblin Smith, Medical Officer of Birmingham Prison and Lecturer on Criminology in the University of that city, sums up the modern view of Lombroso's theory in his *The Psychology of the Criminal*:

" Abnormalities in the shape or size of the cranium may imply the presence of abnormalities in the brain. And these, as well as the other stigmata, indicate either incomplete development or a tendency to reversion to a more primitive type. Although the importance attached to these stigmata is not so great as formerly, and although we no longer hold the exaggerated views which were held by certain of Lombroso's earlier disciples, still the stigmata are of some moment."

IX

Pursue a line of scientific inquiry that is vitiated *ab initio* by a fundamental flaw, and inevitably your line curves and in the end comes full circle. This, most students of criminology hold, is what befell Lombroso's theory in the end.

This came about in a peculiar way.

There are always external pressures and stresses on the individual living in any form of organized society. They come from economic forces, from passions roused by politics or religion, by the actions of those representing the State, and, in its name, imposing tyrannies. Sometimes the outcome is the messianic delusion of a Joan of Arc; at others a great crime, or an act of violence committed as an inescapable necessity.

In the year 1768 there was born, in the pleasant little Norman town of St Saturnin des Lignerets, a child to the impoverished noble house of D'Armont.

The influences that were to mould the character of this child, christened Marie Anne Charlotte, were those of the Church and the established royalist order, presently modified, albeit, by the liberalizing influence of doubtful books carelessly left within reach of the child.

In due course this little girl, who was gentle and mild, was placed in the care of the nuns of the Abbaye aux Dames at Caen. Later, now a child-woman, she was sent to live with an aunt in Caen. There was no other child in the house, so that little Charlotte, newly from the convent, was much alone.

In the rarely used library she came on books that interested her and stirred her mind, and there, forgotten, she passed many hours. Thus she read Voltaire, the Abbé Raynal, Plutarch's *Lives*, and other books not usually put in the hands of a Catholic child at that time.

Mademoiselle Charlotte Corday D'Armont was twenty-five years of age when, in June 1793, the Girondins—the party sympathetic to her liberalism—was overthrown by the forces of the Revolution.

In the streets of Caen, Charlotte saw the fugitives, and she heard from them how they had fled to Normandy in the hope of arousing to their cause its phlegmatic folk. There were lectures, haranguing; and Charlotte, the lonely young woman, much given to musings, began to burn with a dangerous fire.

We know, by inference, from her crime, what thoughts must have formed and unfolded into the dark resolution when, armed with letters to members of the party in hiding in Paris, she made her way there to fulfil her destiny.

At her trial before the Revolutionary Tribunal, Maître Legarde pleaded insanity, but in vain.

Marie Anne Charlotte Corday D'Armont was found guilty of stabbing Marat to death in his bath. So Charlotte Corday, as the world remembers her, died under the blade of the guillotine in the bright sunshine of a July day in the year 1793; and her head, all bloody, fell into the waiting basket.

Many heads fell in Paris in those days, and most have long since vanished in anonymous graves. But the head of Charlotte Corday was kept, and in due time it became a skull.

The years rolled on; then, in 1889, there was held in Paris the first Congress of Criminal Anthropology, and among other objects exhibited to the assembled criminologists was this same little skull of the political assassin. . . .

Thus nearly a century after the crime, our two Italian scientists came to be inspecting three photographs of that skull in the bright light of an Italian July sun.

Well, what was it?

The skull of a lunatic? Of a criminal? Of a saint? Or of a normal being moved to an act of violence by irresistible external political pressures?

In Paris Lombroso had held Charlotte's skull in his hand and had proclaimed it as characteristic of a criminal. It was the skull of a criminal, he asserted, because it was platycephalic and asymmetric.

There could be no doubt whatsoever about it. There they were, all those anomalies associated with the atavistic or regressed criminal. Those tell-tale signs, spelt out in bone, upon which had been erected the vast and impressive structure of mensuration and statistics, this great new theory of criminal man, delinquent woman.

In the skull of Charlotte Corday, Lombroso affirmed ". . . the presence of an extraordinary number of anomalies. Not even the purest political crime, that which springs from passion, is exempt from this law that I have laid down."

The curve in Lombroso's line of investigation had come full circle. But Lombroso did not realize that.

For, as the world saw it dimly then, and as it sees it clearly now, Charlotte Corday was not a criminal. Save for this one murder, she lived a blameless and pure life. And this "murder," was it not, in fact, a justifiable homicide?

What, then, remains of the theory? And what do those

three photographs tell the two men who examine them so minutely but that there, under their eyes, is the refutation of their theory of criminal man, delinquent woman? For here is the skull of a woman who has died for a passionate political conviction; and her skull, say the criminal anthropometrists, is a fine example of the skull of a great criminal!

What might they have found in the skull of Joan of Arc? In the flat face and low brow and prognathous jaw of Socrates?

X

Lombroso's theories have been generally discarded as unsound, or they have been modified. Even the theory of a "criminal type," identifiable by measurement, was disproved in the life-time of its propounder.

Lombroso, whose stature is not to be denied, for he was one of the greatest of statisticians, had become, while still a young man, riveted to a fixed idea. Too often he read into his material that which he desired to find there. It is somewhere about that point that a scientist is in danger of becoming unscientific.

Indeed, there is evidence that this idea of criminality so obsessed him in the end that he actually advanced the theory that insects and even plants can be identified as criminals by their behaviour. When a scientist goes as far as that, prudent men will beware of his teaching.

Lombroso's claim to a place in the hall of fame does not rest upon his work in this field, laborious and long-sustained as it was. He made many contributions besides those to a new science of criminology, based on Positivism. He wrote many pamphlets on such subjects as prostitution, alcoholism, anti-Semitism, and on the cause of pellagra, a disease that was the scourge of the Italian peasantry in his day.

Dr Hamblin Smith has made what is perhaps the just estimate of Lombroso's contribution to the science of criminology.

" There is much in his (Lombroso's) theory of the offender as being an ' atavistic ' survival, which is confirmed by the researches of psycho-analysis. But his theory of the relation between epilepsy and delinquency is now generally abandoned, and was only tenable by giving a very extended meaning to the term epilepsy. The fact, however, that his theories have had to be revised, in no way detracts from the value of the service which he rendered to science, and so to the world. For in Lombroso's work one great principle transcends all the details he gathered. His great glory lies in his insistence on the fact, practically overlooked before his time, that the offender is to be studied in himself, as an individual, and apart from any particular offence with which he might happen to be charged. Like Columbus, Lombroso did not rightly recognize the country which he had discovered. His undying fame rests on the fact that he did lead us to a new country, and opened out a new field for our exploration."

Lombroso's school, sometimes called the Anthropological, sometimes the Continental, continued to exercise a profound influence on the emergent science of criminology until it received at the hands of an English investigator the *coup de grâce.*

CHAPTER TWO

Goring: The Criminal Diathesis

HYPOTHESIS: That there is no " criminal type "

I

ONE day in the year 1903 two men sat discussing a scientific project in the Biometric Laboratory of the University of London.

Their meeting was the outcome of a proposed co-ordination of a prison population biometric survey which had been initiated by Dr Griffiths, of the Prison Medical Service, in Parkhurst Prison.

Recognized generally as being important, the survey had been extended to cover 3,000 prisoners in Parkhurst, Portland, Dartmoor, and Borstal prisons—Borstal being at that date an ordinary prison.

Now, it is one thing patiently to amass scientific data and large quantities of statistical material: it is quite another to interpret them scientifically.

This survey having been completed, the task had been assigned to one of the two medical men whom we find in conference in the Biometric Laboratory of the University of London—namely, Dr Charles Goring.

Dr Goring had succeeded Dr Griffiths at Parkhurst, and, in continuing the survey, had personally dealt with half the total number of prisoners examined—that is, some 1,500.

Because he had thrown himself into this work with such enthusiasm, the Prison Commissioners had assigned to him the task of arranging and classifying the data, and the interpretation of them.

The arrangement was for this work to be done by Dr Goring in the Biometric Laboratory under the Director, Professor Karl Pearson.

Thus these two men came to be talking on that particular

day in 1903. And their theme was the questionable scientific value of the world-wide popular Lombrosoan theory of criminal man.

" And what," asked Professor Karl Pearson, " if Lombroso's theory be established by your analysis, Doctor? "

" I shall accept it," Dr Goring replied without hesitation, " as the foundation of criminology; but I shall none the less condemn Lombroso as a traitor to science."

Professor Pearson smiled. " Indeed," he agreed, " if to disregard the laws of scientific procedure be to commit a grave offence, there has been no greater scientific criminal than Lombroso himself."

" Without denying the genius of Lombroso," Dr Goring went on, " it remains the fact that he never applied the mathematical method, and so was fundamentally unsound."

" I agree," replied Professor Pearson, " and in that connection I recall the poor foundation upon which Lombroso built his theory—the atavistic anomalies in the skull of the celebrated brigand dissected by him. At the risk of appearing trivial, I confess it seems to me that the race of brigands might quite properly resent the implications of the father of criminal anthropology! Indeed, I have no doubt whatever that the skull of that particular brigand in the hands of Lombroso has ever since been a menace to the spirit of sane criticism."

" I have recently made an interesting experiment that bears upon that point," Dr Goring went on. " I prepared a composite photograph of a number of known criminals by the superimposition of negatives; and another of men of the Royal Engineers, and the result revealed many points of resemblance between the ' criminal heads ' and those of the soldiers. And the differences between the two were very small."

" Hence the horns of a dilemma," put in Professor Pearson, " for either the men of the Royal Engineers are potential criminals, or criminals do not differ in head-type from the general population! "

" Much nonsense is talked and more written," observed Dr Goring.

" Yes," Professor Pearson agreed. " And of that truth

Havelock Ellis gave evidence in his treatise *Man and Woman*. In that work Ellis did much to perpetuate some of the worst of the pseudo-scientific superstitions—notably that of the greater variability of the male human being. Ah, I laid the axe to the root of that pseudo-scientific superstition!"

"Nevertheless," Dr Goring said, "Ellis makes a number of interesting points, as, for instance, the physiological factor in female delinquency—the tendency of women to commit offences most frequently during the menstrual period."

Professor Pearson brushed this defence aside.

"I have just read Ellis's reply to me, published—inappropriately, I think—in the January issue of the *Popular Science Monthly*. I see no reason to depart from what I wrote of his work in *Biometrika*; namely, that Ellis does not seem to understand what weight is to be given to scientific evidence as compared with vague generalities."

"Be that as it may," replied Dr Goring, "it shall not be said of this work that I am now undertaking that it is unscientifically performed."

II

From that day forward these two remarkable men became good friends. Goring admired the statistical techniques and brilliance of mind of Pearson; Pearson, on his side, admired Goring, both for his enthusiasm and assiduity, and for the warm humanity of his relations with the convicts who were his "guinea-pigs."

One day the two friends left the laboratory and were walking towards Soho when, near Charing Cross, a terrier-like little Cockney in cap and muffler accosted them.

"You remember me, don't yer, Guvnor?" he asked, holding out a grimy hand and grinning broadly.

Goring hesitated only for a moment.

"Yes!" he said, offering his hand. "Of course I remember you. Parkhurst, wasn't it? A stretch for burglary. You are married and have two children, boy and girl. Is that right?"

"That's c'rect, Doctor," grinned the little man. "It's

done me good seeing yer old chivvy chase agine." Then, with a wink, " An' it's nicer seein' yer 'ere than there."

" A walk with Goring through the streets of London," wrote Karl Pearson, " was almost certain to produce one or more of his prison friends, and the great feature of these meetings was their frank cordiality on *both* sides."

III

Why did Charlotte Corday murder Marat?
Because she was a predestined assassin.
On what evidence?
That of the anatomical anomalies of her skull.
Thus Lombroso made answer, *ex cathedra,* as it were. For him there was no more to be said.

Until the turn of the twentieth century Lombroso's theory of criminal man—upon which was based the so-called Italian or Continental School—remained virtually unchallenged.

One or two critics, nevertheless, declined to accept the teaching, among them Tarde,[1] who observed that one might find by the anthropometrical method anomalies in a large sampling of advocates which would suggest that their pre-destined role was the defence of the criminal.

It remained for the English physician, Dr Goring, to test by methods purely scientific the theory of the Lombroso School.

Lombroso had first formulated his theory while working as a medical officer of a great prison. Goring's work was done in similar circumstances, and when it was concluded much of the Italian savant's monumental life-work lay in ruins.

To say that is not to belittle Lombroso. To him belongs the honour of having opened up a new and little-known scientific terrain by abandoning the sterile preoccupation of the Correctional School, concerned only with the measurement of punishment as a sort of moral medicine prescribed according to the symptom (the crime), without reference to the patient (the criminal).

The old question had been: How many years for grand larceny? How many for rape? And so on.

[1] *La Criminalité Comparée,* 1902.

The new question was: Who is the criminal? What is he? And then: Might not the answer be found in his physical make-up?

Lombroso arrived at that conclusion. Goring, employing the statistical method on his 3,000 English convicts, came in the end to the contrary view.

" The inevitable conclusion," he wrote, " is that there is no such thing as a physical criminal type." And, as though that were not bomb-shell enough, he added: " And there is no such thing as a mental criminal type."

Today Goring's first proposition is generally accepted; but his second has been much modified by the advances made in psychiatry.

IV

Goring's thesis, put simply, was this: the criminal is the constitutional inferior. Who cannot earn, steals; who cannot fight, kills.

" There is no criminal class," he concluded, " but some individuals have elected for the criminal way of life."

Goring's findings, published as a statistical survey (*The Criminal of English Prisons*), did not solve the problem of the nature of criminal man. They did not even help towards the determination of the relative importance of heredity and environment in the etiology of criminality.

Goring was seeking for what he later termed *the criminal diathesis*; that is, the permanent condition of the body which renders it liable to certain special diseases—a constitutional predisposition.

He came to the conclusion that there was no evidence of this. Lombroso's anthropological criminal monster disappears.

" But, despite this negative," Goring wrote, " and upon the evidence of our statistics, it appears to be an equally indisputable fact that there is a physical, mental, and moral type of normal person who tends to be convicted of crime: that is to say, our evidence conclusively shows that, on the average, the criminal of English prisons is markedly differentiated by defective physique—as measured by stature and body-weight; by defective mental capacity—as measured by general intelligence; and by an increased possession of wilful anti-social proclivities—as measured, apart from intelligence, by length of sentences to imprisonment."

And he sums up as follows: " On statistical evidence, one assertion can be dogmatically made: it is, that the criminal is differentiated by inferior stature, by defective intelligence, and, to some extent, by his anti-social proclivities: but that, apart from these broad differences, there are no physical, mental, or moral characteristics peculiar to the inmates of English prisons."

Goring, then, saw the criminal as a defective individual whose defect was usually twofold: physical and mental.

For example, he found that burglars (at that time 90 per cent of the total prison population) were physically inferior to the remaining 10 per cent; and to the population at large. There was, it seemed, no more to be said about " the criminal type " than that.

Publication of Goring's survey marked the beginning of the end of the Continental School of Criminology.

V

The reader may here have a question to ask: Is a sample of our prison population a fair sampling of the total (though unrecognized) criminal element in the community? May not the types observed and measured represent that fraction of the whole *which has been unsuccessful in crime*?

Goring was well aware of this suggested doubt. But he held, nevertheless, to the validity of his conclusions, based on his 3,000 weak and inadequate unsuccessful practitioners of crime. His conclusions may be briefly summarized as follows:

It is the weak and inferior of mind and body who are not adequate to the demands of life. They may have no physical or mental disease, but they will always be found to have inferior endowments of both mind and body. The man or woman who steals as a way of life does so because he or she has neither the requisite physical nor mental equipment, nor sufficient moral toughness, to earn an honest living.

Goring concluded that the relative importance of constitutional and environmental factors was that defective physique and intelligence are major factors in the production of the criminal, and environment only a minor factor.

This last finding astonished Goring himself, as much as it did those who adhered to the generally accepted view of the importance of environment in the etiology of crime.

The finding that there was no evidence that the children of criminals tended to become criminals appeared, at first sight, to constitute a paradox. It was, however, disposed of by Karl Pearson.

Parents of extreme ability produce offspring of marked ability at a far higher rate than do mediocre parents, but the lesser rate at which the latter produce offspring of marked ability is more than compensated for in the total by the very large number of mediocre parents. For example, if 1 per cent of the population be of marked ability, and 30 per cent of their offspring be like their parents, while the remaining 99 per cent of the population produce only 5 per cent offspring of marked ability, it still follows that the bulk of persons of marked ability have mediocre parents.

VI

Goring made a distinction between the mentally defective, or " tainted," stocks and the constitutional inferiors. The term " defect " was seen to be not always synonymous with inferiority. The " inadequate " subject may score high on, say, a Binet–Simon test, yet fail.

Why?

According to Goring, such types fail in life because they are humanity's " lone wolves," in whom is lacking the herd instinct. They are those individuals who are without loyalties, who are incapable of altruism, lacking in self-knowledge, and incapable of self-criticism.

Such individuals are seen as " nature's criminals."

The importance of the new view of the criminal advanced by

Goring was implicit in the question prompted by his findings. For if the theory of " criminal man " was disposed of, the problem reappeared in an amended form.

Lombroso said: The criminal is a type who differs from the normal and may be recognized by certain stigmata.

Goring answered: No! There is no physical difference between the normal individual and the criminal.

Why, then, do some persons become criminal, while the majority abstain from crime?

And presently, as we shall see, many other voices were heard.

There is no criminal class, but some individuals have elected for the criminal way of life.

Society gets the criminals it deserves, since they are stamped out from the social matrix. Poverty, social injustice—these are the prime causes of crime.

Men become criminals because they are weak.

It is the unhappy psychopath who is most likely to develop anti-social trends—the homosexual, the schizophrenic, the hysteric, the epileptic, and the individual of epileptoid personality. . . .

There were many voices, but their theme formed a rough harmony, since all viewed the individual classified by the law as " criminal " as a symptom of the sickness of society, as the resultant of heredity, of socio-economic and emotional strains and stresses.

In a word, the emphasis shifted from the physical make-up and intellectual level of the criminal to his emotional states.

As once Lombroso had examined so patiently the skull of Charlotte Corday for physical indications of abnormality, so the science of psychology turned the direction of research towards the mechanisms of the brain housed in the skull. How does the mind work? What factors determine conduct? And so the biochemist and the endocrinologist come into the field of investigation.

VII

It is a curious omission in the work of Goring that while he lays such stress on the scientific method, he nowhere offers a definition of the word " crime," and so leaves in the air the meaning of the word " criminal."

In all civilizations, in all ages, even so far back as the earliest known Code of Laws—that of Hammurabi of Babylon— certain crimes have been differentiated from others, some being seen to be crimes only because prohibited by the State, while others are recognized as crimes *per se*—offences against Nature— such as murder and rape.

The crime which is *mala per se* is an offence universally recognized by mankind: the crime *mala quia prohibita* is an artificial creation, varying with time and place.

For example, the consumption of alcohol became a crime during the era of Prohibition in the United States. It is so no longer with the repeal of the Amendment to the Constitution. It is probably not putting it too high to say that during the Prohibition period some 90 per cent of the total adult population in that country were, by that criterion, " criminals." And that, as Euclid would say, is absurd.

Ninety per cent of Goring's " guinea-pigs " were not men convicted of crimes *mala per se*, but of the crime of burglary, of the turpitude of which Nature knows nothing, since theft would appear to be a universal mode of life.

Thus, to a great extent, Goring's findings lose their value. Many burglars, no doubt, are otherwise estimable men, home-lovers and good husbands and parents; men who frequently spontaneously display their moral sensibility in their attitude towards the man convicted of gross cruelty to children.

Why should it surprise us to learn that such men differ from the law-abiding only in so far as they are handicapped by a less generous physical and mental endowment?

A survey, such as Goring's, of 3,000 murderers, or sadists, or robbers with violence, might produce very different conclusions.

VIII

When Goring died, the late E. V. Lucas wrote this of him:
" I suppose he was the honestest and most understandingly tolerant man that ever lived. He never trimmed; he rarely

condemned; and he had no fear. No fact was too stark and naked for him; indeed what he wanted was stark and naked facts."

No scientific truth is absolute, because the landscape of knowledge is an ever-changing, ever-expanding, scene. But it is important to walk in the right direction and to wear suitable boots. That is to say, the method must be scientific and unmarred by prejudice.

As Professor Karl Pearson put it:

" The steady collecting of data and the accumulation of measurements, followed by their analysis from the mathematical standpoint, these form the sole path of truth in Criminology as in its parent science, Sociology."

Goring's conclusions, it should be borne in mind, have not been universally accepted. Sir Bryan Donkin estimated that 15 per cent of English convicts are feeble-minded. Dr William Healy put the percentage, including inmates of reformatories, at from 10 to 30 per cent; Dr H. H. Goddard, at from 25 to 50 per cent.

Professor Carl Murchison (1926), using the comparative method with prisoners and recruits in the United States Army, found the former more intelligent than the latter. He got an alpha score of 46·2 of White criminals, and something very near that with the troops. This suggests that an unexpectedly high proportion of young non-criminals are morons.

One thing Goring's survey did, whatever may be the later modification of his conclusions: it demolished the teaching of the Lombrosoan or Continental school.

CHAPTER THREE

Lange: Crime as Destiny

HYPOTHESIS: That man's fate is in his genes

Oh Thou, who didst with Pitfall and with Gin
Beset the Road I was to wander in,
    Thou wilt not with Predestination round
Enmesh me, and impute my Fall to Sin.

I

PELAGIUS, the reader may recall, held that the will of
man is free. St Augustine thought otherwise, his view
being that Adam forfeited this divine birthright of man
by the first act of disobedience in the Garden of Eden. St
Thomas Aquinas put forward a third view; namely, that man
is merely a mechanism demonstrating the infallibility of the
divine causation.

There exists an enormous literature, philosophical and
theological, on the riddle of predestination and freewill. For
where is the man, good or bad, learned or unlettered, who has
not pondered the problem in his mind?

Through the centuries the great debate has continued, nor
has the last word yet been said.

But nowadays the case is generally re-stated in the terms of
science, by the biologist, the social scientist, the psychologist,
and even, as will presently transpire, by the biochemist.

II

Now, if it could be scientifically demonstrated that the
biological inheritance is the governing factor in the production
of the criminal elements of society, then the remedy—eugenic
breeding—would clearly be indicated.

If, on the other hand, type would appear to be moulded
mainly by the environment, then a social system purged of
injustice, poverty, and ignorance should result in the ultimate
elimination of all anti-social beings.

For the scientist the problem is one largely of measurement; of the devising of techniques that will yield the researcher, with a high degree of accuracy, reliable and demonstrably true findings.

How, then, could a piece of research work be so planned as to determine the relative roles of the biological inheritance and of the conditioning environment?

In other words, what human beings could be utilized for this purpose so as to yield a standard of comparative measurement?

" The natural tendencies one is born with, the surrounding world one grows up in—these are essentials, are destiny; and it is also destiny which decides how the environment, with its numberless influences, is going to shape the natural tendencies into one whole."

The writer of these words, Professor Johannes Lange, sought how he might carry out an investigation the object of which would be the isolation of the biological factor from the environmental, so that its importance in the production of criminals might accurately be estimated.

He decided that this might be possible by investigating the life-histories of criminal twins, for identical twins may fairly be regarded as two versions of a single being, two copies from one matrix, with identical genes.

Professor Lange argued somewhat upon the following lines.

If identical twins may be regarded as Nature's duplicates, then, if they are found to respond in a uniform way to the pressures of environment on the mental, emotional, and physical levels, the fair deduction to be drawn would be the dominant influence of inheritance, and the influence of environment could be given its place as of minor importance.

Again, the reactions of non-identical twins could be measured against those of ordinary brothers and sisters. Thus, if non-identical twins showed close similarity of behaviour compared with ordinary brothers and sisters, the role of environment would thereby be shown as increased in proportion.

III

What are identical twins?

Identical twins are two individuals deriving from a single ovum and a single spermatozoon. Ordinary twins are those gestated together from two ova and two spermatozoa.

In the case of identical twins the disposition of the genes is identical in both individuals; in the case of ordinary twins there is the normal variability, such as one sees it in any family of several children, a phenomenon known technically as *segregation*, and which is often expressed in marked differences, though these are most obvious in such features as the colouring of horses, cows, dogs, and cats born of the same parents.

Professor Lange's investigation, then, began in Nature's workshop at the moment of conception, and the first overt act, when the ovum breaches the corpus luteum and, microscopically minute, moves down the Fallopian tube, whose estuary is the waiting womb. It is during this voyage that the ovum encounters the flagellating sperm that has threshed a passage through that anatomical Pillar of Hercules, the cervix, has passed through the womb itself (so soon to enfold a watery world), and so met and become united with the descending ovum, which, now fertilized, beds down upon the wall of the womb, presently to cast forth the lace-like tracery of placenta and embark upon the cellular proliferation and differentiation of gestation.

Such is the normal engendering of a child. But from time to time the ovaries eject from the corpus luteum two ova simultaneously, and, each encountering a sperm, two placentae share the room of the womb and are born as ordinary twins. These twins have shared their mother's hospitality as companions, for they are separate beings, with genes individual to each.

But Nature has another variation yet to play in the drama of gestation and birth.

This is when she makes one ovum serve for two by fission and produces two beings from a single egg—identical twins.

IV

For his material, Professor Lange went to the Institute of Biology and the Institute of Psychiatry of Bavaria; and he had also the co-operation of the Bavarian Ministry of Justice.

In all, Professor Lange investigated thirty-five pairs of twins, fifteen identical, twenty non-identical. He found that identical twins remained similar, but not the non-identical pairs. Identical twins, he found, tended to share hereditary diseases, had closely similar emotional patterns, whereas non-identical twins varied, as do, normally, brothers and sisters. And he concluded that the latter do not share identical inborn tendencies, but only such as might be expected of the children of the same parents. Identical twins were found to resemble one another mentally, and also in functional ways, such as handwriting, voice, gait, and so forth.

The results obtained suggested strongly that biological inheritance plays a part far more important than environment in determining the destiny of human beings.

The investigator saw some of the twins while they were serving sentences of imprisonment, some in his consulting-room, others in their own homes.

V

Georg and Adolf Kraemer were identical twins, so alike as not easily to be distinguished apart. Both had become criminals by early manhood. Both kept out of trouble so long as they kept away from strong drink. Both were dull-witted; neither acquired a trade nor any skill. Both were excessively shy; neither was interested in girls; for both were sexually immature—eunuchoid.

The grandfather was brutal, the father aggressive and alcoholic. Their mother was a decent woman.

Adolf was temperate, but Georg drank. Adolf was a thief; Georg drew his knife when alcohol lent him courage. But since Georg sustained a head injury in early life, the picture is somewhat impaired, because that accident introduced a speculative factor, a hypothetical brain injury which might have played some part in producing subsequent criminality.

Both brothers became criminals, but criminals in different ways. It is fairly clear that both derived their criminal tendencies from a shared biological inheritance and that their criminality was unconnected with their environment.

VI

In the next example—that of Ferdinand and Luitpold Schweizer—Professor Lange had a certain advantage, for both twins were orphaned, adopted by different families, and separated at the age of eight. They thus became excellent guinea-pigs, reacting freely through inherited tendencies in the environment without such influence as might be attributable to close association.

Their father was a drunkard; a brother was also a drunkard. Ferdinand was launched into a bad environment where he was knocked about and neglected. Luitpold was affectionately and well cared for.

During their school years, though living in different towns, both played truant. Ferdinand next ran away and became a vagabond. He had two short sentences for theft. He was conscripted into the Army, and promptly deserted. He received a five years sentence for this, but it was suspended when the First World War broke out. He got through the War without further trouble. After the War he married and sank swiftly into degradation. He was convicted of procuring and conniving at his wife's immorality. He drank, smoked excessively, lived simultaneously with two women, was divorced. He was given a prison sentence for burglary.

Luitpold first got into trouble for truancy. As a boy he smoked excessively. He learnt a trade, but turned vagabond. Before being conscripted, though not convicted, he had been involved in an affray in which he had used his knife. He got an army pension and married, but spent the first night with another woman. He was divorced. He then met with a " tartar," and during his life with her this wife kept him out of trouble, save for one prison sentence.

" On the whole," wrote Professor Lange, " it can be said that the Schweizer brothers clearly reveal the influence of environment.   However, their conduct was not determined by the environment itself so much as by their innate tendencies, which delivered them both up to whatever was the stronger influence of the moment, good or evil.   Their mental make-up probably remains the decisive factor."

VII

Antoine and Amelie Messer were identical twins, so alike that their husbands were sometimes deceived. By their thirties both were stout, excitable, easily elated or depressed to suicidal level.

They came of a family of fourteen, including three sets of twins.   As small girls they were, in the words of their mother, " only half human."   They indulged in breath-holding, grimacing, gesticulating.

Both were quite bright at school, but both played habitual truant.   By sixteen both were in trouble.   They ran away, became vagabonds and promiscuous.   Amelie contracted venereal disease.

Both were sent to a reformatory, and Antoine was referred to a psychiatrist.   Amelie behaved herself at this period, but soon after discharge became a vagabond again, became pregnant, married the father, a drunkard.   She had several children by as many fathers.

She left her husband, but well looked after her children, but she was sent to prison for procuring.

Antoine married, but consorted with other men.   Her husband lived on her immoral earnings.

" A constant sexual urge," comments Professor Lange, " and lack of self-control decided their destinies, which are only outwardly a little different from one another."

VIII

Among the fifteen identical twins investigated both twins became criminals in ten cases.   Among the non-identical twins of thirteen pairs the second twin had been imprisoned in two cases, and in thirteen had not.

" This leads," concluded Professor Lange, " to the following conclusions as far as crime is concerned: monozygotic (identical) twins on the whole react in a definitely similar manner; dizygotic (non-identical) twins behave quite differently.   If, therefore, we attach importance to the Twins Method of investigation, we must admit that so far as the causes of crime are concerned innate tendencies play a preponderant part."

" Innate tendencies " here means biological inheritance, and so suggests that in the Twin Method of Professor Lange there is strong support for the view that individuals such as those investigated are, indeed, the sport of forces dynamic in their unhappy biological inheritance, forces so powerful as to render these unfortunates predestined criminals.

It follows from this that punishment, as that term is normally understood, is inappropriate, and that measures taken against such offenders should never go beyond the object of protecting society, without thought of retribution.   Further, that such " punishment " should be designed to refit the offender to exercise liberty as a law-abiding citizen; and that persons clearly unfitted for liberty should be discovered early in life and permanently segregated.

Like so many other workers in this scientific field, Professor Lange stresses the evil role of alcohol as a major influence for crime.   And he advocates preventive measures to control and dam the tainted biological stream.

" Our Twin method," he wrote, " can only teach us that the tendencies which lead to anti-social behaviour develop in the domain of heredity.   It tells us nothing about the manner in which these tendencies are inherited. . . . The closest study of criminal heredity must go hand in hand with the investigation of the criminal individuals themselves."

IX

The predominant role of heredity as the prime factor in the production of unsatisfactory types has been the conclusion reached by nearly all investigators in this field.

The Eugenists, whose science is biology applied to sociology, hold that some method of control of defective stocks must ultimately be employed.

Professor J. A. Thomson gave the ratio of defective to normal persons as having more than doubled between 1874 and 1896.

The Tavistock Clinic[1] estimated that one in nine of the population of England and Wales have taken the first step towards some form of emotional imbalance, some sort of psychological sickness.

The late Professor Karl Pearson, already mentioned in connection with his work with Goring, carried out an interesting piece of research in this connection.

He drew up a long list of *natural* characteristics, and another of *nurtural* characteristics. He then worked out in each category the coefficient of correlation; that is, the degree of resemblance between the members of the same family in natural and nurtural qualities.

His conclusions coincided with those arrived at by Professor Lange; namely, that the biological inheritance is the predominant factor in the production of type and character. Professor Pearson estimated that the environmental influence is, to the heredity, as one to five, or perhaps one to ten.

X

Nearly all investigators, whatever their angle and method of approach, seem to have come to the same conclusion.

Dr Tredgold wrote: "Again and again in investigating the family history of the feeble-minded, I have found that their brothers and sisters, if not actually defectives, were criminals, prostitutes, paupers, or ne'er-do-wells."

Apropos Professor Lange's condemnation of alcohol, one finds endorsement from quite another quarter; namely, in the late Dean Inge's *Outspoken Essays*, where he observes:

". . . a very different question is whether alcohol should be added to the short list of racial poisons which may affect the germ plasm. . . . The difficulty in this is that alcoholism

[1] The Tavistock Clinic is an out-patient Psychiatric Clinic within the National Health Service.

is usually a symptom or consequence of degeneracy, so that quite apart from any direct possibility of the poisoning of the germ plasm by alcohol, we might expect to see very inferior children from alcoholic parents."

The writer, however, overlooks in this connection the role of the neuroses in the production of alcoholics. It is the common observation of most of us that it is the unhappy who drink to excess, and many of these unhappy ones are individuals of talent, sometimes of genius.

CHAPTER FOUR

Berg: The Sadist

HYPOTHESIS: That some are damned

I

A^{N} argument against capital punishment seldom advanced is that it involves the destruction of valuable clinical material.

The full investigation, by both physician and psychiatrist, of a convicted murderer, carried out over a period of time, might well result in the shedding of some light upon certain types of criminal, particularly those who are referred to in the popular Press as " monsters."

In most trials for murder where psychiatrists are called in to give evidence their knowledge of the psychopathology of the accused is far too superficial to be relied on.

The psychiatric witness may have gleaned sufficient knowledge of the psychopathology of an accused from a number of visits to his cell, made prior to trial, so as to form a fairly reasonable diagnosis—or even a sound one.

But he will remain as much in the dark as the least well-informed juryman as to the etiology of the abnormal state in any given case; for the human mind cannot be plumbed in so casual a manner.

For a complete and rewarding picture an investigation going back at least two generations of the accused's ancestry would be needed; and after that a full record of his life—the domestic, social, and economic circumstances of it. And, in particular, a very detailed knowledge of the emotional experiences of the child and adult.

So far as the writer is aware only one such case has ever been investigated with this thoroughness, namely, that conducted by the late Professor Karl Berg of the Düsseldorf Medical Academy, who was also the founder and director of the

Institute of Legal and Social Medicine of that city, and
Medico-legal Adviser to the Düsseldorf Criminal Court.

As he reads the account of this investigation which now
follows, the reader will recall the view of Dr Goring, and of
Professor Lange, as to the contribution of heredity as the
paramount factor in determining a criminal career as evil
destiny.

II

On April 13, 1931, Peter Kuerten, a labourer, was charged in
the Düsseldorf Criminal Court with no fewer than ten murders.
After a trial lasting as many days, he was convicted of nine of
them.

The crimes of which Kuerten was convicted were, however,
but a small part of a grand total of sexual murders, murderous
assaults, rapes, arsons, larcenies, and theft proved against
him, not by criminal investigation, but mainly by means of
information proffered freely by the criminal himself.

Four medico-legal and psychiatrical-legal experts were
called to give evidence. They had all reached the same conclusion: that Kuerten was suffering from no organic or
functional mental disease, and that he was, consequently,
responsible for his terrible crimes.

Once under arrest, Kuerten spoke with remarkable frank-
ness, Professor Berg being eminently successful in winning his
confidence.

Kuerten was quite truthful, and his accounts of his crimes,
whenever checked, were found to be accurate; and where his
crimes were concerned it was notable that Kuerten's memory
functioned with extraordinary clarity, which indicates the
measure of his pleasure in the deed and satisfaction in retro-
spective contemplation of it. Remorse, shame, a moral sense,
all were completely absent.

III

What were the motives that impelled this terrible being to
his crimes?

It is the criminal himself who supplies the material sought by

his scientific investigator.   In so far as he had any insight into
his own psychology, Kuerten was completely self-revelationary.
He described his feelings of tension before each crime, the relief
which followed its commission.

In all, Kuerten committed sixty-seven crimes, ranging from
murder to arson, and he killed men, women, children, and
even animals, all indifferently.

The psychological and moral riddle posed by this terrible
being was the genesis of such sadistic perversions.   Was it a
bad biological inheritance or bad environment?   Did it
originate out of some encounter or mischance of childhood or
youth?   What processes of deterioration followed upon the
long prison sentences suffered before the beginning of the long
series of sexual murders that turned the great city of Düsseldorf
into a city of dread?   Was it megalomania?   A sadistic
fixation of the libido?   Hatred of society?

Each of these may have exerted some influence upon the
criminal's psychology; but even when taken together, there
remains a fundamental repudiation of the rights of others, a
monstrous and unique egoism.

IV

In personal appearance, Kuerten was a well-built man of
medium height—a typical German peasant.   He dressed
carefully, took great pride in his personal appearance, eschewed
drink.   Alcohol had no part in the deeds that made Düsseldorf
a city perilous for any woman who walked its streets after dark.

Kuerten left his home nearly every evening to seek a victim,
and he generally returned having found one.   In the tenement
where he lived with his childless wife nobody ever suspected
him.   He made no friends, it is true: but that was all.

Only in one respect during the many months that he was in
daily contact with Professor Berg did Kuerten evince any
sort of contrition, and then it was the fantastic admission that
he felt deep regret for being unfaithful to his wife, a reformed
prostitute who had once served a prison sentence for wounding
him.

As he went about his stabbing and slaying, Kuerten dreamed

of how he would one day deliver Düsseldorf from the "monster"; how he would be appointed Chief Police Commissioner. And along with this fantasy of fame, he wove his megalomaniac's fantasy of gigantic catastrophies, the annihilation of whole communities by fire and dynamite.

Investigation showed that Kuerten was immune from all normal emotional reactions, that he was the victim of a sort of spiritual anæsthesia, morally dead.

Finally, seated opposite his wife in a restaurant, Kuerten revealed to her the name of the "monster." At first she did not believe him, but when he had convinced her, she thrust her food away, overcome.

Kuerten was unmoved. He took the second plate and ate both meals.

V

During the ten months he was in prison, between the date of his arrest and his execution, Kuerten ate heartily, slept well, and appeared to be quite content. He had, perhaps, attained one objective: he had achieved a world-wide infamy, and a monstrous egotism was, perhaps, thereby gratified.

Clearly, if one is to get any sort of understanding of Kuerten, one must first enter by force of sympathetic understanding the dark labyrinth of his mind. The part played by the parents must be known, the experiences amid which the infant became child, the child man.

Dr Neustadt, who assisted Professor Berg, investigated the Kuerten family. The father was a drunken moulder. He was sexually uncontrolled, most brutal to his wife. He served a prison sentence of fifteen months for attempted incest with his daughter. This father Peter Kuerten hated bitterly. Perhaps the role of that father in the fate of Kuerten can scarcely be over-estimated.

Peter Kuerten was the third of thirteen children. Three brothers served prison sentences for theft. The family was notorious for violent tempers, megalomania, and arrogance.

The daughters were over-sexed and precocious. The

brothers and sisters of the father were alcoholic psychopaths; endogenous mental disease, however, was not found. The grandfather had served prison sentences for theft; and collaterals included examples of delirium tremens, paralysis, feeble-mindedness, and border-line cases, while throughout the family criminals, alcoholics, and psychopaths abounded.

On his mother's side, Kuerten came of a decent family of normal working-class folk.

Professor Sioli, one of the psychiatrists who gave evidence at the trial, thus commented on this family record:

" This genealogical tree affords a critical commentary on the question of how far hereditary handicaps exert compelling influences on the descendants."

A like thought was in Plutarch's mind when he wrote:

" There is between the generating being and the generated, a sort of hidden identity, capable of justly committing the second to the consequences of an action committed by the first."

Evil, which was Kuerten's portion from birth, suggests a malignancy of fate that amounted to predestination in the sense of the determinist theory.

VI

Consider certain episodes of his childhood.

A dog-knacker who lived in the same tenement showed the small boy Peter how he tortured the dogs before destroying them. He experienced a curious excitement on seeing the dog's suffering, the sight of its blood.

The small boy Peter bathed with some companions in the Rhine. He thrust one of his playmates into the tide, watched him drown.

Of this latter incident, Professor Hubner, of Bonn, a witness at the trial, observed: " Many children, otherwise nice, do such things."

Later the boy ran away from home and lived as a vagabond, thieving, robbing from the person, choosing as victims chiefly women and girls.

He was arrested for theft and sent to prison—the first of

seventeen sentences which were to take up twenty-seven of his forty-seven years of life.

On coming out of prison he committed his first sex murder. Is it significant that this crime came after two years of sexual deprivation? It was in his prison cell that Kuerten developed his sadistic fantasy-weaving. He courted punishment in order to be free to conjure up in the darkness of the solitary cell the delights of his perverted imagination.

When a prisoner died, Kuerten offered his services in the mortuary, carrying out his gruesome duty with evident enjoyment.

While serving a seven-year sentence for desertion from the army Kuerten suffered an attack of prison psychosis: he became for himself a cocoon.

Prison, it would seem, must come fairly high among the causes which made Kuerten what he became.

VII

Writing of this fearful disintegration of character under prison conditions, Prince Kropotkin said: " Prisons are the nurseries for the most revolting category of breaches of the moral law."

Dostoevski, writing of his own prison experiences, said:

" During so many years, I ought to have been able to seize some indication, however fugitive, of regret, of moral suffering. I have perceived positively nothing. Seclusion and excessive work only develop among these people a profound hatred, a thirst for forbidden pleasures, or a terrible indifference."

A trained prison psychiatrist would not have been likely to have missed the significance of Kuerten's behaviour, the prison psychosis, his avidity to lay out the dead. But few prisons have been adapted for the cure of criminal abnormals, the roots of whose ills lie buried in the subconscious; and there can be no cure for the psychopathic criminal without an understanding of the processes that are the destructive dynamic forces. And perhaps, it might be added, no reform is possible save in that small category of cases where a secret punishment appetite has to be satisfied, without penal reforms so radical as to amount to the abolition of the institution of the prison as now understood.

VIII

Kuerten was found to be devoid of the sense of guilt that is characteristic of the neurotic criminal. He had moral suffering only right at the end. He then asked for a priest. As Stekel somewhere remarks, every fear is the fear of the punishment of God.

A man may commit a criminal act to satisfy a need—the need for moral suffering that alone can bring self-forgiveness. This is the psychic mechanism, perhaps, of the sadistic medallion in reverse.

Again, we may say that man, psychologically considered, is a pyramid whose apex is represented by the thin layer of his recently acquired culture. As we proceed downwards to the base of the structure of his being we come, with pardonable reluctance, to the unflattering truth. It is that man is the victim of his racial past, and that every human life must resolve itself into a single combat against the ghostly army of primitive man.

When in that unequal combat the collapse of the moral structure is complete, we say of such a man: He is a throwback, atavistic, *à la* Lombroso. But how strange: there are no physical stigmata!

If, as Professor Berg concluded, Kuerten presents no novel aspect of psychopathology, he does raise in an unmistakable way urgent problems in penology. For it is not possible to study this product of a bad heredity, plus twenty-seven years of prison life, without pondering the effect of prison in changing a pervert and psychopath into an arch-criminal and an enemy of his kind.

Kuerten remained impassive to the end. He confessed that when Professor Berg's woman doctor assistant entered his cell the desire to strangle her was almost irresistible. And when he knew he was to die at the hands of the executioner on the following morning, he asked, almost eagerly: " Shall I hear the gush of my own blood? That would be the pleasure of pleasures ! "

D

CHAPTER FIVE

Schlapp: The Criminal Imperative

HYPOTHESIS: That the criminal is the victim of his glands

I

ALICE C was thirty years of age when her criminal behaviour brought her to the consulting-room of Professor Max Schlapp, neuropathologist, of the New York Post-graduate School. She had been repeatedly caught stealing from department stores, and always the same type of article—handbags.

Alice C's husband was a wealthy man with whom she lived happily with their only child. Like most American women, she was somewhat spoiled, given complete freedom of action, and kept well supplied with spending money. Nobody in the family circle had ever noticed any signs of a repressed yearning or other psychological conflict.

After she had been caught several times her family took measures to prevent further thefts, since it was inevitable that, sooner or later, a store would insist on prosecuting and refuse compensation without legal remedy.

Despite the vigilance of those aware of her propensity, Alice C contrived to shake off her guardians and get into a New York department store, where she stole a handbag.

She was detected and arrested. When she came before the court she was released on condition that she submit to medical treatment. She was referred to Professor Schlapp.

Why did Alice C repeatedly steal handbags for which she had plenty of money to pay and which were of no use to her?

Because she was a kleptomaniac, is the unenlightening answer, unenlightening because it leaves unanswered the further question of why Alice C had become a kleptomaniac.

Many cases of this kind have been referred by the courts, both in England and America, for medical report, and the text-books yield a rich harvest of cases in which the strange impulsion, which Schlapp terms the " criminal imperative," developed.

The explanation most frequently offered comes as the psychological interpretation of conflicts whose roots go back to childhood or even infancy, and remain suppressed, but dynamic, in the subconscious mind. And these psychological interpretations often have the beauty of an art form, and carry the conviction of a mathematical solution. Can the facts be interpreted in some other way equally impressive?

Let us see how Professor Schlapp went to work on the investigation of Alice C.

<h1 style="text-align:center">II</h1>

Her medical history revealed the circumstance that at the age of thirteen, when she began menstruation, she became moody and restless, and prone to give way to impulsive acts of an imprudent kind that led to embarrassment.

After marriage Alice C became more steady and stable, but soon after the birth of her child the former instability returned. She became moody, erratic, and unaccountable.

Then she began to steal—to steal handbags, nothing but handbags.

Physiological tests yielded the following information. Alice C had an abnormally high basal metabolism; that is, of the changes undergone by nutritive material in the body. The sugar tolerance was also abnormally high. The suprarenal glands were found to be over-active, while the case-history pointed to glandular abnormalities.

The suprarenal glands are associated with the sex glands, and it was at two points in Alice C's life when the sexual function was affecting the body radically, that is, at the onset of menstruation and during gestation, that the emotional disturbances appeared.

Alice C was treated in the light of this diagnosis, one that ignored psychological causation and based itself on the idea of the body as a mechanism, a mechanism that had got out of order, as the engine of a car gets out of order.

The treatment, which proved to be quite successful, was the employment of sedatives, with ovarian, suprarenal, and other gland extracts.

III

Schlapp holds that a large proportion of criminality could be prevented by the correction of glandular defects, and he bases his opinion on twenty years' experience in the Post-graduate Medical School and Hospital of New York, and of the New York Children's Court Clinic. He is, therefore, entitled to be heard with respect; and he says this:

" We shall attempt to demonstrate that the vast majority of all criminals, misdemeanants, mental deficients, and defectives are the product of bodily disorders, that most crimes come about through disturbances of the ductless glands in the criminal or through mental defects caused by endocrine troubles in the criminal's mother."

Certain categories of offence are excepted; namely, crimes due to trauma (injury to vital parts of the nervous system), to psychoses (insanity), drugs, toxic infections, epilepsy, and criminality of " the true hereditary type."

IV

The realm into which this exponent of man as an adaptive mechanism takes us is full of wonders, and its central marvel is the cell.   How is the cell nourished, or not nourished?   How does it do its job of storing and giving out energy, of proliferating?

Who conducts this corporeal orchestra, whose instrumentalists are the cells of its parts and members, to produce a harmony?

What prompts gland-cells to secrete, nerve-cells to give out their energy?   It is the release of electro-chemical forces.

The layman can follow fairly well the scientific materialist, and still ponder the source of the *élan vital*, the nature of the controller of the machine.

The endocrines that assume nowadays so great an importance in medical science are ductless glands.   They are little factories whose products are hormones, those internal secretions that pass into the blood and stimulate organic activity.

For example, diabetes is a disease that results from the failure of the cells of a part of the pancreas, known as the Islands of Langerhans, to change superfluous glucose into glycogen and store it for future use.   This process is the job of the hormone.

There are ductless glands throughout the body, and for health they must produce the appropriate amount of the chemical peculiar to each.

The activities of these glands are affected by the sympathetic nervous system: they respond to external stimuli, such as anger, fear, shock, and so on.

The importance of the role of the endocrine glands can be seen in truly dramatic form in cases of hypothyroidism; that is, lack of the thyroid hormone.   Before treatment the eyes of the patient bulge and he will display other physical and even mental and emotional symptoms.   Corrected by the artificial supply of the deficient hormone, the physical and all other symptoms at once vanish; to reappear only if treatment is stopped.

Schlapp's mechanistic theory of criminality rejects the biological and environmental hypotheses as causations, and, excluding the categories enumerated above, attributes all crime to defective bodily function.   The body is viewed as a mechanism that reacts chemically, automatically, and may be conditioned by the artificial correction of defects.

The " criminal imperative " is seen as the impulsion to the criminal act as the result of forces purely material; no weakness of the will, no *mens rea*, or evil intent, but the inevitable and predictable consequence that follows in obedience to physicochemical laws.

An example of how the endocrinologist can predict the trend towards crime of a gland case is cited by Schlapp in his book *The New Criminology*.

V

Arnold Anderson was the second of five children, the son of a pious Brooklyn tailor in a small way of business.   The other children were superior types, and the atmosphere of the home was religious.

A thorough investigation of the family history disclosed no evidence of hereditary taint. The history of the lad disclosed no contamination through environment, early emotional shock, or other adverse experience.

Yet Arnold Anderson became a criminal, and the moment arrived when Professor Schlapp, giving evidence at the trial of this youth for burglary, prophesied for him the terrible fate that, lacking treatment for gland deficiency, the burglar would end as a murderer.

VI

As a child Arnold Anderson was a solitary. As a small boy of four he was a persistent thief of sweets and other pleasant edibles. He began to stay away from home, and by the age of nine did so for quite long periods.

His behaviour was erratic. He would behave properly for weeks, and would then break out again. After each outbreak and the reproaches of his pious father, he showed signs of remorse. His father punished the boy, but never excessively, and only with the view to his good. But by the time Arnold was ten years old he was too much for his parents, and they sent him to the Truants' School, from which, after a time, he was discharged uncured.

Home again, Arnold began to behave badly, as before. He stayed out and went about with bad companions. Presently he appeared in Brooklyn Juvenile Court. The judge sent the boy to Professor Schlapp. He was then only thirteen.

The diagnosis was the defective functioning of many glands, in particular the suprarenal. There was also detected a tendency towards homosexuality.

The treatment consisted of sedatives and gland extracts. For this purpose attendance at the clinic was necessary. After two months Arnold got tired of it. He threw the pills away and stopped taking the treatment.

Soon after this the boy ran away again, joined forces with a vagabond stranger, and landed up in a Home of Refuge.

He then became a burglar, was caught, and sent to Sing Sing prison.

After serving his sentence he committed another burglary, was again caught, and sentenced to five years' imprisonment.

In prison he made strange false confessions. He was again sent to Professor Schlapp.

Arnold Anderson was then brought before the court, following the investigation of the false confessions, and once more Professor Schlapp gave evidence. He stressed the following points: that the youth was an *emotional* criminal of a dangerous type; that his glandular disease was progressive; that unless he was forced to take treatment in prison he would proceed from crimes' against property to murder.

The folly of keeping such a case in prison was stressed, and the dire consequences that might be predicted from a place where already the youth had learnt so much evil.

This plea, however, fell upon deaf ears.

Arnold Anderson was released in April 1924. In August of that year he broke into an apartment in Jersey City, was intercepted by the householder, a real-estate dealer, whom he shot and killed.

He was caught, tried, convicted, and condemned to death. He had confessed to his pious father, who had—after, one may well believe, a fearful inner conflict—denounced his son.

Public opinion being against the death sentence, Arnold Anderson was sentenced to life imprisonment.

VII

Could appropriate treatment have saved this young criminal from further crime, and so have saved the life of his victim?

Perhaps the answer to that question is implicit in the case of James Blank, who also came into Professor Schlapp's clinic.

James Blank served in the Navy in World War I, and had experience of a submarine attack. After the War he got employment as a Wall Street broker's clerk. He lived with and supported his mother. They were able to live only by the strictest economy.

Presently James Blank became friendly with a man who was

a professional crook, though James did not know this.   Little by little his loyalty to his employer was undermined, until he was persuaded that he could justify the theft of the firm's money for a " cert " known to his tempter.

One day he was sent to the Bank to draw out 1,000 dollars. He did not return, and passed the money to his " friend."

Taxed by his employer with the theft, he confessed what he had done.   He was forgiven and kept on, under an arrangement whereby he should make restitution over a period of time.

Though this composition of the wrong was an act of kindness, its effect was to increase the economic pressure which had been the original cause of the crime.

Now worry obsessed the wretched man.   He could not sleep, but walked the floor at night, churning over his problem. Sometimes he failed to turn up for work; sometimes he refused food.

At that time there were many hold-ups in New York.   These were prominently featured in the Press and were the subject of talk.

One morning James Blank left the apartment where he lived with his mother, but did not go down to Wall Street.   Outside a garage he saw a piece of iron pipe lying on the ground.   He picked it up and, holding it behind him, went into a pawnbroker's shop.

The pawnbroker was called to answer the telephone, thus turning his back on the shop, whereupon he was struck down by a blow from the iron pipe.

Having done this senseless thing, the foolish assailant lost his nerve completely, threw the weapon down, and dashed out of the shop.

He was easily captured, and duly brought up in court. There, since there seemed to be something strange about him, he was referred to Professor Schlapp's clinic.

Carbohydrate tolerance tests showed a high pathological curve; oxygen consumption was abnormally high.   He was given appropriate treatment for these glandular deficiencies, and soon gave normal test reactions.

The emotional disturbances now subsided, and after some

part of his sentence had been served, James Blank was put on parole. He gave no further evidence of criminal impulse, and was regarded as successfully cured.

In the above causes it would appear that the abnormal functioning of the glands, and the effect both of deficiency and correction by hormone treatment, suggest the mechanical view of the body as an entity that responds automatically to physical and chemical forces.

As with the doctrine of Freud of the sexual etiology of many forms of psychological imbalance, this mechanistic theory of man is one that is instinctively rejected because it is unflattering, not to say, humiliating; and again because, by implication, it rules out so much that has become precious to mankind in religion, ethics, and philosophy.

VIII

" The great mother of all living," wrote Professor Schlapp, " has been at work countless millions of years upon her machines. With the tyranny of Time for her ally, she has had infinite hours for her labour, constructing everything, from fly-traps to Pleiades. Perhaps if we can muster enough detachment and impartiality we may yet be overtaken by the discovery that she concentrated her mechanical wizardry in the fabrication of our noble selves."

In the quarter of a century which has passed since the above words were written the science of endocrinology seems to have gone further towards the idea of man as machine, what time the new science of cybernetics produces machines that acquire, more and more, the attributes of man, the thinking reed.

But it is not to be expected that there will be any general acceptance of the implications of much new knowledge concerning the role of the body's chemistry in determining character and conduct. For man, caught up between heaven and earth, has need to regard himself as a creature of flesh and blood apart from the lower animals, as a well-ordered organism, or one not so well ordered, but, in any case, captained by a soul.

IX

The appearance of a " black sheep " in the family has long been something of a riddle of heredity, to be accounted for, perhaps, by some quirk of the genes or the chromosomes in the germ-cells.

Why should worthy parents with a happy brood produce a criminal type? Why should families with excellent histories suddenly be plunged in shame by the appearance out of the same stock of some blackguard or irreclaimable criminal?

There is an aspect of Schlapp's theory which offers a possible explanation of the " black sheep " of the biologically sound family.

As we have seen, he holds that the correction of glandular defects and deficiencies can be brought about by the artificial use of gland extracts. And he goes further by suggesting that those defects are present because of defective chemical conditions in the body of the mother during the period of gestation. In short, the criminal is made what he is destined to become in his mother's womb; the period of gestation is the point of departure, not the ancestral rootstock.

Thus, one might have a mother producing four healthy children during pregnancies completed in good health, but thereafter, suffering a chemical imbalance, fail to pass to a fifth child the blood and lymph necessary for a healthy new life.

It is put forward merely as an idea—an idea that may account for that odd black sheep that has broken so many parental hearts.

CHAPTER SIX

Wertham: *The Show of Violence*

HYPOTHESIS: That the criminal may also be the victim

I

GINO, an Italian boy of seventeen, stabbed his mother to death in her bed in a New York tenement, inflicting thirty-two stab-wounds.

Asked what impelled him to do so terrible a thing, he replied without emotion: " Because she dishonoured my family."

At Gino's trial for murder Dr Fredric Wertham, a former Professor of Psychiatry at Johns Hopkins University and, at that time senior psychiatrist in the New York City Department of Hospitals, testified that Gino was insane by legal definition.

The jury accepted that diagnosis, and Gino was committed to a State asylum for the criminally insane.

When Gino said that he had killed his mother because she had dishonoured his family, he gave a reason that was not true, though it was the true reason for Gino when he gave it.

What was the real reason?

It was from this point that Dr Wertham began his search for the murderer's true motive.

Here was a case of matricide, a rare crime: what had the literature to say upon the subject? Curiously enough, very little. But in such cases as were unearthed there was found to exist a remarkable similarity of pattern. These matricides were nearly all young, all greatly attached to the mother slain; indifferent to girls. In each case the crimes were committed in the mother's bedroom, and with outstanding ferocity of attack: never by poison.

II

Gino's mother, after her husband's death, neglected her children, of whom Gino was the eldest, became the mistress of her brother-in-law, and of two other men.

53

The family had returned to Italy for a time, and there the father had died. Very soon Gino knew that his mother was sleeping with his uncle, Aiello. Gino was then eleven years of age and he understood the situation. He then made an oath: " God, I swear some day my right hand must be cut off at the wrist if I do not kill her some day! "

Gino went to his father's grave, kissed the earth, and swore: " Some day I will avenge your name, our name. Give me the strength to vindicate our honour! "

The happy days of his father's lifetime were done. Now the widow neglects the children. She beats Gino. When he is thirteen, the family return to New York. Other lovers soon occupy Gino's mother—first Cerretti, then Manello. The boy sees things, and he understands.

" I loved my mother before I knew all these things. Afterwards I never kissed her," he told Dr Wertham.

Now the boy dreams of his father, who comes, urging him to avenge his honour, albeit to do no violence.

All this, and much more, Gino told the psychiatrist long after the crime and the trial.

III

The interest of Gino's crime, psychologically considered—indeed, humanly considered as Dr Wertham traced it to its hidden emotional source—lies in the parallelism of its pattern with the Orestes legend; and also with many points of resemblance with Hamlet.

In the *Chœphoroe* and the *Eumenides*, the second and third plays of Æschylus's trilogy, Orestes goes, at the direction of Apollo, to avenge the murder of his father, Agamemnon, dishonoured by the crimes of his brother, Ægisthus and his wife Clytemnestra.

Orestes obeys, and kills his mother.

The points of resemblance between the Greek drama of the fifth century BC and the American tragedy of the twentieth century AD are remarkable, as Dr Wertham shows.

Orestes goes to his father's grave: Gino goes to his father's grave.

Orestes swears to avenge his father: Gino swears to avenge his father.

Orestes listens to the oracle of " Our father—I mean, not mine, but the great Sun god Apollo." Gino listens to his father's commands in his dreams.

Orestes defends his crime by reference to his duty to his fellow citizens. Gino said: " I think she [his mother] deserved it."

Orestes said: " I hate thee not, thy sin destroyeth thee." Gino said: " That is God. He made her pay."

Orestes contemplated suicide, but refrained. Gino did likewise.

IV

Was the motive of Gino's crime, tendered by him to Dr Wertham after his trial and conviction, the true one; or was it a rationalization, and something quite different from a five-years' conscious urge to avenge his father's honour?

Long after this tragedy of a New York tenement had faded from public memory, the real motive of Gino's terrible crime (and that of Orestes?) was uncovered by the questing psychiatrist as an obsession with incestuous fancies and desires.

There are in the literature of psycho-analysis and psychiatric investigation many brilliant analyses. But in the *Dark Legend*, the story of Gino, the loving matricide, Dr Wertham has added to literature a study as revealing and important as Freud's uncovering of the Œdipus situation.

Since matricide is so rare a crime, Gino's case, and Dr Wertham's brilliant unravelling of its secret significance, might do no more than demonstrate the psychological truth that informs the great Greek tragedies; namely, that escape from the intolerable situation is by the dark, predestined path of crime.

In another case—that of a simple woman who kills her two small children—Dr Wertham notices the points of similarity with the Greek tragedy, Euripides' *Medea*. But here, it seems, the parallel is far less striking than in the case of the boy Gino.

V

One fine day in the Spring of 1941 Mrs Y set out to picnic on Bear Mountain with her two small sons. Mrs Y was a devoted mother who kept her sons clean and, as one neighbour put it, " sees that they eat good." The home consisted of a tenement room five feet by seven. Life was hard for Mrs Y, and more than once she had asked for help from the City Welfare Department. She complained that the two boys " were driving her nuts."

Had Mrs Y been a bad mother the city authorities would have acted; but she was a good mother and there was, therefore, no ground to justify taking over the care of the two boys.

Out on Bear Mountain, Mrs Y found a pleasant clearing for a picnic, and there she killed both boys with an axe. Having murdered both her children Mrs Y returned quietly home.

At her trial, Dr Wertham gave evidence for the defence. He testified that Mrs Y was sane in law, but he pleaded for clemency on the ground of emotional stresses and hardship. Feeling against Mrs Y ran high; but the court passed the minimum sentence, and later Mrs Y, deemed to be no longer a menace, was released on parole. She at once turned to the man who had put the circumstances of her case, from the psychological viewpoint, before the court.

Why did this woman, who had killed her two children, turn to the psychiatrist? Perhaps, because more than anything else, she needed friendship, as do many for whom life has proved too difficult.

Mrs Y found Dr Wertham in a small basement below the church house of St Philip's Church, Harlem. It was a low-ceilinged and windowless place, cut up by movable partitions into cubicles. Into one of these the paroled murderess followed the tall, white-coated doctor.

" Well, how are things going Mrs Y? " he asked, as one might inquire after the health of one absent.

" I'm starting a new life, Doctor," Mrs. Y replied.

" Is your work hard?"

" Oh, no. I worked in gaol, too. But I have to learn to be with people again."

The Lefargue Clinic was not opened in its modest basement quarters in Harlem primarily to give after-care to criminals. It was founded in the face of official obstruction and professional indifference to give psychiatric facilities to the people of New York's Negro Ghetto. Thus an interview between psychiatrist and murderess was unusual, an experience unlikely to occur twice. But the potential criminal, the potential murderer, too, now and then casts his twenty-five cents into the plate provided for " voluntary subscriptions "—or, if in need of bus fare, takes what he needs—and shuffles behind the screens into one of the small treatment cubicles, there to unburden himself to a patient and understanding listener.

What forces produce the potential killer?

Dr Wertham postulates three conditions: the negative emotion, the death wish, the catalyst.[1] There is also the personality as a whole; what Dr Goring might have referred to as the " murder diathesis ".

Pushkin's two characters in the play *Mozart and Salieri* are seen by this psychiatrist as apposite in this connection. For Mozart life and music were one: for Salieri the achievement of supreme virtuosity was the be-all and end-all. And so his life narrowed down to a single, all-consuming ambition, and thus envy led on to murder.

The cases of Gino and of Mrs Y reveal how great crimes, seemingly impulsive, frenetic, may be the culmination of a long period of incubation.

" Nothing," wrote Dr Wertham, " has a longer preparation than the impulsive act." This may appear a paradox, but common experience bears it out.

Murder is often seen as an act of this quality. So, too, is religious conversion, as Starbuck has shown in his *Psychology of Religion*. In both cases the overt act is the fruit of a long seed-time.

The practical question is this: Can the traveller who sets

[1] Catalysis: a change, as in a chemical reaction, by the presence of a substance which itself undergoes no change: in crimes of violence, alcohol, poverty, easy access to a weapon.

out upon the road to Mycenæ—that road which ends in the murder of mother or child, or of any fellow creature—be halted and turned back? Can the mirror of Psyche, that reflects for the potential murderer the secret truth concerning the masked motive which impels to the deed, be held up by the psychiatrist before the fatal moment of catharsis? Had the boy Gino understood, would he have struck: had Mrs Y not encountered the intolerable situation, would she have killed the two sons she loved?

Or we may put these questions in another form and ask: What can society do for those seen to be heading for spiritual disaster; what is the culpability of that society which fails to act?

VI

The Lefargue Clinic is a small organization. It operates without State or municipal financial aid. It is staffed by lay and medical volunteer workers, White and Coloured, among the former, Dr Hilde Mosse, a well-known woman psychiatrist. Compared with the London Tavistock Clinic, or with the Institute for the Study and Treatment of Delinquency, this Harlem centre of mental healing may seem of small account. Yet its work must be rated as altogether disproportionate to its modest size. It is a clinic for psychological healing; it is also a field research station for the study of social evils, poverty, ignorance, racial discrimination. The clinic acts also as a sieve that catches the potential criminal and so saves him from himself. Out of this work has already come a terrifying study of one evil, the " crime Comic," *The Seduction of the Innocent.*

In Dr Wertham's opinion nearly all murders committed by the insane and by sex maniacs, could be prevented, since these are types that are recognizable long before the commission of their crimes. " Instead of quibbling about insanity after the event," he wrote, " we should provide treatment or guidance before."

In the concluding chapter of his *The Show of Violence*, Dr Wertham writes:

" The real problem is prevention.   That requires not only
the changing of man but the changing of conditions, the modification not only of individual impulses but of social institutions
and rationalizations.   The question is not only why one does
it but how one justifies it to oneself.   The dangers of violence
that threaten us come not from the heads of individuals but
from social circumstances.   Murder is an embolus.   The
disease lies elsewhere.   It is not a matter of episodic violence,
but of a continuous violation of the principle of the dignity and
value of human life.   Actually in our society respect for
human life is only a professed theoretical ideal.   We must
vigorously remove the obstacles that prevent it from becoming
a practical reality."

VII

Dr Wertham holds that the psychiatrist must understand
the patient's personal and biological history, if he is to uncover
what he calls the *micro-dynamic* factor, by which is meant the
inter-personal relationships of an individual, his family, his
employer, fellow workers, and associates; and the *macro-
dynamic* relationships, by which is meant the relationships of
patients to their particular group, and that group's relationship
to society in general.

In the case of the American Negro it is the racial group that
constitutes the chief factor of its members' attitude to society
as a whole.   And though at times the harshness of life stimu-
lates a perfervid religiosity that seeks the solace of an anthro-
pomorphic god and a heaven of fish frys, it more often produces
neuroses, psychoses, and criminality.

Is the high incidence of crime in Harlem due to qualities
inherent in the Negro character?

The verdict of the Lefargue Clinic is that this is not so.

" Discrimination and poverty," says Dr Wertham, " cause
as much mental confusion and neuroses as the bewilderment of
possessing several million dollars.   The exploitation of racial
groups is a much more serious cause of disorder in the development of personality than sexual maladjustment or similar factors
stressed in the text-books."

E

Harlem offers material almost unique for the field study of sociology, and for the psychological investigation of the effects, in terms of misery, mental sickness, and crime, of men, women, and children subjected to group segregation and discrimination.

A group of Negro children were asked who were kind and who unkind to them?

" It's only the plain Americans who are unkind," was the unanimous, but mystifying reply.

" And who are the plain Americans? " they were asked.

" The ones that aren't Poles, Italians, Germans, Dutch, Jews, or Roman Catholics," was the disconcerting reply.

Harlem is overcrowded, and its coloured people are riddled with tuberculosis. It is cursed by unemployment, poverty, crime, vice, and—not least as evil—superstition. There are over two hundred so-called Spiritualist " churches " offering true messages from the departed for ten cents a session; and on the crowded sidewalks quacks offer love potions and wonder-working talismans for dimes. It is a rich quarry for the psychologist investigating the effects of racial group segregation and discrimination upon those subjected to these forms of injustice and inhumanity.

VIII

In the Lefargue Clinic the reactions of men and women and children to this racial bias against them is being broken up into case-histories. The techniques used are not academic, but practical, and one of the first considerations of those giving treatment is to convince many anti-social patients, and potentially anti-social patients, that this floating hostility arises, not from prejudice or any other genuine belief in the inferiority of the Negro, but for reasons of economic exploitation. This, it has been found, lessens hostility, and thus brakes the tendency of maladjustment to culminate in acts of aggression.

In the Lefargue Clinic the youthful patient ranks as the most important, for Harlem's 400,000 people provide 53 per cent of all Manhattan's juvenile delinquents—and Manhattan has a population of 1,600,000.

Dr Wertham cites the address given by an eminent criminal

lawyer to the American Society of Medical Jurisprudence. The speaker sketched what one might term the "chain reaction" that culminates in the act of murder.

Thus: an adolescent likes to have a girl; in order to have a proper standing with her, he has to have a car. He steals one. To entertain her, he needs money. He sees all round him false prototypes of what a real girl wants.

He learns about guns. He shoots.

IX

A bright-looking boy of fourteen is brought to the Clinic.

"Do you think your stealing had anything to do with the comic books?" he is asked.

"Oh, no," comes the quick reply; "in the comic books it's mostly murder."

A bright boy of ten is asked: "What do you want to be when you grow up?"

"I want to be a sex maniac," he replies.

A youth of seventeen sits facing the doctor. He has been referred to the Clinic by the Juvenile Aid Bureau, for though the municipality of New York does not support the Lefargue Clinic, social welfare organizations and the courts frequently turn to it for help.

This lad has stabbed a boy of thirteen.

"Do you read many comics?" he is asked.

"Oh, no," he protests, "I don't read many comic books. I like crime comics. . . . Sometimes they kill the girl."

Now it is a worried mother.

"My boy," she complains, "used to be a good boy, but lately he's been playing hookey. . . ."

"Where is he now?"

"Outside."

"Let me have a talk with him."

The boy comes in. He, too, has complaints.

"Ma makes me stay in the house or on the porch . . . the other fellers have started calling me a sissy."

"And you're not a sissy, are you?"

"Course not. I play hookey more'n any of 'em. . . ."

" You're going to show them, aren't you? "

" You bet, Doc."

For all such this so eminently practical psychiatrist has his own particular kind of group therapy. It is the Hookey Club, out of whose cogitations it gradually emerges that playing hookey is a stupid proceeding.

Such boys are often at the point of departure for delinquency, their progress being somewhat like this: hookey, petty theft, window-smashing, the gang, a sex escapade, and so on.

A thwarted boy, an over-anxious mother: no long-term psycho-analysis for these. For the boy's frustration the simple remedy of Scouts, a summer camp, a creative hobby, plus some insight given into the mainsprings of foolish actions. How splendid, how moving a thing is compassion in action! How precious when the compassionate one has knowledge that heals.

X

In England there has been a certain complacency in the contemplation of this great American problem, and much criticism of the injustices perpetrated against the citizen of colour.

Now, with the steady arrival of large numbers of Jamaican Negroes in search of work, England will soon have to face the social and economic challenge of a Negro racial group.

Already the pattern is taking shape, and, as it does so, it approximates to the American pattern; namely, the unofficial hostility of organized labour to the Negro worker, and the unadmitted social ostracism suffered by him *unless he has ample means*, which is very, very seldom.

In England, if his numbers increase, the Negro is likely to encounter that handicap which arises from free-floating hostilities, from frustrations, poverty, and overcrowding.

If the Negro in England turns—as the streets of London's West End suggest he is already turning—from honest work to become pimp and whoremaster, where should be laid the ultimate blame?

" The Negro," observes Dr Wertham, " has to be shown

that he must have the will to survive in a hostile world; otherwise he will be sunk by hopelessness, social fear, worry, frustration, and the extremes of poverty."

He will also, in those circumstances, make a disproportionately high contribution to the criminal elements of society.

XI

Violence is as contagious as measles, says Dr Wertham. And among the young it is on the increase today on both sides of the Atlantic.

A twelve-year-old New York boy kills his young sister.

A thirteen-year-old boy operates as a burglar and carries a gun.

A New York public school has to be patrolled by two policemen to prevent violence.

A schoolmaster has to have a policeman in the classroom during examinations.

Three youths set out on a winter's night in New York to " hunt bums." They find a Negro vagrant asleep on a park bench. They apply lighted cigarettes to his bare feet, beat him up, throw him into the Hudson to drown.

None of these three was found to be sub-normal; one, indeed, was of superior intelligence. But all had been nurtured on that literature which is, in Dr Wertham's phrase, "the pornography of violence."

In Britain the same trends are discernible.

In London a gang of boys drag a little girl of fourteen into a dark passage and violate her.

Gangs of Teddy Boys terrorize local cinema audiences, carrying such weapons as razor-blades, cycle chains, and daggers: and using them.

Two youths, one an epileptic, shoot it out with the police on a roof, and one is hanged, though he was not the one who fired the shot.

A gang of Teddy Boys raid a club that has been organized and is run for precisely such young people as themselves. They smash up the furniture and terrorize the occupants.

A boy of sixteen, before the Juvenile Court, unwatched for a moment, throws himself from the balcony in the court-house and kills himself.

In all these cases there is present the element of violence, but there also is frustration, lack of leadership, and the example of a world given over to violence and talk of it.

SUMMARY

Though Lombroso's positivism is now mainly discredited, he remains the father of criminology, since he was the first man of science to study the criminal rather than the crime. He thus stimulated scientific interest in the right direction, though retarding it by an untenable theory of criminal man.

The examination of the respective roles of heredity and environment in the production of criminality now points to the former as the paramount factor in the formation of the " criminal diathesis." The criminal is merely the inferior man.

Modern criminological research is concerned with the mind, emotions, body chemistry, personal and family history of the criminal.

Research also suggests that the integration of the individual into the group, and the group into the community, are essential if psychological maladjustment, which may proceed from mental suffering to crime, is to be checked.

As postscript, that there are criminal types, the so-called " monsters," who suggest that there may be such a thing as a " spiritual deficiency disease " which condemns the victim to pass beyond the realms of good and evil into an outer spiritual night.

PART TWO

THE CRIMINAL: CAN HE BE CURED?

CHAPTER SEVEN

Beccaria: *Of Crimes and Punishments*

HYPOTHESIS: That pleasure and pain are the sole springs of action

I

ON the evening of October 13, 1761, Jean Calas, grocer and Protestant—that is to say, Huguenot—of Toulouse, sat down with his family to the simple evening meal of an austere household. The set table was candle-lit, the atmosphere sombre.

The Calas shop, in the rue des Filatiers, with its barrels and bins and shining brass scales, was closed. The double doors between shop and warehouse had been made fast and all business for the day was done.

The shadow of fear is long, and it lay, day and night, upon the Protestant grocer's family like an unmerited curse.

About the table there were seated Jean Calas, aged sixty-four, his wife, Anne Rose, nearing fifty—she was a distant relative of Montesquieu—and two of their three sons. Marc Antoine, the eldest, aged twenty-nine, who, though qualified as an advocate, was precluded from practice, since he lacked the requisite priest's certificate attesting due performance of his Catholic duties; and Pierre, the younger son, who was an apprentice. There was also present a guest, M. Lavaysse, a friend of the eldest son.

The youngest son, Louis, was absent, for he had elected to leave his father's house—that of a heretic—on being converted to Rome by an aged servant.

Jean Calas had been a citizen of Toulouse for some forty years. His character was without blemish, other than his detested heresy, that is to say; but with his family he suffered the disabilities, the odium, and the hatred that were the portion of a Protestant family in eighteenth-century Catholic France.

The Calas family had few friends, for the Protestant community was small. Neighbours bought in the shop, for people will go where they are honestly served, but there was little neighbourliness and not a little hostility against the heretic family.

II

On this particular evening the customary sober atmosphere of the Calas *ménage* was more marked than usual, for Marc Antoine had given way to one of the moods of depression which overwhelmed him from time to time since he had been debarred from the practice of the law. He had become a melancholy figure behind the counter of his father's shop.

The night outside for these socially isolated people must have been peopled with the intangible images of a hostile world. But in that small candle-lit room there could have been no forebodings of impending tragedy, nor of the long-drawn-out Calvary that lay before the heretic grocer and his family when Marc Antoine pushed back his chair, abandoned an unfinished meal, and went silently into the adjoining kitchen. It probably seemed merely that his moods were getting worse.

In the kitchen the servant quizzed the young master curiously.

"Is it, then, cold in there?" she was heard to ask. "Are you cold?"

"No, no, I am not cold. I am burning! Burning!" he was heard to reply.

The meal continued in silence. Then presently M. Lavaysse —a trifle uneasy, perhaps—remarked on his friend's long absence.

"Why does he not return?" he asked.

"He has probably gone to play billiards," suggested his father. "He often plays, and that is, no doubt, the simple explanation."

Presently M. Lavaysse rose to go.

"I will light you through the shop," said Pierre, taking up a candle from the table.

A moment later the older people heard their voices.

" But this is very strange! " Pierre was heard to ex-
claim.

" The shop door is open, and I most certainly left it shut! "

" Let us go in," M. Lavaysse suggested.

Holding the candle aloft, Pierre entered the shop, followed by
M. Lavaysse.

In the uncertain light shed by the candle he saw that the
folding doors between shop and warehouse, which he had left
shut, were now open.

From one was suspended the body of his brother, Marc
Antoine.

The young men would not allow Madame Calas to enter
the shop.   They cut the suicide down and M. Lavaysse ran for
the Sieur Camoire, the surgeon.

Evil tidings travel fast.   Before M. Lavaysse returned with
the surgeon a crowd had collected outside the shop, and, as
though they had been awaiting the event, the Sieur de
Beaudrique, the *Capitoul*, or magistrate, and his assistant were
already at the door.

The crowd was hostile, the magistrate suspicious.

The body of Marc Antoine now lay on the floor of the shop.

" How did he come by his death? " demanded the
magistrate.   " Answer! "

But the Calas family, grief-stricken, secretly ashamed of the
act of their son, were evasive, curiously reticent.   It was their
fatal mistake.

Only an accusation was required to put in motion the
machinery of the law: it came, as a voice from the crowd.

" Marc Antoine has been murdered by his father because he
intended to embrace the true faith! "

It was enough.

The whole Calas family, the servant, and M. Lavaysse,
were immediately put under arrest and hustled through the
hostile crowd—for whom they were already guilty—to the
lock-up.

A few days later, while Jean Calas was suffering the first
of many tortures to be inflicted on him, the body of Marc
Antoine, the pathetic suicide, was borne with pomp through

the streets of Toulouse to the Cathedral of St Stephen, followed by 20,000 of the faithful.

Was not this an unfortunate young man who had met his death at the hands of his heretic father, and so died for the true faith he had just embraced?

III

Jean Calas was put upon his trial before the *parlement* of Toulouse, and by a majority vote of seven to six convicted of murder and sentenced to death.

Already horribly tortured in futile attempts to extort a confession from him, Jean Calas was now sentenced to have his bones broken and his body stretched on the wheel until death. This torture the poor man endured for no less than two hours before expiring.

How, then, on the facts, easily established, could a conviction have been secured against the heretic grocer?

The short answer is: only by what Voltaire called " the jurisprudence of the Inquisition."

It was, in effect, the total usurpation by the ecclesiastical body of the function properly belonging to the civil judicature.

Under this system it was possible, and it happened frequently, that an accused was induced by torture to make false confession, or was tortured to death, unconfessing.

Judges and magistrates acted as prosecuting counsel in trials that were secret, on charges secretly brought against the accused, who had no legal aid, and who was subjected during trial to torture.

There was no burden of proof upon the prosecution, as proof is understood in the criminal courts of our time. Truth, as the end-object to be sought, had no place whatsoever in the eighteenth-century criminal courts of any State in Europe; while in France, land of logicians, it was regarded as a sort of entity, or unit, that could be assembled from fractions making up the whole.

Thus, a rumour might be deemed to be one-eighth of the truth, a witness's opinion a quarter, the completion of the unit being held sufficient to justify conviction.

It was by such means that Jean Calas was tried and condemned, ostensibly, for the murder of his son, actually for the " crime " of heresy.

Were the Calas case no more than an example of judicial methods in eighteenth-century France it would have only an historic interest today. But it is much more than that. It is an example of the extent to which a society can deviate from the upright administration of justice when prejudice and passion rule.

Even as this book is being written the United States offers the world an example of the same evil forces in action. For there a White citizen has been sentenced to a ferocious term of imprisonment for aiding and abetting a Negro family in the " crime " of acquiring a freehold home in a quarter exclusively White. The indictment, however, did not define the offence so simply.

IV

In France the evils of the criminal law and the inhumanity of punishments moved noble minds in protest. There, in a group of liberal thinkers, Voltaire, D'Alembert, Diderot, and Buffon were outstanding.

Even so, it was from Lombardy that there came the greatest single contribution to the cause of reform and humanity—namely, the Marchese di Beccaria's treatise, *Of Crimes and Punishments*.

This seminal work cleared the air of long-established error by a concise statement of first principles, to which its remarkable author added concrete proposals for remedies. Within a few years, translated into no fewer than twenty-six languages, this small treatise had completely transformed the climate of opinion concerning the nature of justice and the true purposes of punishment throughout the civilized world.

In France, Beccaria's treatise crowned the labours of the French reformers, of whom he wrote: " I owe everything to French books. They were the first to stir up in my mind feelings of humanity, which had been stifled by eight years of a fanatical education."

In particular Beccaria paid tribute to Montesquieu's *The Spirit of Laws*, whose author spent no less than twenty years upon it. He was also, no doubt, familiar with the *Persian Letters* that so pleased the Pope that he offered Montesquieu and his family perpetual dispensation from all fasting, concerning which an amusing story is told.

Presented with the bill for the customary fees, the thrifty Frenchman declined to pay. "The Pope is an honest man," he said; "his word is enough for me, and I hope it will be enough for my Maker." Having said which, he handed back the parchment and the bill which had been offered with it.

Beccaria's treatise coloured the revolutionary code in France, and in England it greatly influenced Bentham and Romilly, and was examined with astonished admiration by Blackstone.

In Russia, the Empress Catherine II came under Beccaria's influence; while Peter Leopold II, Grand Duke of Tuscany, put down *Dei Delitti e delle Pene* ("Of Crimes and Punishments") to issue a decree abolishing capital punishment in his Duchy.

It is a common dictum that no man can escape from the framework of his age; yet Beccaria not only did that, but may be said, in some respects, to have been ahead of our own.

V

Yet Beccaria's treatise might easily have been still-born, for it was originally written without thought of publication, and only as some part of a very extensive survey undertaken by him as mathematician and social thinker, with a group of like-minded friends, into the social and political questions of the time.

In 1762, under pressure from his friends, Beccaria agreed to publication; but on condition of anonymity.

In eighteenth-century Lombardy the critic of existing institutions published at his peril; and Beccaria was not of the stuff of martyrs.

Two years later, D'Alembert received from Frisi, an Italian Liberal friend, a copy of *Dei Delitti* in Italian. Though at that date the authorship was still unacknowledged, the French mathematician recognized the treatise as a work of the greatest importance as an indictment of the criminal laws and of the barbarous methods of punishment, and, even more important, as a lucid statement of first principles.

Following the execution of Jean Calas in 1762, D'Alembert had been closely associated with Voltaire in a campaign to clear the name of the judicially murdered Protestant grocer, and to secure compensation for his family. He therefore sent a copy of *Dei Delitti* to Voltaire, upon whom it made an impression equally profound.

In 1766, Beccaria was persuaded to acknowledge authorship. He was astonished at the great noise his small book had made in the world.

Three years had then yet to pass before Voltaire's campaign secured the annulment of the verdict of the Toulouse *parlement* against Jean Calas and 30,000 *livres* compensation for the family. But it so happened that Beccaria's work came into Voltaire's hands at his home in Ferney at a moment when he was deeply moved by a judicial crime committed in his near neighbourhood. He was, therefore, in a frame of mind to read it with special interest.

We know from Voltaire himself that it was this tragedy that moved him to write his Commentary on Beccaria's treatise— one equal in length to the book itself.

" Having read," he wrote, " with infinite satisfaction the little book on Crimes and Punishments, which in morality, as in medicine, may be compared to one of those few remedies capable of alleviating our sufferings, I flattered myself that it would be a means of softening the remains of barbarism in the laws of many nations; I hoped for some reformation in mankind, when I was informed that, within a few miles of my abode, they had just hanged a girl of eighteen, beautiful, well made, accomplished, and of a very reputable family.

" She was culpable of having suffered herself to be got with child, and also of having abandoned her infant. This unfortunate girl, fleeing her father's house, is taken in labour, and without assistance is delivered of her burden by the side of a wood.

" Shame, which in the sex is a powerful passion, gave her

strength to return home and to conceal her situation. She left her child exposed; it is found the next morning; the other is discovered, condemned, and executed.

" The first fault of this unhappy victim ought to have been concealed by the family, or rather claimed the protection of the laws, because it was incumbent on her seducer to repair the injury he had done, because weakness hath a right to indulgence; because concealing her pregnancy may endanger life, because declaring her condition destroys her reputation, and because the difficulty of providing for her infant is a great additional misfortune.

" But because a child is dead, is it absolutely necessary to kill the mother? . . . Where charity is wanting, the law is always cruel."

This judicial atrocity was brought home in a peculiarly intimate way to Voltaire, for he had taken into his home and had adopted an impoverished girl, Renie Philiberte de Varicourt—his well-beloved " Belle et Bonne."

On the Calas case alone Voltaire published no fewer than five closely argued pamphlets, and between the years 1762 and 1777 at least twenty-one papers came from his pen in defence of individuals falsely convicted in the priest-ridden courts.

Voltaire's Commentary gave Beccaria's *Dei Delitti* a final imprimatur: both book and author were famous.

VI

Much of *Dei Delitti* has ceased to have importance for the modern penologist or reformer, since many of the evils against which Beccaria wrote, in particular judicial torture, no longer exist in any civilized State. Many of the evils attacked by Beccaria were abolished, or first recognized as such, within a short time of the publication of *Dei Delitti*, and as a direct consequence of it. But the principles laid down remain as valid now as then, since they are principles for all time, flowing from his first general proposition that the end object of all laws is the greatest happiness of the greatest number.

The characteristic extracts that follow show how well

Beccaria's theory of crimes and punishments have worn. They might have been formulated in our own time. They have been selected, condensed, from that part of the treatise which has value and importance for our own time.

Laws are the conditions under which men, naturally independent, unite themselves in societies. They sacrifice one part of liberty for peace and security, vesting the sum of the liberties of the individual in the hands of the sovereign in whom are vested sanctions against trespasses.

Every punishment which does not arise from absolute necessity is tyrannical.

Every act of authority of one man over another, for which there is not absolute necessity, is tyrannical. It is upon this that the sovereign's right to punish crimes is founded.

Punishments are just in proportion as the liberty, preserved by the sovereign, is sacred and valuable.

No man ever gave up his liberty merely for the good of the public. Every individual wishes, if possible, to be exempt from the compacts that bind the rest of mankind.

Observe that by JUSTICE I understand nothing more than that bond which is necessary to keep the interests of individuals united, without which men would return to their original state of barbarity.

All punishments which exceed the necessity of preserving this bond are in their nature unjust.

The laws can only determine the punishment of crimes, and the authority of making penal laws can only reside with the legislator, who represents society united by the social contract.

If every individual be bound to society, society is equally bound to him by a contract which binds both parties. This obligation descends from the throne to the cottage. Its violation leads to anarchy.

Judges in criminal cases have no right to interpret the penal laws because they are not legislators. The sovereign is their lawful interpreter.

The office of the judge is to determine if an accused is guilty of an action contrary to the laws.

F

When the rule of right is a matter of controversy, not of fact, the people are the slaves of the judicature.

One would have everything to fear if tyrants were to read books: but tyrants never read.

Obscurity in the laws is an evil. It will be greater if the laws are written in a language unknown to the people.

Crimes will be less frequent as the code of laws is more universally read and understood.

It is not only the common interest that crimes should not be committed, but that crimes of every kind should be less frequent in proportion to the evil they produce on society.

Punishment should be greater in proportion as crimes are destructive of safety and happiness. Therefore, there ought to be a fixed proportion between crimes and punishments.

A scale of crimes should be formed of which the first degree should be those tending to the dissolution of society; the last, of the smallest possible injustice done to an individual.

Any action not included in the above scale will not constitute a crime.

The history of nations and their laws show that the ideas of virtue and vice, the good or bad citizen, change with the revolution of ages.

The passions and vices of one age are the foundations of the morality of the following. Hence our uncertainty concerning the nature of honour and virtue.

Pleasure and pain are the only springs of action.

Men often with the best intentions do the greatest injury to society, and with the worst, do it the most effective service.

Public utility is the foundation of human justice.

Crimes concern the relations of man with man: *sins* those between God and man. Sin cannot determine the degree of crimes; if otherwise, man might punish where God would pardon; pardon what God condemns.

Crimes are to be estimated only by the injury done to society. They fall into three categories: those immediately destructive of society or its representatives; those that attack the private security of life, property, or the honour of individuals, and those that are contrary to laws made for the general good of the community.

The crime of the highest degree is high treason.

Every crime injures society, but every crime does not threaten its immediate destruction.

That the individual has the right to do anything not contrary to the laws is a sacred dogma without which there can be no lawful society. By this alone minds become free, active, and vigorous; by this alone is inspired that virtue that knows not fear.

Crimes against the person or against liberty are crimes of the highest degree; they include murder and robbery, whether perpetrated by private citizens or by those who abuse power in public office or by wealth.

Every member of society should know when he is a criminal and when not.

The purpose of punishment is not to torment the criminal nor undo his crime. The end of punishment is to deter others from like offence.

The appropriate punishment is that which makes the strongest and most lasting impression on the minds of others with the least suffering to the criminal.

The credibility of evidence is in proportion to the interests of the witness in declaring or concealing truths.

One witness against an accused is not sufficient; for while the accused denies while the other affirms, truth remains suspended, and the right that everyone has to be believed innocent turns in his favour.

The credibility of a witness is the less, as the atrocity of the crime is greater, from the improbability of its having been committed.

When the proofs of a crime, taken separately, prove nothing, or when all proofs are dependent upon one, the number of proofs neither increase nor diminish the probability of the fact; for the force of the whole is no greater than the force of that on which they depend. If this fails, all falls to the ground.

When the proofs are independent of each other, the probability of the fact increases.

Moral certainty is only probability. The certainty which is essential to decide guilt is that which determines every man in the most important transactions of his life.

It is an admirable law which ordains that every man shall be tried by his peers.

All trials should be public, so that opinion, the cement of society, may curb the authority of the powerful and the passions of the judge.

An oath administered to a criminal to secure truth involves a contradiction between the laws and human nature. As if a man could think himself obliged to contribute to his own destruction! For this reason oaths become a mere formality.

The swifter punishment follows crime, the more just and useful it will be. More just, since it will spare the criminal the pains of suspense.

All punishments should be contrived to have the maximum effect on others, with the minimum of suffering to the criminal.

An immediate punishment is best, since it brings close the two related ideas: *crime* and *punishment*, clearly seen as cause and effect.

The punishment should fit the crime in order that it may lead the mind of the criminal to consider the crime from a different point of view from that seen when it promised advantage to him.

Men do not in general commit great crimes deliberately, but in some sudden gust of passion, and seldom consider the punishment.

Crimes against the person merit corporal punishment. None should be exempt this law, for punishments should be assessed solely by the injury done society without reference to rank.

Robbery, unaccompanied by violence, should be punished by fine, since he who would enrich himself by the property of another should be deprived of some part of his own. In this case the appropriate punishment is the labour of the thief.

Robbery with violence should be punished by corporal punishment and forced labour.

Painful punishment should not be applied to fanatics who take pride in persecution: ridicule is the weapon against them.

Crimes are more effectually prevented by the *certainty* than by the *severity* of punishment.

The certainty of a small punishment will make a stronger impression than the fear of one more severe, but uncertain to follow upon the act.

Mankind is terrified at the approach of the smallest *inevitable* evil, but hope offsets apprehension of *the greater*, but *more remote*.

States with the harshest punishments for crime are those in which the most atrocious and bloody crimes are common. In them the hand of the lawmaker and the assassin share the same spirit of ferocity.

As punishments become more cruel, the minds of men grow hardened. It is enough if punishment demonstrates that the *evil* it occasions exceeds the *good* expected of the crime.

Human nature is limited, no less in evil than in good. Excessive barbarity can never be more than temporary.

Punishment of death is a war of a whole nation against a citizen whose destruction is considered necessary, or useful for the general good. It is neither useful nor necessary, save, when living, the criminal endangers the security of the State. Even then, only when a State is already in jeopardy.

The punishment of death has never deterred men from injuring society.

It is not the intenseness of pain that most affects the mind, but its continuance. Senses are more easily and powerfully affected by weak but repeated imperfections than by violent but transient impulse.

The death of a criminal is a terrible but a momentary spectacle, and less efficacious as deterrent than the continuing example of a man deprived of liberty and consigned to hard labour to repair the wrong done by him to society. "If I commit such a crime," ponders the spectator, "I shall be reduced to that miserable condition for the rest of my life."

That is a greater deterrent than death, held by all men in distant obscurity.

The severity of a punishment should be just sufficient to deter others.

The punishment of death is pernicious to society from the

example of barbarity it affords. Laws which are intended to moderate the ferocity of mankind, should not stimulate it by examples of barbarity.

Is it not absurd that the laws, which detest and punish homicide should, in order to prevent it, publicly commit murder themselves?

Almost all nations in all past ages have punished certain crimes with death; but the force of these examples vanishes when opposed to truth: the history of mankind is an immense sea of errors in which a few obscure truths may here and there be found.

Adultery is a crime which owes its existence to two causes, viz. pernicious laws and the powerful force of sex. There is a considerable difference between adultery and all other crimes. Adultery proceeds from an abuse of that necessity universal in human nature, one more ancient than societies. Unlike all other crimes, it does not tend to the destruction of society.

Conjugal fidelity is always greater as marriages are more numerous and less difficult.

To every crime that remains frequently unpunished, the punishment is an incentive: surmountable difficulties embellish the object, spur pursuit. The mind fixes itself upon the most agreeable aspect, avoiding every idea that disgusts.

Homosexuality is not the consequence of debauch, but of education. Schools where ardent youths are segregated from the other sex stimulate sex in a way useless to mankind.

It is better to prevent crimes than to punish them. This flows from the first principle of good laws that have as object the maximum happiness and the minimum of misery among men.

To prevent crimes laws should be clear and simple. They must be of benefit to all, and should be feared, but nothing else.

Would you prevent crime? Let liberty be attended by knowledge. A daring impostor, always a man of some genius, is adored by the ignorant, but despised by men of understanding.

A man of enlightened understanding, given judicial office, is the greatest blessing a sovereign can bestow on a nation.

Such a man is accustomed to behold Truth and not to fear it.

Another method of preventing crimes is to reward virtue. Upon this subject the laws of all nations are silent.

The coin of honour is inexhaustible and abundantly fruitful in the hands of a prince who distributes it wisely.

Finally, the most certain method of preventing crimes is to perfect education.

From what I have written results this general theorem: that a punishment may not be an act of violence, of the one, or the many, against a private member of society; it should be made public immediately, with the fewest possible details of the crime.

VII

The treatise from which the above extracts have been taken was written by a man twenty-six years of age who had no formal training in law or philosophy; who was, primarily, a fine mathematician, and an earnest student of social conditions.

What manner of man was this Lombard nobleman who had so tremendous an influence on his age, and from whom, after nearly three centuries, it is still possible for us to learn?

Cesare Bonesana, Marchese di Beccaria, came of a line of Church dignitaries, judges, and soldiers. He received his education in the Jesuit Academy of Parma, and reacted strongly from that rigid discipline.

The turning-point in his intellectual growth came when, at twenty-one, he read the *Persian Letters* of Montesquieu, who from that time forward was his hero, and to whom he refers as " the immortal Montesquieu " in the Introduction to *Dei Delitti*.

Beccaria became an admirer of the French Encyclopædists and a student of the institutions of his times, the laws, the social usages.

Lombardy was then under Spanish domination, and disfigured by licensed cruelty and corruption. With a group of like-minded young men, he formed the Accademia dei Pugni, a society which might be likened, perhaps, to the Fabian Society in our day.

Dei Delitti was originally written to be read in this small circle. It was translated into French by the Abbé Morellet. An invitation to visit Paris followed from the Encyclopædist group. Beccaria went, but because of his shyness, the visit was a failure. He could not bear to be a day away from the wife he adored.

Beccaria was probably a neurotic. His moods swung significantly between depression and elation. " My tyrant imagination," he complained, " does not allow me to enjoy the sights of nature or of art." Like Bentham, he shrank from the crowd, feared the rough-and-tumble of life.

It was, indeed, fear of the possible consequences to himself that led him to shield his work for two years under the cloak of anonymity. He gave that as his reason to his translator, the Abbé Morellet, when pressed by that friend to come out into the open.

" I must confess," he wrote to him, " that in the course of my writing I had before my eyes the examples of Machiavelli, Galileo, Giannone. I heard the noise of chains, shaken by superstition and fanaticism, stifling the utterances of truth. The vision of this horrible spectacle obliged me to veil sometimes the light with clouds. I was desirous of defending truth, without becoming myself a martyr."

Reformers always arouse hostility in the minds of the stupid and of those incapable of entertaining new ideas. Beccaria came in for his full share. *Dei Delitti* was condemned by the Church and by the legal profession in both Italy and France, its unfortunate author being berated as contumelious of the Church, a fanatic, a madman, and a seducer of the people.

No reasoned or well-argued reply came from legal critics, but abuse only. The great advocate, Muyart de Vouglans, denounced in violent and undignified language Beccaria's humanitarianism. He demanded not less, but more punishment, including, of course, torture.

As we shall presently see, a somewhat similar situation arose in England when Romilly was pressing for the reform of the criminal law and was opposed by a strange lawyer turned priest.

Despite much venom, *Dei Delitti* shed a light not easily put out. Its influence was profound, far-reaching. In England Blackstone, Romilly, and Bentham were greatly impressed by it, the first named paying tribute to the Italian in his famous *Commentaries*.

But the tide was turning, and many were persuaded and won over to Beccaria's principles of penology and his proposals for reform.

VIII

From earliest recorded history, the problem of crime and punishment has occupied the minds of lawmakers.

The subject was codified by the great Babylonian Justinian, King Hammurabi, 2,000 years before the birth of Christ.

In the Athens of Plato, society had made only the smallest advances against cruel laws and cruel punishments; for were not the criminal laws such that they could be invoked to put to death one who was, in Plato's phrase, " the wisest and the best of men "?

The light of the Renaissance broke over Europe after a night of 2,000 years; but the age of Leonardo and Dante was also the age of the Inquisition and the multiplication of crimes and the development of the barbarous techniques of punishment.

Small wonder that men such as Beccaria, centuries later, learnt discretion, became perhaps unduly prudent wherever a matter of debate slipped over into the great theological reserve.

Dei Delitti went a long way, but not all the way. Its author does not inquire when, and to what degree, a criminal is to be held morally responsible for his crime. He takes no part in that celebrated theological disputation which has continued ever since St Augustine and Pelagius debated the enigmatic issue of predestination and free-will in a world presumed to be governed by an omnipotent deity.

Today other sciences make contributions—biology, psychology, sociology, biochemistry, and several more. For Beccaria it seemed more simple. He saw the final solution in education, knowing nothing of the role of biological inheritance in the moulding of men's lives.

It was another great Italian, Cesare Lombroso, who widened the field of inquiry and formulated a theory of criminal man that was to misdirect criminological research into a scientific *cul de sac* where it stuck for many years. .

Lombroso, as we have seen, approached the subject from the anatomical point of view.

Why, he asked, did Charlotte Corday murder Marat? Answer: Because she was a predestined assassin. Upon what evidence? That of the anatomical anomalies of her skull.

CHAPTER EIGHT

Bentham: The Panopticon Panacea

HYPOTHESIS: That appropriate punishment promotes
reform

I

As that word is used today, there were no prisons in
eighteenth-century England. As Howard's exposure
revealed, the gaols were revolting institutions where
men and women were locked up, rather as tiresome or
dangerous animals are kept under restraint. And since
Assizes had ceased to be regular and frequent, a wretched man
might be held for years untried.

Thus a number of accused persons were held in Hull Gaol
for no fewer than seven years, during which period not a single
Assize was held in that city.

II

There were two types of prison: the county gaols, in which
debtors, accused persons, and those awaiting judgment or
execution were herded together.

Next there were the Bridewells. These were for prisoners
sentenced to be confined as a punishment. They were as bad
as the county gaols and made scandalous by the many abuses of
those in authority.

In 1718 a third type of penal institution was introduced—
transportation to the plantations of North America. As with
the prisons, there was as yet no thought of punishment as a means
to reform, but only an impatience to be rid of a social liability.

Under this old system, which came to an end temporarily
with the end of the American War of Independence, convicts
were handed over to a contractor, rather like animals that are
sold in the market-place, for transportation for the term of their
sentence.

If the system did nothing to make safer life and property, it frequently changed criminals into decent citizens. Many a decent man, transported for an offence arising out of the evil social and economic conditions, lived to complete his sentence in the New World, and thereafter to do well as a law-abiding citizen.

This system of ridding the country of its unwanted citizens was brought to an end with the Declaration of Independance in 1776. Consequently, new methods had to be devised, new prisons provided.

III

There were at that time a number of ships of the line unfit for service. The bright idea occurred to somebody that they might be converted into floating prisons. And this plan was adopted, the converted ships being known as hulks. There were three such ships moored in the Thames. Into them were crowded men, women, and children. And, inevitably, from them presently descended upon London swarms of cut-throats, street thieves, and robber gangs, to terrorize the City.

The hulks, it was clear, provided no solution.

Two years after the Declaration of Independence, and mainly as the result of Howard's evidence before a parliamentary committee, as mentioned in a later chapter, the Hard Labour Bill was introduced by Mr William Eden, later first Lord Auckland. Blackstone had a considerable part in the drafting of this Bill. Law by 1779, the Act authorized the building of two prisons—the first ever contemplated with a view to adding the object of reform to that of punishment.

But though a site was selected at Millbank, by the Thames, and supervisors were appointed, including Howard, nothing was done about it; and for nineteen further years, following Cook's discovery of Australia and the reintroduction of transportation to the new colony at Botany Bay—convict galleys, or hulks, were moored in the Thames and in use as prisons.

Though the Hard Labour Act of 1779 had no material result, it did stimulate general interest in the problems of crime and punishment. It also called forth from Jeremy Bentham a characteristically searching and acute analysis, *A Criticism of the Hard Labour Bill*, before the passing of the Bill.

For some time Bentham had been preoccupied with the theory of punishment. He had read with enthusiasm Beccaria's *Dei Delitti*, and had apostrophized its author as " My Master, the first Evangelist of Reason."

IV

Bentham applied to the problem of the nature of crime and punishment the method he employed in the philosophical examination of every subject which entered the mill of his extraordinary mind.

John Stuart Mill called him " the great questioner of things established . . . the great subversive . . . the critical thinker of his age and country."

Let us see, then, how Bentham, as criminologist, applied his method; how he took a subject to pieces, like the works of a clock, scrutinized each part, and then proceeded to classify everything according to his criteria of its nature.

It was nothing to Bentham that throughout the ages all civilizations had condemned murder; that a truth might long have been accepted as self-evident. He ignored all that, and proceeded, *ab initio*, to examine minutely the grounds upon which the proposition stood.

First, he drew up a list of all the evils or mischiefs that might ensue upon the commission of murder. These he classified into three groups: the first, second, and third order.

To Number One he assigned all *evils* caused to the victim, and the victim's personal connections. To Number Two all *dangers* arising from the bad example, and the *alarm* or nervousness in the community. To Number Three, the *discouragement* to industry and useful pursuits consequent upon that alarm, and the loss arising from precautions taken to provide against the danger.

This meticulous process of dissection of the crime and its consequences into its several parts, Bentham followed by a quantitative analysis. He took up his balances, as it were, and weighed goods against evils. Thus, measuring the evils

caused to the victim and his connections against the goods
reaped by the criminal, he found the former far outweighed
the latter.

The reader might say that anybody could have told Bentham
that and saved him a lot of trouble. But that was the way
Bentham's mind worked.

Had this been found otherwise, the philosopher argued,
punishment of the crime would have been unwarrantable.

Why go through all this intellectual rigmarole to demonstrate
that which had always been known?

Bentham had a ready reply to that: " There are truths," he
said, " which it is necessary to prove, not for their own sakes,
because they are acknowledged, but that an opening may be
made for the reception of other truths which depend upon
them."

Bentham called his the " exhaustive method." But it was
not really new, for it is similar to that of Plato in the *Socratic
Dialogues*. Everything not germane to the subject under
examination is winkled out, eliminated, until what remains is
reckoned to approximate to reality or truth.

Can such a method yield the truth—knowledge of all the
properties and aspects of the object? Mill thought not. And
he made the point that Bentham rejected the conclusions of all
minds that went before him, and also the general opinion of
mankind, considered as an aggregate of the conclusions of all
minds.

V

Bentham concluded that all crimes proceed from one of
three causes: incontinence, hatred, rapacity. Punishment had
but one object: the furtherance of the greatest happiness of the
greatest number, as Beccaria said somewhat before him.

Of prevention he wrote: " Never use a preventive means of
a nature to do more evil than the offence to be prevented.
Punishment that goes beyond the limit of necessity is a pure
evil."

Bentham advocated pecuniary damages for pecuniary
offences, the fine to be proportionate to the wealth of the

offender and the gravity of the offence. (One is left a trifle uncertain as to how this covers the punishment of the man of straw.)

He holds with retributive justice and regards judicial leniency as an encouragement to crime, condemning judge-made law.

With regard to punishment, Bentham believed that a would-be offender would be restrained if the penalty likely to ensue involved more suffering than the pleasure promised by the act. He envisaged the criminal act as a *rational* act, as did those judges who framed the M'Naghten Rules.

That many crimes are irrational, resulting from emotional states, was a possibility overlooked not only by Bentham, but also by all writers on criminology until a much later date.

Bentham considered the true purpose of punishment to be prevention, and that a necessary punishment ought never to be remitted.

On the nature of punishment he quotes Horace, Montesquieu, and Beccaria: it should be made to fit the crime.

The evils of the punishment must exceed the gains of the offence; the non-effectual punishment is an evil, serving no useful purpose. Where punishment is uncertain it should be severe, and vice versa.

Punishment should follow closely on the offence. When of two crimes one is greater than the other, but the punishment is the same, the wrongdoer will choose the greater.

Heavy punishments are inappropriate for small offences: they resemble a high price paid for a trumpery article.

An offence should not inevitably carry the same penalty, since circumstances alter cases. For example, a fine which may scarcely be felt by a rich offender, may ruin a poor one.

VI

Of the general qualities necessary for punishment Bentham suggests three: variability, equability, and commensurability. He held that an offender should be punished where it touches most closely his moral infirmity; for example, avarice, lust, idleness.

All punishments should be as apparent as justice to become exemplary. But punishments must have popular approval: and unpopular punishment defeats its own end, since it shocks public sentiment.

Next, Bentham holds that a punishment is preferable in so far as it inclines to reform the offender, such punishments being those that study *motive* in order to weaken it. And from that proposition he proceeds to this: that all prisoners should have individual treatment in prison, an ideal now being slowly achieved, here and there, in modern prisons.

Next the philosopher considers the nature of prisons: how should the ideal prison be constituted?

He saw those of his own time as sources of physical and spiritual infection; no work—lacking which even a good man rots—no exercise, bad and inadequate food, vile, fever-breeding surroundings. " They are schools," he wrote, " in which only wickedness is taught—they are the academies of crime."

Bentham held that to free a convict after imprisonment under such conditions was to abandon him, weakened, to want and temptation. He therefore advocated prison labour, segregation, and moral instruction. Thus, as he saw it, a man would come out of prison with some skill and knowledge to serve his need.

Next, from prison he would pass, not to complete freedom, but to an auxiliary establishment with qualified liberty, choice of occupation, and payment for work done against lodging charges. It was a system designed to enable the offender to earn to compensate the person wronged by him. And, always the Utilitarian, Bentham adds that it would also be an economy.

VII

To the issue of capital punishment Bentham applied his customary method of analysis. His conclusions may be summarized thus:

Arguments for : Capital punishment prevents the offender ever offending again. It removes the fear engendered in society by his continued existence. It is the most exemplary of all punishments.

Arguments against : Capital punishment is not compensatory. It is uneconomic, since it removes a production unit from society. But since most criminals are drones in the human hive, this is not important. But imprisonment and hard labour might be preferable and result in reform. Further, capital punishment lacks degrees and is an absolute punishment, whereas the turpitude of the act may differ in degree widely from crime to crime.

Finally, the death penalty is irrevocable and unpopular for crimes other than murder. This leads to reluctant witnesses and juries, and prevarication by judges.

To this point Bentham quotes a case in illustration.

It is a prosecution for theft, subject-matter thirty-nine pieces of gold, carrying, of course, the capital sentence.[1]

The Judge : Gentlemen of the jury, find the value thirty-nine shillings. . . .

" Observe that juryman in a blue coat," whispered one Old Bailey judge to another. " Do you see him ? "

" Yes."

" Well, there will be no conviction of death today."

Thus, comments Bentham, perjury became meritorious as the child of pity and defeated the intended ends of the laws, at the same time bringing them into contempt, and, finally, perjury increases crime, since it makes punishment appear to the offender as less certain.

On balance, Bentham found against capital punishment. And in support of this view he gives an example from his own time, that of the experience of the Grand Duke of Tuscany, who, after abolishing the death penalty from his duchy, found that the number of murders had actually *decreased*.

Prolonged hard labour and solitary confinement, Bentham considered, are more dreadful in contemplation, and a more effective deterrent than the death penalty; but he omits Beccaria's strong argument of the lasting impression of life-imprisonment, contrasted with the momentary impression left upon the mind by an execution.

[1] At that date the theft of goods of or above the value of £2 was punishable by death.

G

"The policy of a legislator," Bentham wrote, "who punishes every offence with death is like the pusillanimous terror of a child who crushes the insect he does not dare to look at." And he adds what every Home Secretary might well take to heart, "Be slow to believe in death."

"By disusing death as a punishment you will prevent it as a crime; for when men are placed between two offences it is desirable to give them a sensible interest not to commit the greater. It is desirable to convert the assassin into a thief, and to give him a reason for preferring a reparable to an irreparable offence."

VIII

Many of Bentham's writings on crime and punishment are full of sound sense and humanity; it was his undoing that he attempted ways and means of implementing them. For this he had few of the essential qualifications. He had a hawk's eye for anomalies and for what is irrational in institutions, and he had the courage to point them out. Like Socrates, he is the Great Refuter, the exposer of things false. But he knew nothing at all about human nature.

When, as a young Chancery barrister, he found that it was customary to make a client pay for three attendances in the office of a Master in Chancery when only one was given, he was disgusted at the "sinister interest" behind the *laisser-faire* attitude of the profession, whose members were content to leave the evil as they found it so long as it offered profit.

Every lawyer, attorney, or barrister, every Master, knew all about the chicanery that vitiated every activity of the Chancery Court. Bentham alone had the moral strength to swim against the tide of opinion upon which the less ethically fastidious were content to drift at ease. Bentham failed at the Bar, not because he was not good enough, but because he was too good.

IX

In 1791, by which time it was evident that the much-discussed Hard Labour Act was not to bring into being the first English prison designed to reform as well as to punish, Bentham published a plan upon which he had been working for four years, a plan for the perfect prison.

The Paper, entitled *Panopticon or the Inspection-House*, ran to some 40,000 words, and a copy of it was laid before George III.

The opening words of its preface reveal both the enthusiasm and the high hopes of the scheme's " inventor."

" Morals reformed—health preserved—industry invigorated —instruction diffused—public burthens lightened—Economy seated, as it were, upon a rock—the Gordian knot of the Poor Law not cut, but untied, all by a single idea in ARCHITECTURE."

The scheme for the Panopticon was to occupy Bentham for nearly twenty-five years, to absorb the best part of his considerable patrimony, despite a parliamentary grant of £20,000, and to end in final disappointment in 1811.

X

In 1787 Bentham went to White Russia, where his brother, an engineer of genius, was organizing the shipyards of Cherikov.

With the idea of devising a method of perpetual observation of the work in progress, the engineer had drawn a plan for a great building so designed as to enable him to observe all the workers from one central site.

Bentham seized upon this idea as one equally applicable to other purposes :

"Whether it be that of punishing the incorrigible, guarding the insane, reforming the vicious, confining the suspected, employing the idle, maintaining the helpless, curing the sick, instructing the willing, training the rising race in the path of education; in a word, whether it be applied to the purposes of perpetual prisons in the room of death, or prisons for confinement before trial, or penitentiary-houses, or houses of correction, or workhouses, or manufactories, or mad-houses, or hospitals, or schools."

Since Bentham's scheme for the Panopticon came to nothing, it has little more than a museum interest for the penologist of our time.   Even so, it is truly remarkable, and had an influence on the theory of prison architecture and on the theory of punishment.   For these reasons it may be briefly described.

The Panopticon prison was to be a circular building, the cells occupying the circumference, and so set in radii as to prevent prisoners seeing one another.

At the centre was to be the apartment of the Inspector, who, by means of reflectors, would have every prisoner always in full view, while remaining invisible to them.

As the artificial Ear of Dionysius made audible to that tyrant every word spoken in his palace at Syracuse, so in Bentham's Panopticon an invisible eye would watch perpetually the activities of the prisoners.

The cost of maintenance of the prisoners was to be transferred from the public purse to a contractor, who, in exchange for free labour and its products, would undertake to feed and look after the well-being of the workers, and to assign to each work appropriate to his capacities.

In this arrangement we see Bentham's childlike innocence of the world in general and of contractors in particular.

Bentham worked on his plan with a passion for detail that came near the pathological.   He pondered every aspect of the building itself—form, materials, dimensions, and so on—and then, with the same passion for regulation, the activities of the prisoners.

Though in the end the Panopticon scheme came to nothing, it had great merits, and contained the seed of a number of ideas that are now commonplace in penology.

For example, the provision of decent cells, adequate food, and proper sanitation—rudimentary requirements not always to be found even in a modern prison—were revolutionary notions in his day.

But the cellular system ignored the basic fact that man is a social animal, and by imposing isolation on the prisoner cut him off from the satisfaction of this instinct.

XI

It is said that the King disliked Bentham personally, and scotched his plan, even after it had been authorized by Parliament and a site for its erection selected at Millbank.   The record of the parliamentary manœuvres against him suggests strongly its sabotaging. It is said that Bentham wept like a child when he finally realized that this scheme, to which he had devoted more than twenty years and the best part of his fortune, was never to fructify.

Perhaps Bentham would have suffered even more had his Panopticon materialized with himself as Inspector, which had been the promise made to him. For Bentham was a theorist, a sort of " closet philosopher," rather like those contemporaneous geographers who mapped the undiscovered parts of the earth from their studies rather than in the cabins of exploring ships.

Mill, who knew him well, wrote of Bentham after his death : " He never knew prosperity and adversity, passion nor satiety; he never had even the experience which sickness gives; he lived from childhood to the age of eighty-five in boyish health. He was a boy to the last."

It was perhaps Bentham's misfortune that he had no misfortune : a Xanthippe might have made of him a deeper philosopher and a broader, even if battle-scarred, human being.

" Bentham's idea of the world," Mill goes on, " is that of a collection of persons pursuing each his separate interest or pleasure, and the prevention of whom from jostling one another more than is unavoidable, may be attempted by hope and fears derived from three sources—the law, religion and public opinion."

And Hazlitt, who missed so little, remarks of him in *The Spirit of the Age* : " Mr Bentham relieves his mind sometimes after the fatiguing study by playing a fine old organ, and has his relish for Hogarth's prints." He had, as a matter of fact, a piano in every room in his home, The Hermitage, in Queen Square Place, where, by the favoured few, the great Utilitarian philosopher was to be seen from a very different angle, *en pantoufles*.

XII

For most who made the pious pilgrimage to the home of the great criminologist and honorary Citizen of the French Republic the experience was a disagreeable one.

" Pray tell your master," Mr Richard Lovell Edgeworth, father of the great Maria, bade Bentham's servant, " that Mr Richard Lovell Edgeworth, desires to see him."

" Tell Mr Richard Lovell Edgeworth," replied Bentham by his servant, " that Mr Bentham does *not* desire to see him."

Nor did the distinguished and the great fare much better. Madame de Staël sent by her servant a most flattering message —she had for so long ardently desired to meet him, she was among those to whom his illustrious and illuminating writings had meant so much in inspiration, and so forth.

" Tell her," snorted the ungallant little man, " that I certainly have nothing to say to her, and that I cannot see any necessity for an interview for anything this lady may have to say to me."

Those who penetrated this barrage of incivility were rewarded. Their host revealed himself, undersized and puny, but dynamic, dressed shabbily in old-fashioned clothes.

He would, at the first opportunity, introduce Sir John Langborn very ceremoniously, that being the name of his favourite cat.

Then there were the numerous mice that were encouraged with crumbs to play on the floor of his study, thus raising, one imagines, a moral problem touching the thesis of the greatest happiness of the greatest number, Sir John having decided views about mice, as his master about criminals.

If the call was about tea-time the visitor would also meet Dicky.

" I make Dicky sing," Bentham would explain, caressing his teapot; " I do it by means of a flame and spirit-lamp."

This he considered a little jest that could not be too often repeated.

Then, if the mood was on him, he would bring out Dapple and proceed to confer the accolade of knighthood on some favoured visitor, Dapple being a curious-looking walking-stick.

Let Mill sum up:

" He had the freshness, the simplicity, the confidingness, the liveliness and activity, all in the delightful qualities of boyhood, and the weaknesses which are the reverse side of those qualities

—the undue importance attached to trifles, the habitual mis-measurement of the practical bearing and value of things, the readiness to be either delighted or offended on inadequate cause. . . . All through his life, we may truly say, Bentham remained a child."

If his own country would have none of his panacea, the Panopticon, Bentham fared better abroad. He became an international consultant on prisons and penology, advising, at one time or another, the governments of Russia, Switzerland, Spain, and Portugal.

In the United States the Penal Code of Louisiana was based on Bentham's work, and his influence persists to our own time.

CHAPTER NINE

Romilly : The Wisdom of Ancestors

HYPOTHESIS: That certainty of punishment deters the
criminal

I

THE scene was the House of Commons; the day,
February 9, 1810; the occasion, the introduction by
Samuel Romilly, KC, of the three Bills to abolish the
death penalty for stealing privately from a shop goods to the
value of five shillings, of the value of forty shillings from a
dwelling or ship, and a great many more venial offences then
punishable by death.

An excited young Member, the younger son of a noble lord,
afflicted with a stammer, accosted the introducer of the three
Bills in an agitated manner.

Romilly was a man of noble presence, tall and dark, with an
aspect of benevolence not associated in the popular mind with a
great lawyer.

" I am against your Bill," the young Member stuttered.   " I
am for hanging them all ! "

Romilly, always remarkable for an exquisite courtesy,
remained calm.

" You mean," he suggested urbanely, " that the laws ought
to be executed, as *certainty of punishment* affords the only prospect
of suppressing crime ? "

"Oh, no, no ! It is not that ! There is *no good* done by mercy.
They only get worse.   I would hang them all up at once ! "

Such was the reaction of many Members of Parliament when
the first great criminal law reformer moved against the abuses
and cruelties of the time.

II

The French Revolution had two opposed effects upon
English political trends. It engendered in the ruling classes

fear of all reform, and consolidated their resistance to any kind of innovation.

In the contrary direction, it stimulated radical aspirations towards projects for reform, in particular for sweeping reforms of the criminal law, and the Draconian penalties exacted for minor crime.

Economically, as culturally, a wide gulf divided the nation. On the one side was wealth founded on the Agrarian Revolution, the flow of treasure from India, and the new fortunes being made by the first of the industrialists. On the other side were the dispossessed, the submerged masses, a peasantry driven from a destroyed village economy by the Enclosure Acts to serve the machines of the new industrial towns at wages so low that, even with the labour of small children, combined family earnings were often not enough for a bare subsistence.

In this arid economic soil flourished the social weeds of crime and vice, whose origin is to be seen, not in the turpitude of individuals, but in abuses tolerated by the State.

Penalties for offences were ferocious, but the detection of crime was uncertain, and the death penalty, prescribed by law for some two hundred offences, might be, and frequently was, remitted by humanitarian judges. And since remote risk of severe punishment—even punishment of death—is less terrible in contemplation than a less, but certain punishment, there existed at that period a dangerous state of lawlessness and a general contempt for the criminal law.

This general situation was epitomized by Romilly's three Bills; and the hostility to them, as exemplified by the House of Commons incident quoted, are recorded by Romilly in his *Memoirs*.

III

A psychologist might find in the childhood experiences of the youngest son of Peter Romilly, the Soho Huguenot jeweller, the explanation of the man he became. And he might say something like this: Here you have a delicate and sensitive ninth child, deprived of much of his mother's tenderness by her chronic invalidism, who is left much in the company of an ignorant Methodist maid who selects for his reading the *Newgate Calendar*, and for his bedtime tale whatever horror tale came into her foolish head. Such a boy may well carry those childhood memories all his days, and be by them conditioned in his reactions to cruelty and injustice.

" In my earliest days," Romilly tells us in his *Memoirs*, " my imagination was alarmed and my fear awakened by stories of devils, witches and apparitions; and they had a much greater effect upon me than is even usual with children. . . . The images of terror, with which those tales abound, infested my imagination very long after I had discarded all belief in the tales themselves, and in the notions on which they are built . . . I thought myself present at executions, murders and scenes of blood; and I have often laid in bed agitated by my terrors."

Perhaps here is the explanation of Romilly's revulsion against the barbarities of the criminal law and of his sacrifice of his career as the most brilliant Chancery barrister of his time to devote his abilities to the humanitarian crusade for penal-law reform.

There was terror and cruelty in plenty in the world in which Romilly grew up. England might hypocritically claim that torture had no part in her penal system, as sanctioned in France and elsewhere on the Continent, but in all but name it did.

Debtors were left to rot in gaols for years without hope. Persons found not guilty by the criminal courts were continued in gaol for inability to pay the exorbitant fees demanded by the gaolers. There were stocks for the sport of brutal mobs and torture for the pilloried. There were public hangings of men, women, and children; and still on the Statute Book were certain crimes for which the criminal law prescribed embowelling and quartering of the living victim.

There were children of five or six years of age working seventeen hours a day in those mills for breaking the machinery of which men and women were hanged.

Inevitably, being the man he was, Romilly strove for the reform of the criminal law, for decent, clear-cut judicial procedure, for the repeal of ancient statutes, the abolition of barbarous punishments, and the recognition of reform as part of the purpose of punishment.

His exposition of the purpose of the Bills referred to was clear and simple, and when he addressed the chamber a noble spirit gave tongue in noble utterance, and the goodness and sincerity of the speaker moved even his most bitter opponents.

IV

Reading the record of what Romilly achieved, it may seem that it was little enough until the climate of opinion of his time is conjured up, when it becomes impressive.

In the history of criminal law reform, as of prison reform, it has generally been the men and women of noble character who have, whatever the limitations of their achievement, exerted the greatest lasting influence upon progress. They have been, as it were, sowers of ideas, of ideals, that have germinated and thrived long after the lives of their originators.

" A very transient view," Romilly wrote, " will suffer to discover the absurdity and inhumanity of the system, if that name can with any propriety be given to a mass of jarring and inconsidered laws, which are severe when they should be mild, and mild when they should be severe, and which have been for the most part the fruits of no regular design, but of sudden and angry fits of capricious legislation."

Close on the event, Romilly believed and hoped that the French Revolution would stimulate a demand in England for criminal law reforms. But it had the contrary effect.

Parliament, by a series of new statutes, increased the already over-long list of offences, many, as Romilly objected, " scarcely deserving corporal punishment," for which the death penalty was prescribed.

Already enacted or new statutes made punishable by death between 200 and 300 offences. It was a capital offence for a debtor to withhold from his creditor assets exceeding £20; to pick a pocket of money or goods exceeding in value one shilling and a farthing—to give but two examples.

In fact, as late as 1831 a boy of nine was sentenced to death for breaking a shop window and stealing two pennyworth of paint. (He was reprieved, following the public clamour.) Even so, only two years previously another boy had been hanged in public at Chelmsford for firing a house. The flogging of seamen and soldiers was very often, in effect, the punishment of death, or death preceded by the torture of a thousand lashes, since no human frame can survive such treatment—and sometimes the number inflicted exceeded even that.

On the other hand, certain crimes involving grave turpitude ranked only as misdemeanours, and were comparatively lightly punished. For example, murderous assault and housebreaking in the early hours of the morning in summer.

Anomalies and absurdities of criminal law procedure vitiated criminal trials as judicial processes. Thus, for example, the accused was not permitted to give evidence on his own behalf; nor to be represented by counsel when charged with felony; nor to see the indictment against him before his trial nor to subpœna witnesses on his own behalf—that being a Crown prerogative.

The result of this state of things was a widespread revulsion against capital punishment for venial offences. It led also to judicial chicanery to secure verdicts contrary to the weight of the evidence, or to do so by means of fictions.

One Bridget McAllister was accused of stealing a £10 Bank of England note. The jury convicted her, but added a rider to the effect that the value of the note was thirty-nine shillings, thus saving the woman's life.

Another consequence of the failure of the criminal law to change with public opinion was the frequent refusal of persons to prosecute; many preferred to sustain wrong or loss rather than be instrumental in the judicial killing of some petty thief or cheat.

By the ninth decade of the eighteenth century it had become the practice of judges to offer the alternative of transportation to the death penalty as prescribed by Statute. Thus hanging was tending to go out of fashion, and by 1784 the annual number of executions in London had dropped to fifty-one, a striking contrast to the 2,000 in a single year of the reign of Henry VIII.

Natural law, common humanity, and common sense, too, were tending to soften the ancient asperities when there appeared a tract, *Thoughts On Executive Justice*, by Martin Madan, a lawyer who had abandoned the law for the Church.

V

Madan's tract embodied some part of the teaching of Beccaria, but only to pervert it. Beccaria held that *certainty* of punishment, as deterrent, was more effective than *severity* without it. Madan adopted the first part of this proposition, but rejected the other.

He opposed any reduction in the number of crimes for which death was prescribed, advocating *certainty* and *severity* as the remedy. Madan argued for the restoration in all cases of the death penalty wherever prescribed by law. He criticized the judges for their humanity, whereby, he averred, they betrayed the office of magistrate by surrendering to their instincts as men.

The operation of the criminal law, he held, must be as cause and effect in the physical world : it must ensue upon the offence as inevitably as a burn from fire.

Judges, too, were untrue to their oaths, in that they frequently acquitted the guilty. In consequence of these defects, certainty, as a deterrent, had become no longer effective, and so crime increased, and would increase, until the law, as it stood unaltered, was enforced with full vigour.

Such was Madan's thesis, and though the tract had little worth as a serious contribution to the problem of the conquest of crime, it exerted a surprisingly powerful influence both on Parliament and upon the judges themselves.

Within a year of the publication of Madan's tract, executions in London had risen to ninety-seven.

Another publication that exerted a great influence about this time was Archdeacon Paley's *Principles of Moral and Political Philosophy*.

Paley also followed Beccaria in that he asserted that the

object of punishment is not retribution, but deterrence, both of the offender and others likely to offend.

Where punishment was uncertain, he argued, it should be more severe, and severer in proportion to ease of commission. He held that criminal code best that " sweeps into the net every crime which, under any possible circumstances, may merit the punishment of death," but which resorts to that extremity only in certain circumstances.

Paley reasoned that the greater number of crimes carrying the death sentence, and the certainty of it, cast the shadow of terror over the potential criminal, and so exerted a powerful deterrent force. But at the same time he put forward the incompatible proposition that the essence of deterrence lies in certainty of punishment. He disapproved of the weight given by the criminal courts to the element of doubt, deeming the innocent man, wrongly condemned and executed, as one who immolates himself for his country—a strange proposition indeed.

This venerable don, whose fame as author of the *View of The Evidences of Christianity* has suffered since his death from the disclosure that that work was a plagiarism, deemed hanging an inadequate punishment in really bad cases, and suggested that the malefactor should be cast into a den of wild beasts to be devoured, where, his sufferings being unseen, nobody's sensibilities would be hurt.

These two writers, Madan and Paley, exerted an influence on their time which today seems completely inexplicable.

Of Madan's tract, Romilly tells us in his *Memoirs*:

" It was very much read, and certainly was followed by the sacrifice of many lives, by the useless sacrifice of them; for though some of the judges, and the Government, for a time, adopted his reasoning, it was only for a short time that they adopted it; and, indeed, a long perseverance in such a sanguinary system was impossible."

Whenever he was opposed by the plea that the criminal law of that day represented the " wisdom of our ancestors," Romilly retorted that, however that might be, those laws were: " absurd and barbarous notions of justice, which prevailed for ages, have been exploded, and humane and rational principles have been adopted in their stead." And he summed up the large body of ancient statutes, long since overdue for repeal, as " bloody monuments of our history," making the point that " the antiquity of the law is not really worth inquiring into, the more ancient any criminal law, the less likely is it to be founded on just and rational principles."

Throughout his great career Romilly's parliamentary record was remarkable for the high courage of his sustained advocacy of unpopular measures of penal reform.

First returned for Queenborough shortly after the Mutiny at the Nore, Romilly at once raised the character of the ferocious floggings in the senior service.

In the same year he backed Fox in efforts to end the Slave Trade. He secured the passage of Bills to amend and humanize the bankruptcy laws; and attacked the notorious abuses of the Chancery Court. He supported with great eloquence Whitehead's Bill for the establishment of parochial schools, holding illiteracy to be one of the causes of crime. The purpose here, he pointed out, was not to give poor children knowledge, but the means of acquiring it.

In the matter nearest his heart—the reform of the criminal law—Romilly brought in a number of important measures. He introduced a Bill for the compensation of wrongly accused persons; and another to raise the value of goods for the theft of which death was the penalty. He secured the abolition of the death penalty for simple theft from the person; the repeal of an Act of Elizabeth which provided capital punishment for what today is known as being " absent without leave." He also supported a Bill for the abolition of flogging in the Army.

VI

In 1786 Romilly published his *Observations on a late Publication* (*1786*). This was a reasoned counterblast to Madan's tract. Therein Romilly refers to Beccaria's *Dei Delitti*, and to the Continental trend towards the humanization of punishment, a reform that followed the principles enunciated by the Italian.

Romilly warned his countrymen against opinions contrary both to humanity and to the new spirit of the time.

Romilly's theory of the purposes of punishment may be summarized briefly.

Punishment, he laid it down, has three purposes: (1) the deterrent effect on the community through terror; (2) the sequestration, for a period of time, or permanently, of the offender; (3) the reformation of the criminal.

These three heads, it will be noticed, are merely three techniques for reaching a single end: deterrence. They were not so much new as little known. Bentham, influenced by Beccaria, had already written on similar lines, and how closely Romilly's theory of punishment harmonizes with that of Beccaria may be judged from the quotations from Romilly's writings, and of those speeches of which there are written records.

Of Incompatibles

A sum of money and the life of an individual are incommensurable.

Of Deterrence

The prospect of evil which men know to be possible, but believe to be highly improbable, has seldom much influence in determining their conduct.

Of Terror

If authority, instead of considering its own will as the standard of right, would deign to look back and profit by the experience of the past ages; if it would stay for a moment to reflect upon the miseries which have in vain been inflicted by man upon man; if it would imagine what good has resulted from burning, from impaling alive, from the rack, from the wheel, from tearing limb from limb, less reliance would be placed upon those supposed beneficent effects of terror.

Of Greed

When vice is tempted by the certainty of gain and the certainty of immediate gain, it will have recourse to every expedient to indulge its depraved propensities: it deludes itself with the chance of concealment, with the hope of flight, with all the vain deceptions which misguided passion is ever prone to discover when bent upon gratification.

Of Reform

We must depart from old ways when it is just and useful to do so . . . they who reverence too much old times are not of most service to the new.

Of Punishment

All punishment is an evil, but is yet necessary to prevent crimes, which are a greater evil. When the legislature therefore appoints for any crime a punishment more severe than is required to prevent the commission of it, it is the author of unnecessary evil.

To impose the same punishment on a man who picks a pocket as on a man who murders his own father is to confound all ideas of justice, and to render the laws objects of horror and aversion.

Of *State of Prisons in England and Wales*, Howard's famous book, Romilly recorded his admiration:

" What a contrast might be drawn between the painful labours of this man, and the ostentatious sensibility which turns aside from the scenes of misery and with the mockery of a few barren tears, leaves it to seek comfort in its own distresses."

Of Romilly, his biographer, the late Dr Colman Phillipson, wrote:

" In his lifetime he—a daring pioneer—reaped scanty fruit; his successors, however, gathered and are still gathering a rich harvest due to his sowing. He made it infinitely easier for the generation coming after him to dispel the old errors, prejudices and tyrannies, to shake off the bondage of noxious traditions, and to introduce in criminal law numerous salutary changes of an almost revolutionary nature. Accordingly, his work occupies a place of supreme importance in the evolution of English jurisprudence."

H

CHAPTER TEN

Howard: *State of Prisons in England and Wales*

HYPOTHESIS: That cruel punishment is the crime of society against the criminal

I

TWENTY years before Romilly introduced his three famous Bills in the House of Commons, and so aroused the spleen of the stuttering young Member, there died in Cherson, a town on the Dnieper, another man whose name will forever be associated with reform. Romilly attacks evils found in the courts; John Howard those he discovered in the prisons of England.

Emerson says somewhere that, to succeed, a man must be a man of one idea. Few men illustrate this truth better than John Howard. He was a man of one idea, and he succeeded greatly. Yet he made no contribution to the theory of punishment. His great achievement was in the moral sphere: he awoke the slumbering conscience of England to the state of her gaols.

It seems improbable that Howard was influenced in any way by contemporary thinkers, or by earlier reformers, though, as we know from the great Utilitarian philosopher himself, he influenced Jeremy Bentham.

"This is a quarry," said Bentham, after reading *State of Prisons in England and Wales*, adding, characteristically, "but a quarry is not a house."

And it is true that Howard's celebrated work, exposing the horrors of the prisons of England, was purely factual. But its facts were the yeast that leavened the inert mass of public indifference to and ignorance of the conditions of the gaols and baked the bread of public opinion.

Bentham was well aware that the appalling catalogue of facts compiled by Howard, his indictment of injustice, cruelty, jobbery, and vice, demanded a plan related to fundamental principles of penology. It might be necessary to *feel*; but it was even more important that one should *think*.

" My venerable friend," continued Bentham, on the *State of Prisons*, " was more usefully employed than in arranging words and sentences; his kingdom was a better world—the labours of the legislator, or the writer are as far below his as earth is below heaven."

It was true Howard's famous book had no literary merit. Moreover, it needed none, any more than do the annual statistics issued by the Home Office of the year's crime. The book was a stark indictment; and few more terrible have ever been levelled at society.

Howard belonged to no school, and his intercourse with Bentham was concerned with the communication of facts rather than with the reception of ideas. Culturally, they had no common language, but in morals they spoke the same tongue.

Howard was the son of a London tradesman. From his father, a successful man of business, he inherited a small estate that made him independent. He was indifferently educated, of simple faith, natural piety, transparent purity of heart, and singleness of purpose. By definition, he was an Evangelical Humanitarian, and if it was pity that first moved him, it was chance that determined the object of his compassion. This was a personal experience.

II

At nine o'clock on the morning of November 1, 1755, the people of Lisbon heard a thunder-like rumbling. The sky was clear, the day serene. It was curious, this dull rumbling as of distant thunder.

A moment later the ground upon which that beautiful city stood shuddered as though the earth had heaved a great sigh, and then subsided, at which moment the city of Lisbon collapsed in ruins.

It was the hour of Mass. The great cathedral and the churches were full. In a moment they became vast graves. This, the first of twenty-two shocks that followed, killed 30,000.

Then the sea rolled back, mustered the might of its waters, and smote at the stricken city, engulfing it beneath a vast wave sixty feet in height.

Before nightfall 60,000 lay dead. First the earth, then the sea, and, finally, fire. The ruins of Lisbon went up in flames.

It so happened that at this time Howard had recently been widowed. He was free and independent, but without either occupation or purpose in life. He read accounts of the Lisbon disaster and was deeply moved; indeed, so moved that he determined to do something about it himself. He accordingly took passage for Portugal in the packet *Hanover*.

During the voyage French privateers came up with the unarmed packet and captured her. Ship, passengers, and crew were brought in to Brest. And it was in that ancient port that Howard suffered the personal experience that determined the subsequent course of his whole life; for he was thrown into a dungeon and nearly starved and nearly frozen to death.

He later described how the only food given the captives who shared that dungeon for six days was a leg of mutton thrown into it by a gaoler. Later Howard was moved to a number of other prisons at Morlaix and Carpaix, and in those he found the conditions just as bad as those in the Brest gaol. All were airless, dark, damp, without sanitation, fever-ridden, and inhabited by sick and half-starved prisoners.

Were all prisons like these? he must have asked himself—those in England, too?

III

Thus Howard never gratified his desire to play the Good Samaritan to a stricken Lisbon's decimated population. Finally released by the French, he returned to England and to the small property at Cardington which he had inherited from his father.

Many of the cottages on the little Bedfordshire estate were in bad repair; Howard set about repairing them, and in the process of putting his property in good order, he bought more land and more cottages and reconditioned the whole.

Howard regarded landed property as a trust—a view

common now, but unusual in that day, as one may judge from the biography of him by his contemporary, Hepworth Dixon.

Dixon referred to Howard's views as " a very extraordinary heresy . . . some will think subversive of the very principles of political economy. Such heresies arise from studying the Bible instead of *The Wealth of Nations* and may be classed with other deplorable results of an imperfect education."

We may feel that it was his biographer, and not Howard, who laboured under the handicap of an imperfect education.

For eighteen years Howard occupied himself in making his a model estate, occasionally travelling abroad. At close range Howard must have been something of a trial to less pious persons, for his brand of piety was perhaps just a trifle self-conscious.

The following apostrophe, for example, in a letter written from Italy, announcing his return home, has a slight smell of morbidity.

" Oh! why should vanity and folly—pictures and baubles— or even the stupendous mountains, beautiful hills, or rich valleys, which ere long will all be consumed, *engross* the thoughts of a candidate for an everlasting Kingdom . . . ? "

Unction, redeemed by sincerity.

IV

In 1773, eighteen years after his first personal experience of prison, Howard was nominated High Sheriff of Bedfordshire, a surprising appointment, considering that he was a Dissenter, and so was unable to comply with the requirements of the Test Act.

In the eighteenth century a High Sheriff seldom took his office seriously, valuing it mainly for the social *cachet* it conferred. The High Sheriff would sit on the Bench beside the Assize judge, or dine and wine with him, and generally make his weight felt in the county.

But High Sheriff Dissenter John Howard, who even by accepting office exposed himself to heavy penalties, took another view of his office.

True, he went in state to meet the Assize judge and sat beside him in court. But he also paid close attention to the cases that came up for trial. And presently he was asking himself: What happens to those tried and convicted and sentenced when all this is over?

Then it must have been that memories of Brest and Morlaix and Carpaix flooded in. Howard decided to find out for himself what kind of places the English prisons were; and he was in due course appalled at what he found.

Thus it was that Howard's dark Odyssey among the gaols of England and Europe began—there, in Bedford Gaol, where once Bunyan lay for twelve long years.

" The distress of prisoners," he wrote, " of which there are few who have not some imperfect idea, came more immediately under my notice when I was Sheriff of the county of Bedford; and the circumstances which excited me to activity in their behalf, was the seeing some, who, by verdict of juries, were declared *not guilty*—some of whom the grand jury did not find such an appearance of guilt as subjected them to a trial— and some whose prosecutors did not appear against them— after having been confined for months, dragged back to gaol, and locked up again until they should pay sundry fees to the gaoler, the Clerk of Assize, etc. In order to redress this hardship I applied to the justices of the county for a *salary* to the gaoler, in lieu of his fees. The bench were properly affected with the grievance, and willing to grant the relief required; but they wanted a precedent for charging the county with the expense. I therefore rode into several neighbouring counties in search of a precedent; but I soon learned that the same injustice was practised in them; and looking into prisons, I beheld scenes of calamity, which I grew daily more and more anxious to alleviate."

V

When Howard began his investigation of the prisons of England all gaols were the property of the Crown under Common Law. But nobles and bishops had their own gaols. For example, one of the most horrible prisons investigated by

Howard was the property of Bishop Mawson, in the episcopal city of Ely.

In this gaol prisoners were chained *on their backs* on the wet stones by iron bars that were passed over them. Spiked iron collars were fastened round their necks, and a heavy iron bar was fixed over their legs. Thus, they were virtually crucified in the horizontal position.

Howard found conditions in the gaols were but one aspect of many gross defects in the administration of justice. For example, a debtor imprisoned for debt did not regain his liberty by its discharge. He had to pay fees to both gaoler and turnkey, and to the Clerk of Assize; and until these fees were paid, the debtor, no longer a debtor, was kept in gaol, *sometimes for years.*

Nor was that the worst of which the system was capable. A man might be tried at Assizes for a crime and found not guilty; but he was still held for an indeterminate time in gaol until he paid the fees demanded; for both gaoler and prison staff got their livings out of the prisoners, who thus became for them a source of revenue. There were gaols in which the turnkeys were found to have paid money to secure their jobs.

VI

In travelling through England Howard found everywhere conditions similar to those prevailing in Bedford Gaol. Having completed his survey he published, at his own expense, and through a modest local printer, the book that was to shake the nation out of its complacency and to galvanize Parliament to consider measures to end the inhumanity of the country's gaols.

The *State of Prisons*, though written laconically, constituted a terrible indictment of man's inhumanity to man. It has upon the reader a cumulative effect of horror that no emotional or highly coloured writing could have produced.

Here, as an example of his style, is Howard's description of the gaol at Chester.

" This castle is the property of the King. The first room is a hall.   There are two staircases leading up from it to the four rooms for master's-side debtors.   Down eighteen steps is a small court, which was once common to debtors and felons. It is lately divided; but the high, close pales which separate the two courts, now so very small, deprive both debtors and felons of the benefit of fresh air, and the keeper has no view of the felons' court or day-room, in which men and women are together. . . . Under the pope's kitchen is a dark passage, twenty-four feet by nine; the descent to it is by twenty-one steps from the court; no window; not a breath of fresh air; but only two apertures lately made with gates in the ceiling into the room above.   On one side of it are six cells (stalls) each about $7\frac{1}{2}$ feet by 3, with a barrack bedstead, and an aperture over the door about 8 inches by 4.   In each of these are locked up at night sometimes three or four felons.   They pitch these dungeons two or three times a year.   When I was in one of them I ordered the door to be shut, and my situation brought to mind what I had heard of the Black Hole of Calcutta."

Was that the worst of which the system was capable? Far from it!

In Plymouth, Howard visited a gaol which had a dungeon for felons called The Chink.   It was seventeen feet long and eight feet wide, *but only five and a half feet high.*   It had neither air nor light, save what could penetrate a wicket five inches by seven in the door.

Howard was informed that three men had been kept in The Chink for two months while awaiting transportation.   They maintained life by taking turns to crouch at the door aperture, the sole source of air.

When Howard demanded admittance, he found there a prisoner who had been slowly dying for seventy days, and who told him that he would prefer being executed at once to being buried alive any longer.

VII

Though publication of the *State of Prisons* swung public opinion no less than Parliament in the direction of reform, there were those also who looked upon Howard as a crank.

The general argument of these was, briefly: Prison is horrible? Then let people take care to keep outside.

To such Howard replied: " They forget the vicissitudes of human affairs, the unexpected changes to which men are liable, and that those whose circumstances are affluent may in time be reduced to indigence, and become debtors and prisoners. And as to criminality, it is possible that a man who has often shuddered at learning the account of a murder, may, on a sudden temptation, commit that very crime."

It is a curious circumstance that while philosophic thought, as voiced by Montesquieu, Beccaria, Bentham, and others, was gradually shaping the science of penology, there was a contrary trend towards the intensification of harsh punishments and the making of new laws more cruel and stupid than the old.

It was the false reasoning of such men as Judge Heath that represented the sentiments of many people opposed to the humanization of both punishments and gaols.

" If," said this reactionary judge, " you imprison at home, the criminal is soon thrown back upon you hardened in guilt. If you transport, you corrupt infant societies, and sow the seeds of atrocious crime over the habitable globe. *There is no regenerating a felon in this life.* And for his own sake, as well as for the sake of society, I think it better to hang."

The power of words! Such men as Judge Heath talked of " felons " as they might have talked of tigers or sharks, forgetting entirely that felons were men, not greatly differing from themselves, save through misfortune.

VIII

In 1774 Howard was examined by the House of Commons, and had the exceptional honour of being formally thanked for his work on behalf of prison reform.

It was directly as the result of Howard's exposure that the Hard Labour Act of 1779 was passed, that measure to which Bentham devoted so long and so acute an analytical critique.

This Act called for separate confinement, for work, and for religious and moral instruction. It was followed by a further

Act in 1781. This measure transferred to the Justices new duties—namely, to provide separate accommodation for men and women, and thus the first local gaols, designed to reform as well as punish, were built. The earliest were those of Horsham, Petworth, and Gloucester.

As we shall presently see, Bentham did not approve. He held such prisons to be uneconomic.

The gaols, as remodelled by these Acts, were attempts to embody two principles of penology. First, classification—that is, the separation of the sheep from the goats—as a remedy against contamination of the less bad by the worse. Secondly, separation—that is, the isolation of each prisoner from his fellows.

But experience soon showed that the sorting out of prisoners into categories did not do much to end disorders or to obviate contamination.

In 1832 Parliament found against the system as introduced by the Act of 1779.

Howard, who assisted in drafting the new conditions of separation, was, as we have observed, little concerned with theory or doctrine. He saw a practical need for the separation of felons from debtors, the guilty from the innocent, men from women, and children from adults—for in the eighteenth century small children were thrown into gaol for the most venial of offences, and were as eligible for Tyburn as any cut-throat adult.

That two schools of thought emerged from these trends—that advocating separation (the Associated System), and that advocating Classification (the Cellular System)—does not belong to this short account of Howard's labours for prison reform.

Unlike many legislators and judges of his time, Howard did not look upon the inmates of the gaols as other than men, women, and children in trouble, and little different from those outside the grim walls. And his deep humanity was a better guide than any learning.

IX

Howard left England for the last time in 1790. He died in Russia while investigating the conditions under which Russian soldiers served, which proved to be as bad as anything the old gaols of England had to show—or should one write hide?

Howard died, as it were, in harness, and was buried on Russian soil. He requested that his funeral should be without pomp and his grave marked only by a sundial, and that no memorial should be erected to his memory.

He was accordingly given a funeral of great pomp, and a memorial that may still be seen in St Paul's Cathedral, near the choir screen. It is an effigy of himself. The inscription is long and laudatory, and though undesired by the object of it, well deserved. For, to quote its concluding words, Howard had indeed " trod an open but unfrequented path to immortality in the ardent but unintermitted exercise of Christian charity."

CHAPTER ELEVEN

Elizabeth Fry: The Common Touch

HYPOTHESIS: That love is the key

I

ONE bleak morning early in March 1813 two ladies, blue with cold after a long journey by coach, presented themselves to the Governor of Newgate Gaol.

They desired, they said, to be shown the women's quarters.

The two ladies were Mrs Fry, well advanced in pregnancy, and her sister-in-law, Anna, sister of Sir Fowell Buxton, MP.

The Governor was polite. The proposed enterprise, well meaning as no doubt it was, would be ill-advised. The women's quarters in Newgate were no fit place for any gently nurtured woman.

But Elizabeth Fry had no intention of returning to her home, Plashet Hall, Essex, without seeing that which she had come to see; and so, the two women being adamant, the Governor capitulated.

" If you are determined on it," he warned them, " then I beg that you leave your gold watches and any other valuables you may have about you with me, for otherwise they will most surely be stolen from you."

Thus properly warned, the two ladies advanced into the shadows of the prison.

II

Newgate Gaol was at that period a comparatively new prison, having been built on the site of the old, damaged by fire in 1780 during the Gordon Riots, of which Dickens gives so vivid a picture in *Barnaby Rudge*.

The new prison incorporated none of the novel ideas made current by Bentham. There was no separation of prisoners, except by sex, no work, no decent living conditions, proper food, instruction, nor attempt at reformation.

On the contrary, the new prison perpetuated all the defects of the old plan and tolerated all the evils of the old régime; for the new Newgate had been designed to serve precisely the same purpose as its predecessor—namely, as a place of confinement for prisoners of both sexes awaiting transportation to the American Colonies, for those awaiting trial, and those under sentence of death.

Newgate had been built to accommodate 500 prisoners. It had, on an average, 800 inmates.

The quadrangle of the gaol was divided into three courts. In the first were prisoners able to pay three shillings and sixpence a week for a bed; in the second were the penniless ones; in the third the women and children.

III

It was into this third court that the Governor of Newgate conducted Mrs Fry and her companion.

At once a vile stench assailed their nostrils and the clamour of many voices filled the foul air with language equally foul. There were about 300 women and children in the court. They had no furniture, no bedding, no water supply. Some of the women were very drunk, for the gaoler and his son, who had sole charge, dealt in gin and did very well out of the trade. Other women were brawling, and others again were contriving to attend to their small children and babies.

Here no distinction had been made between old and young, between the cut-purse and cut-throat, the hardened whore and petty-thieving little household drudge. It was a female company of the doomed and of the damned.

But it was now that something very curious happened. The entry of the well-dressed pregnant lady produced a dramatic effect. A silence fell upon the court.

Many, if not most, of the women and children in that Newgate court were not really criminals, but unfortunates, and victims of bad social conditions, of poverty and drink. They had good grounds for feelings of hatred against the more fortunate of their sex. Thus Mrs Fry must at first have appeared, standing amid that squalor, as the symbol of wealth and privilege. Yet not a single voice that day was raised in insult.

The power which Mrs Fry exerted on that occasion, and throughout her years of work in the prisons of England and Europe, was that which can be derived only from a spiritual source. This is not a legend woven long years after her death, but a fact attested to by many of her contemporaries who had occasion to observe it.

She had a fine presence, a melting voice, a command of words. From her also flowed the power of love, which is the key that unlocks the prison of the human heart.

Was she a sentimentalist? No. She was a practical woman, with powers of organization rather like those of Florence Nightingale. Mrs Fry saw Newgate as a job of work, and within the quite clearly defined limitations of her intellect, which was in no way remarkable, she set about doing it. She had no insight into the real causes of the evils she so passionately wished to end, and her unsophisticated religion—that of a convert to the Society of Friends—gave her a very exaggerated idea of the value of religious instruction, isolated from a fair deal in this world.

IV

Mrs Fry began by collecting clothes for the destitute women of Newgate. Would Anna Buxton enlist the sympathies of her brother to raise the matter in Parliament? Could pamphlets be written to arouse the public conscience? To excite indignation?

There was always some obstacle, and so Mrs Fry decided on direct action. But when she unfolded her plan for a committee of ladies to visit and teach and generally befriend the women in Newgate, she came up against the opposition of the City Fathers.

" It is vain," said one, " to expect that such untamed and turbulent spirits will submit to the regulations of a woman armed with no legal authority, *and unable to inflict any punishment*."

Mrs Fry's answer was terse.

" Let the experiment be made ! " she demanded.

Thus the Ladies Prison Visiting Association was formed. It was composed of eleven Quaker women and a clergyman. . . .

On that day when Mrs Fry first saw the third court of Newgate, she had employed the silence so effortlessly secured to take out her Bible and read therefrom the Parable of the Vineyard, and from it to preach a sermon.

Such a proceeding for most people would have been both futile and idiotic. But in her case it was not so, for by this means she paved the way for what was to follow. And what was achieved by these women came as a revelation to men familiar with the gaol over the years, and they marvelled greatly.

Mrs Fry instituted discipline without fear of punishment. She did away with the filth of the place. She put an end to gin-drinking, tackling the gaoler and his son as Florence Nightingale tackled the complacent military authorities in the Crimea. She separated the young from the old, instituted the first of all prison schools. She introduced crafts, managed for the prisoners the sale of prison-made products, and so provided an incentive to industry.

Every day two members of her committee visited Newgate. They taught patchwork, spinning, and knitting. Over 100,000 articles were made in this strange factory, not one being stolen. She organized everything, appointing from the better sort matrons, ward women, and a yard woman who acted as a kind of orderly to keep order in the court. Nor did Mrs Fry's work end there. She instituted after-care for the discharged, thus foreshadowing the work which was later to be organized by the Prisoners Aid Society and the Probation System.

And what of those Sheriffs and City bigwigs who had opposed her plan? Of them Mrs Fry wrote:

" They saw no more an assemblage of abandoned and shameless creatures, half naked and half drunk, rather demanding than requesting charity. The prison no more resounded with obscenity and imprecations and licentious songs; and to use a coarse, but just expression of one who knew the prison well, this ' Hell on earth ' exhibited the appearance of an industrious manufactory, or a well-regulated family."

V

Naturally, word of these strange goings-on in Newgate got about and widespread interest was aroused as to the work and as to the woman.

The United States Minister of the day came to Newgate to witness the wonder. He saw Elizabeth Fry, Bible in hand, the centre of a silent and orderly, if ragtag and bob-tail brood.

" Two days ago," he wrote afterwards, " I saw the greatest curiosity in London, aye, in England, too, compared to which Westminster Abbey, the Tower, Somerset House and the British Museum, nay, Parliament itself, sink into utter insignificance. I have seen Elizabeth Fry in Newgate effect true Christianity upon the most depraved of human beings. And these wretched outcasts have been tamed and subdued by the pure eloquence of Mrs Fry."

Making allowance for hyperbole, this is surely a tribute such as few earn in a lifetime of good works.

Elizabeth Fry's journals are matter-of-fact and do not exploit the feelings of the reader. Indeed, no colouring was needed to make the reader shudder: the plain facts were enough, as the following extract from the *Journals* serves to bring home to the reader:

" I have just returned from a melancholy visit to Newgate," she wrote, " where I have been to see Eliza Fricker, previous to her execution tomorrow. Her hands were cold and covered with something like the perspiration preceding death. She was distressed and tormented in mind. The women who were with her said she had been so outrageous before my going that they thought a man must be sent for to manage her.

" Beside this poor young woman there are also six men to be hanged, one of whom has a wife near her confinement (also condemned) and several young children. Since the awful report came down he has become quite mad from horror of mind. A strait waistcoat could not keep him within bounds;

he had just bitten the turnkey; I saw the man come out with his hand bleeding as I passed the cells."

Such were the sights and sounds to which this remarkable woman exposed herself. Who, then, was she?

VI

Elizabeth Gurney was the daughter of a Norwich banker. At adolescence she experienced " conversion." In 1797, when she was seventeen years of age, she wrote this in her diary: "I am like a ship put out at sea without a pilot. I feel my heart and mind so over-burdened I want someone to lean upon. I believe I am going to be religious or something."

Her conversion followed the hearing of a long sermon by a well-known American spellbinding Quaker, then visiting Norwich, one William Savery.

Returning home in a state of exultation, she wrote in her diary: " Today I have felt there is a God. If I were to grow a preacher I should be able to preach to the gay and un-believing better than to any others, for I should know their hearts."

Elizabeth Fry's conversion at adolescence was a distinctively adolescent phenomenon, as both Starbuck and James concluded in their respective studies of religious experience.

From being a gay little person, Elizabeth became very serious, practising unselfishness as a sort of self-imposed penance that may well have had in it just a little of the morbidity associated with that age-level and emotional state.

Elizabeth Fry was thirty-three years of age and the mother of eight children when she began her life-work for women and children in the gaols of England.

She was by that time a minister in the Society of Friends. Indeed, it was two Friends, Stephen Grellet and William Forster, who had first entreated her to visit Newgate.

Before failing health and her husband's bankruptcy ended her work, Elizabeth Fry had followed in the footsteps of Howard through much of Europe, inspecting the prisons and exerting herself on behalf of their inmates. Everywhere she was received with honour. The Dowager Empress of Russia

I

permitted her son, Nicholas, to convert the royal palace into a model prison when he had come under the influence of Elizabeth Fry. She was received by King Louis Philippe of France and by the King of Prussia.

Towards the end she extended her work beyond the prisons, developing an activity which had begun in a small way in the very hard winter of 1819–20, when she read with horror of the death of a boy found frozen in the street.

Though contemporaneous with it, Elizabeth Fry's crusade against the barbarities of the prison system was no part of the Evangelical Revival.

Many notable men and women had been drawn into that movement, including Howard himself, and Raikes, Hanway, Wilberforce, Granville Sharp, and that curious character, Hannah More. The movement was a reaction from the selfish self-complacency of society, and of the Church of England, whose record was tartly summed up by Leslie Stephen as that of an organism with its central organ in a permanent state of paralysis, the lackey and lickspittle of the ruling classes.

The people of the Evangelical Revival visited the gaols, conducted Sunday schools, taught the Three Rs, helping the children of pauper parents. They also doughtily fought the abominable slave trade.

They were people who exemplified virtue and goodness rather than intellect. They addressed themselves to evils the root causes of which were obscure to them; they were not so much the physicians of the disease of society as a hard-working first-aid party.

Elizabeth Fry had no theory of crime and punishment, and there is nothing in her *Journals* to suggest that she had in any way concerned herself with the underlying causes of the squalor and misery amid which she laboured so long and so honourably.

Her contribution was direct action, without which whole libraries of theory get nothing done. But most of all it was love in action which gave her power. Of her the last word is this: she had the common touch.

CHAPTER TWELVE

Philadelphia and Auburn: Two Rival Systems

THE PHILADELPHIAN: That solitary confinement day and night fosters reform

THE AUBURN: That silence and hard labour foster reform

I

IN England prison history may be dated from 1779, when the first Prison Act was passed, with its three main objects, separate confinement, hard labour, secular and religious instruction. Prisoners were to be grouped, or classified, as Bentham had advocated, with the object of separating the sheep from the goats.

In 1818—that is, seven years after the final abandonment of the Panopticon scheme—an ingenious individual, Sir William Cubitt, invented two devices to further the new methods of penology. Both were worthy of an inquisitor. They were devised for prisoners sentenced to hard labour under the Act.

In 1824 Cubitt's first treadmill was installed in an English prison in Horsemonger Lane, Brixton, South London. The machine was a large hollow wooden cylinder on an iron frame set around its circumference with steps. The prisoner trod these, grasping a handrail, and thus turned the wheel by manpower.

Imagine yourself ascending the descending side of an escalator, and doing it for a long working day, in semi-darkness and damp, and you have some slight notion of what Cubitt's treadmill involved by way of torture.

Despite the cruelty of this infernal machine, it remained in use for many years, and that without greatly troubling the public conscience.

By The Prison Act of 1865 all male convicts over the age of sixteen had to do three months hard labour on Cubitt's mill.

The worthy inventor's other device was the crank.   This was a small hand-wheel turning in a case and operated by the convict.

Both these survivals of medieval torture were in use up to the end of the nineteenth century, a circumstance that gives us the measure of the snail-like progress of prison reform in England, the last machine ceasing to be revolved by man (and woman) power as late as 1901.

II

The prisons built on lines provided for by the Prisons Act of 1823 were on a plan that reflected to some extent the basic idea of Bentham's Panopticon.   The governor's house was at the centre, with blocks radiating from it.

The system was a failure, and so discredited by two parliamentary inquiries in 1832 and 1836 that new legislation was passed.

In 1835 a number of officials—English, French, German, and Belgian—went to the United States on a reconnaisance, for much had been heard in Europe of American penal methods. These were the Auburn and Philadelphia schools, the first advocating the Silent System, the other the Separate System.

The latter of these two schools found favour with the English investigator, and an Act of 1839 made legal, permissively, the adoption of that system.   It provided for solitary confinement of prisoners, hard labour, and moral and religious instruction. A number of prisons at once adopted the plan.

Indeed, it was out of this movement that came the first " model " prison in England: Pentonville, a building consisting of five wings or galleries of cells to accommodate 520 prisoners.   These were to be men between eighteen and twenty-five years of age under sentences of transportation.

III

Since early American penal techniques determined the course of English practice, a few words about them are in place.

The Associated system was first employed in Auburn.   It

provided for the isolation of each prisoner at night, but for work in association by day, with, however, a Trappist rule of silence, for the infraction of which there were brutal punishments.

In Philadelphia, the Separate System provided for total isolation of the prisoners, day and night.

There were fatal flaws, flowing from ignorance of psychology, in both systems. Silence could be maintained only by drastic punishments. Total isolation brought about rapid mental and physical deterioration.

By chance we have a very clear picture of what life was like in these institutions, since an English traveller, Captain Basil Hall, with the sharp eye of a Cobbett, visited both.

" The Auburn plan," he wrote, " consists in the strictest solitary confinement at night, in hard labour, but in hard labour, in rigid silence, by day, and always in company, though under constant superintendence. In solitary meals, under lock and key; in regular marchings to and from their workshops; in subjecting the prisoners to stripes for infractions of the prison rules; and in their never being placed in absolute solitary confinement, except as a punishment of a temporary nature; in having prayers morning and evening said regularly by a resident clergyman, with whom alone the prisoners are allowed to converse, and that only on Sundays.

" The Philadelphia plan is widely different from this. It is intended that the prisoners shall be subjected, during the day as well as at night, to separate confinement, either in solitary idleness, or in solitary labour; along with which they are to be allowed not more exercise than what they may themselves choose to take in their little courts. The keeper is the only person, besides the clergyman, who is ever to see them, and a Bible is to be placed in each cell. By these means, it is expected that while many of the prisoners will be reformed, a salutary terror will be spread over the evil spirits of the State, and crime will thus be doubly prevented.

" I heard in Philadelphia one curious argument in favour of the solitary system: It was said to be so dreadfully severe that it would frighten all the rogues liable to its action, out of the

State of Pennsylvania altogether! But if this, which was gravely stated to me, were justifiable, fire, or any other process of torture, would be preferable, because, while equally effectual, it would be more transient in its operation, and if it stopped short of death, less horrible to think of, from being applied to the body, not to the mind."

Thus, very clearly, Captain Basil Hall described the two systems.

IV

The Philadelphia System was largely the outcome of Quaker activity, and it was really remarkable for its complete lack of understanding of human problems and for its unconscious cruelty. This manifestation of religious zeal, directed to a social end by the Pennsylvania Puritans, was a Quaker version of the spirit of the Inquisition.

For, surely, the long-drawn-out and refined tortures inflicted in the name of religion on the immured convicts of the Philadelphia penitentiary, were as terrible as those of the dark torture chambers of the Holy Office, though passive in character.

In early times solitary confinement—the *detrusio in monasterium*—had been the usual punishment under the Canon law. In Renaissance times solitary confinement was still the ecclesiastical method of punishment, but reserved for noble malefactors.

Following the publication of Beccaria's *Dei Delitti*, and largely as a consequence of its argument, the idea of solitary confinement as retribution came to an end in France; and in 1789 the Declaration of the Rights of Man sounded the beginning of the end of " *le prison perpetuelle*," sentence of which was so often the last heard of the unfortunate offender.

It was Mirabeau whose report defined the new idea of prisons as *maisons d'amélioration*. Therein he outlined innovations such as regular labour in place of the ghastly ennui of unending empty hours, segregation, and rewards for good conduct, and even a system similar to ticket-of-leave.

But the line of least resistance mars the history of English penal methods.   The loss of the American dumping ground, following the loss of the War, stimulated activity for a time and produced the Hard Labour Act of 1779.

The discovery of Australia by Captain Cook in 1770 provided an alternative dumping-ground to the one lost, and thus there began the transportation of convicts to the newly founded hell of Botany Bay.

In the American plantations men had a chance of rehabilitation, and in Australia the day came when discharged convicts could make a new start on Australian soil.   But before that came to pass conditions became utterly inhumane.

They were described in that terrible book *For the Term of His Natural Life*, by Marcus Clarke, who wrote from first-hand knowledge.   Two other novelists did much to awaken the public conscience.

Dickens, who had attacked the Old Marshalsea and, elsewhere in his novels—as, for instance, in *Barnaby Rudge*—had fought for social reform and the reform of the penal laws, also had something trenchant to say by way of criticism of the American penal experiments, which were, let it be said, no better and no worse than our own.

It was Dickens's strictures on the two prisons mentioned that brought down upon his head the wrath of the American people.

Writing of the state of the prisons as he saw them in 1842, he wrote of Philadelphia, in the *American Notes*:

" The system here is rigid, strict, and hopeless solitary confinement.   I believe it, in its effects, to be cruel and wrong. In its intention, I am well convinced that it is kind, humane, and meant for reformation; but I am persuaded that those who devised this system of Prison Discipline, and those benevolent gentlemen who carry it into execution, do not know what it is that they are doing.   I believe that very few men are capable of estimating the immense amount of torture and agony which this dreadful punishment, prolonged for years, inflicts upon the sufferers, and in guessing at it myself, and in reasoning from what I have seen written upon their faces, and what to my certain knowledge they feel within, I am only the

more convinced that there is a depth of terrible endurance in
it which none but the sufferers themselves can fathom, and
which no man has a right to inflict upon his fellow creatures.

" On the haggard face of every man among these prisoners
the same expression sat. I know not what to liken it to. It
had something of that strained attention which we see upon
the faces of the blind and deaf, mingled with a kind of horror,
as though they had all been secretly terrified. In every little
chamber that I entered, and at every grate through which I
looked, I seemed to see that same appalling countenance."

Such passages might be read with that moderated compassion one expends upon tragedies long past, were it not for
the discomforting fact that solitary confinement has not even
yet been banished from the gaols of the world, not entirely
even from our own.

V

In the year 1854 a lad named Andrews, a quiet, neglected,
and inoffensive creature in dire poverty, stole a piece of meat,
being famished. He was caught, tried, and sentenced by the
Birmingham bench to three months imprisonment.

There, in a weakened state, he was put on a five-pound crank,
which is said to have been equal in resistance to one of twenty
pounds. Because he could never do the impossible task set
him, the lad was starved and jacketed, put in a black cell and
punished.

Finding his condition more than he could bear, he hanged
himself in his cell.

Charles Reade took this character and wrote round this
victim of a ferocious penal system his celebrated novel, *It Is
Never Too Late To Mend.* Josephs, the central character of
that novel, is none other than the unfortunate Birmingham
boy.

Following the suicide of Andrews, a Royal Commission had
been set up to inquire into the running of Birmingham Gaol,
and the publication of its Report coincided with the publication of Reade's novel. The result of the two exposures was a
storm of public indignation.

But public indignation is as short-lived as public memory. It is one of the unavoidable consequences of prison punishments that the victims are out of sight, and the emotion of moral indignation, easily aroused, is as short-lived as it is shallow: the sufferings are unseen, and so, forgotten.

CHAPTER THIRTEEN

Osborne: *Society and Prisons*

HYPOTHESIS: That prison must give the prisoner some power of choice

I

A FIEND bent on devising the ideal method for the destruction of a man, body and soul, might have hit on the idea of the Separation System, but would have been unlikely to have improved upon it. Yet this was the system adopted after much thought by Parliament, following its recommendation by Mr Crawford, who had been dispatched to America to observe it in practice.

To implement it the great cellular prison on Millbank was built, and soon thereafter Pentonville, and within six years fifty-four more prisons, all to the same plan.

What does the Separation System involve? It involves the complete, absolute, and utter isolation of a human being for a long period. In England the period was limited to fifteen months; in America it was unlimited.

The convict thus immured saw no other human face save that of his gaoler, the only human being with whom he had contact, if one excepts the periodic visitations of the prison chaplain. Even when he was taken from his narrow cell for exercise, he walked with his face covered by a mask, so that none might see his features or register any sign from him. All that nourishes the human spirit—work, the opportunity to serve, the love of wife and children, the beauty of the world— was taken from him. And, to mock him, his sole reading was the Bible, with its strangely inappropriate teaching of brotherly love.

And the object of it all? Not to destroy a man, but to improve him!

Of course, prisoners had been cast into solitary confinement in England and elsewhere long before the system was officially adopted.

There was, for example, the case of John Bernardi, who died in Norwich Gaol in 1736. He had lain there for forty years. Of this unfortunate Macaulay wrote that his name derived a melancholy celebrity from a punishment so strangely prolonged that it at length shocked a generation which could not remember his crime.

II

How does a man feel, subjected to this system? That is something that should be known, for otherwise we know not what we do. But such knowledge is not easily come by, though it does so happen that, thanks to a great American, we have in full the dossier of one remarkable and deeply moving case.

If the story of Canada Blackie is set out fairly fully here it is not to import sensation for sensation's sake, but to show, through the sufferings of one man, how punishment itself may become crime: the crime committed by the community against the criminal.

Canada Blackie was born in the Dominion. His mother died when he was young. His father was a brutal man. The boy ran away from this unhappy home, he wandered about, picking up a living, now a circus performer, now a cowboy; then, as he slipped into crime, a train robber, and finally a " big shot " crook organizing bank robberies and not stopping at violence.

Swarthy and very powerful, Canada Blackie took part in a bank robbery at Cobleskell, New York, in which a night watchman was killed. He was given a life sentence, though he denied any part in the murder, and was sent to Clinton Penitentiary to serve his sentence.

For seven years Canada Blackie was a model prisoner, but then there came a change. Prison psychosis? Probably, but such psychological states did not interest those who saw the change that converted this model prisoner into a dangerous man whose fits of violence unnerved the guards.

Once Canada Blackie attempted to escape. He had made with amazing ingenuity and patience some sort of gun. He

shot at and wounded a guard. This necessitated a trial outside the prison, and he was duly sentenced by the county court
to an additional ten years' imprisonment.

Back in the prison, he was thrown into a dark cell and kept
permanently in solitary confinement. There, in the dark, he
lived for a year and eight months. He had neither bed nor
bedding, summer or winter: he slept on a stone floor without
covers.

At the end of twenty months, Canada Blackie was brought
forth into the light of day. He had gone blind in one eye. He
was tubercular.

Now he was put into a light cell, but still kept in solitary
confinement for no less than three years. That suffered, he
was again brought forth, manacled, and taken by train to
Auburn Penitentiary—that institution upon which our prison
system was modelled.

There for yet another year the tubercular, one-eyed prisoner
was kept in solitary confinement.

III

Here it was easier not to go mad, for there was light, and so
objects upon which to rest the eye, from which to engender
thought. This must have seemed very wonderful to Canada
Blackie, this child of the prairie and the vast spaces of the
Dominion.

In the dark cell, Canada Blackie had had only one object:
to fight insanity. This he did by means of a game, played as
follows, day after day, week after week, year after year.

Having torn buttons from his shirt, he threw them over his
shoulder. He then turned round and started simultaneously to
search and to count aloud. If he found all the buttons before
reaching a certain number, he won. If not, the buttons won.

Such was this new prisoner who entered Auburn in the year
1913, to continue along this long and lonely road whose bourne
was death.

IV

In that same year Thomas Mott Osborne, a well-to-do
industrialist, was appointed Chairman of the Commission on

Prison Reform set up by the Governor of New York. Most men take such appointments in their stride, discharge the duties laid on them, and there rest content.

Thomas Mott Osborne was not constituted that way. How, he asked himself, could one deal wisely with prison problems when the inside of a prison was an unexplored realm?

So, feeling that he could discharge his duties only if he knew the meaning of imprisonment, Thomas Mott Osborne arranged to be received into Auburn as a prisoner.

Seventy-one years after Charles Dickens had walked these same stone corridors and peered into these same cells, this new prisoner, registered by Warden C. F. Rattigan as Tom Brown, heard the clank of a cell door and found himself alone.

The suffering began almost at once. The term was to be a short one, and though it was the gentleman's agreement that Tom Brown should have absolutely no privileges, no crying off was thinkable, or perhaps possible, under the terms of the agreement.

" I am a prisoner," he wrote, " locked, double-locked. By no human possibility, by no act of my own, can I throw open the iron grating which shuts me from the world into this small stone vault. I am a voluntary prisoner, it is true; nevertheless, even a voluntary prisoner can't unlock the door of his cell—that must be done by someone from outside.

" I am perfectly conscious of a horrible feeling of constraint —of confinement. It recalls an agonized moment of my childhood when I accidentally locked myself into a closet. . . . This is a cell in one of the oldest parts of the prison. It has a concrete floor and plastered walls and ceiling, and looks clean. The electric bulb hangs from the hook in the centre of the arched ceiling, and my head nearly touches it. . . . I look forward to only six nights in this stone vault; but how about those who must look forward to an endless series of nights, month after month, year after year, five, ten, fifteen, twenty years, life? "

V

This sensitive observer desired to shirk nothing. He therefore broke a rule in order to learn the manner of punishment in Auburn. He was sentenced to the " coolers."

Here is how he described the experience:

"A large key opened a solid iron door in the wall; the officer in charge of me led the way along the corridor leading to the execution chamber. Just before we reached the door to that terrible place, another iron door to the right was opened and we entered the jail. . . . The jail is admirably situated for the purpose of performing the operation of breaking a man's spirit; for it has on one side the death chamber, and on the other the prison's dynamo, with its ceaseless grinding, night and day. . . . I had never imagined anything so terrible; and yet it is difficult, if not impossible, to describe to anyone else exactly why they are so. I ended in no very great discomfort myself—although a bare floor does not make a very comfortable bed, when you are unused to sleeping in that fashion; yet at the end of only fourteen hours confinement I came out feverish, nervous, and completely unstrung."

VI

During the week Tom Brown struck up a friendship with a convict named Jack Murphy. Both were working in the basket shop, where a certain amount of talking was tolerated.

Murphy was interested in prison reform. They talked together on the subject, the convict and the Chairman elect of the Commission on Prison Reform, alias Tom Brown; but his true identity known to the other.

Murphy was saying that the Sunday afternoons were the worst of the week, since all the prisoners were then locked in their cells.

"But you can't ask the officers to give up their day off— and you don't think the men could be trusted by themselves, do you?"

"Why not? Why, look here, Tom, I know this place through and through. I know those men. I've studied 'em for years. And I tell you that the big majority of these fellows in here will be square with you, if you give 'em a chance. . . . Of course, there are a few who won't."

"Do you really believe, Jack, that the Superintendent and

the Warden could trust you fellows in the yard on Sunday afternoons in summer? "

" Sure they could! And there could be a band concert, and we'd have a fine time."

" Yes. Then in rainy weather you could march to the chapel and have some sort of lecture or debate. What about those bad actors who don't know how to behave? "

" But don't you see, Tom, that they couldn't do it without putting the whole thing on the bum, and depriving the rest of us of our privileges? . . . Or why not let out only those who have a good-conduct bar? That's it Tom, a Good Conduct League! "

It was the birth of a big idea; and the discussion out of which it was born was set down by Tom Brown as it has been set down here.

VII

After that, it was a matter of ways and means that matured in the Auburn Penitentiary as the Mutual Welfare League, officered by prisoners elected by the vote of their fellows.

On December 26, 1913, a free election was held in the prison and a committee of forty-nine was chosen. No. 33,33X, Thomas Brown, was made chairman. All, it was agreed, should be eligible until proved unworthy. A sub-committee drew up by-laws. The object of the League was defined as being " To promote in every way the true interests and welfare of the men confined in prison." The motto: Do Good—Make Good.

Was the Mutual Welfare League a success? The answer to that question brings us back to a one-eyed tubercular man in a solitary confinement cell.

By some sort of osmotic process, intelligence penetrates prison walls, soaks through them, even to the cells of those in solitary confinement. And so, quite soon, Canada Blackie knew a good deal about what was going on in the great world of the prison—for all things are relative, and to the prisoner in solitary confinement the prison is a wide world of freedom.

In this way, then, Canada Blackie came to know all about

the Mutual Welfare League; and the question arose in his hungry heart: Was it for such as he, a man said to be violent and evil?

It must have seemed " screwy " to Canada Blackie that the Chairman of the Commission on Prison Reform should come often to his cell and talk with him, even calling him " old fellow."

Strangest of all it must have been to learn that this big shot had voluntarily submitted to serve a week in that very prison that he might taste the bitter medicine served to other men.

VIII

One day in June 1914 the Chairman of the Commission on Prison Reform got a message that Canada Blackie wanted to see him. He went, and both men were at once locked in the cell.

" There's something I want you to do for me," Canada Blackie began. He then produced a talcum tin, and pulling out and unwinding a cotton rag, drew something out.

" That key," he said, displaying it, " fits the door of my cell. I don't believe there's another man in prison could have made that key."

He next drew from a hiding-place a short, home-made knife. This, too, he handed over to Mr Osborne.

" I intended to use that," he admitted; then: " Well, I want you to give those to the Warden, and tell him that I feel so deeply what he and you are trying to do for the men in this prison that I want him to know he need have no further anxiety about me. . . . I'm going straight."

Next day Canada Blackie walked beside this wonderful friend in the open air of the prison yard. A week later he was transferred to a regular cell in the north wing. Even more wonderful, he was appointed as assistant sergeant-at-arms of the League.

Later he was elected a delegate. He achieved immense popularity.

" By September," wrote Mr Osborne, " he was one of the most trusted men in Auburn prison, and justly so; for his voice was always raised on the side of right and common sense. No man in prison wielded a greater influence, and he always used it to strengthen the League, the essential principles of which he grasped with the same keen intellectual force which had formerly made him a bold and determined criminal."

IX

Some time later, Mr Osborne was offered the Wardenship of Sing Sing. He was undecided, felt the need of counsel. Whom could he consult? He decided to put the question to a number of men then serving sentences in Auburn, including Canada Blackie. It was on their majority vote that Mr Osborne accepted the appointment.

Canada Blackie was now a dying man, and as Sing Sing, on the Hudson, has a milder climate than Auburn, it was arranged that he should be transferred there.

The newly-appointed Warden of Sing Sing did not assign a cell to Canada Blackie, but gave him a pleasant bedroom in his own quarters, overlooking the river.

There, on March 20, 1915, Canada Blackie died, having received, shortly before his death, a pardon from the Governor of New York.

By what mysterious motion of the soul did this man, so wronged, tortured, and ruined by society, in the end display the cardinal virtues, purge his heart of all rancours, and die with a prayer on his lips?

Was it that Canada Blackie experienced a sort of secular conversion? That for him the Mutual Welfare League had become a religion?

To state that this man died praying may sound perhaps somewhat unconvincing, yet it was so. But he did not pray for himself. He prayed for three lusty young men who were due that day to be electrocuted. And the words of that prayer have been recorded.

But was there not here an unfiled indictment, one that should have been preferred by one Canada Blackie against the State of New York?

K

X

Tom Brown House is the New York headquarters of two organizations which have been merged as The Osborne Association. The first is the Welfare League Association, an aid society for discharged prisoners; the other the National Society of Penal Reform, which works from field studies for practical reforms.

In 1949 Kelly Prison, Alabama, was surveyed by Dr E. Galway and A. H. MacCormick, for the Osborne Association. They found that flogging with heavy leather straps was a routine punishment. Open gambling was permitted; and the Warden himself claimed that some prisoners had several thousand dollars " stashed away."

" One afternoon," states the report, " we saw in the prison hospital a man who had been stabbed in the lung. That night we saw the man who stabbed him wandering around the cell block as free as a lark. He had been flogged, and then turned loose. He took down his clothes and showed us what the strap did to him. He was a wild-eyed psychopath, and unquestionably had already obtained another knife and was ready to use it."

Influential prisoners, they found, had an easy time. One man, convicted of murder, had private rooms where his wife and business associates were allowed to visit him. He went home for week-ends.

The chief evils were summarized as public indifference, lack of money, low-standard types of personnel, enforced idleness, lack of leadership, political domination, and too large prisons.

XI

The conclusions reached by Thomas Mott Osborne, based on personal knowledge and wide experience, are valid for any State.

Here are his main conclusions:

Constant confinement for long hours in unhealthy cells seven and a half feet by three and a half feet makes for physical, mental, and moral degeneration. Overcrowding and long hours of cellular confinement result in homosexuality. There is no incentive to honest work; and work is assigned without regard to suitability to individuals. It is slave labour. The silence rule deprives prisoners of an essential function, and can never be fully enforced. Monotony leads to waves of nervousness when, about once a month, an execution takes place. Espionage by guards induces unstable nervous equilibrium. Guards fear assaults upon themselves and by one prisoner on another. Trusties become spies and create an atmosphere of suspicion, and sometimes murderous assaults on the tale-bearer. Guards are too often brutal, because they are afraid. This sometimes leads to secret torture. The denial of initiative, withholding of responsibility, exposes the absurdity of the theory that bad men are made good by inertia, by giving them nothing to think about, nothing to hope for.

XII

Of the system introduced by him into Auburn Prison through the Mutual Welfare League, this great reformer laid stress on personal honour.

" One's natural prejudices," he wrote, " would lead one to form the theory that of all men the convicted criminals of a State prison are unfitted for even the smallest amount of self-government. Yet the facts are otherwise; for we have given them a considerable measure of self-government *and the thing works.*"

As for Canada Blackie, there could be no parallel between Bunyan in Bedford Gaol, and Canada Blackie in Clinton and Auburn, the one being a " good " man, the other " bad "; but prison suffering did not damage the " good " man to make him " bad," but did something to the " bad " man to make him good.

Perhaps the spiritual gulf between these two victims of society was less wide than that which yawned between the wicked and the bosom of Abraham.

No judge knows what he is about when he sentences a prisoner. He cannot. That what he does segregates an

individual from society—that, of course, he knows.   But beyond
that the judge knows nothing.   There are no painful memories
of physical or mental suffering in the judge's mind.   He thinks
in terms of numbers, putting a price upon the crime in terms of
years.   Even a judge of sensibility (and with usage all sensibilities become blunted), even a judge who has troubled himself to exert his imagination or is anguished by the duties of his
office, can have no notion of the nature of the suffering that
must ensue upon the sentence : only personal experience could
yield him that.

Thomas Mott Osborne submitted voluntarily to a personal
experience of prison as a necessary preparation for the exercise
of his office as chairman of a Prison Reform Commission.
How much more does the judge who passes sentence need
personal experience of the other side of the prison wall?

XIII

What Thomas Mott Osborne did was to challenge long-
accepted ideas of penology and by demonstration to prove
them not only bad, but also cruel and useless.   And it is from
his work, and to a great extent because of it, that prison
reform has taken the direction which it has in recent years.

Osborne's argument was based on simple propositions
touching human nature.   He reasoned that since all real
discipline is self-imposed, external discipline, being coercive, is
effective only while the coercive power persists.

It follows from this now generally accepted proposition that
to be of use to society a good prison must be one that gives an
offender some power of choice between alternatives, as was
done in Auburn with the setting up of the Mutual Welfare
League, available to all but those who elected to be " bad
actors."

This experiment was one of the early steps towards the
" honour " system and the modern prison without walls.   For
the prisoner who can, but does not break and run when on
his honour, has already achieved true discipline; and when
he returns to prison of his own free will he does so as one who
pays his debt to society, as an honest debtor pays off his debt.

It has been wisely said that a man is not sent to prison to be punished, since the prison is the punishment; and it may be said that the best and most useful prison is one that least stresses punishment but emphasizes the social re-education and character improvement of its inmates.

But, as Kant observes somewhere, " from the crooked timber of humanity no straight thing was ever made," so that to suggest that the time may come when such institutions will no longer be necessary would be but foolish optimism.

" Of all the methods by which a prison régime may hope to inculcate self-respect and self-responsibility and in other ways prepare the prisoner for a normal life in society, the open institution appears to be proving the most effective."

So wrote Sir Lionel Fox after a lifetime's experience of administration.

And Kenyon J. Scudder, superintendent of the California Institution for Men, the most successful experimental prison on the " open system "—that is, " minimum security "—has this to say:

" If we can successfully adjust men in prison after they have run the whole gamut of the law, if we can get them over the fear of work, if we can send them back to society a little better than when they entered, then how much more sensible it would be if we could reach these cases earlier in life before the damage has been done; reach them in the early years of childhood before they become delinquent, before we allow them to enter on a criminal career. We make our criminals in this country. They are not born into crime.

" When prisoners revolt, seize hostages, set fire to prison buildings, and resist armed force, it does not, as some district attorneys suppose, demonstrate the innate wickedness of such men, but the badness of the prisons into which society has thrown them."

One man may find himself able to withstand the conditions of prison life, but another may succumb to prison or " cell " psychosis from time to time, curl himself up in his cell, believe himself a grub within its enveloping cocoon. That is one way of escape adopted by the organism lest insanity befall.

There are, on the other hand, cathartic explosions in which the ringleaders are always the less psychologically robust. For example, in one recent prison riot—that in Block 15, Jackson Prison, USA—the ring-leaders were a high IQ but graded homicidal psychopath, a handsome young man known as Crazy Jack by his fellow-prisoners, and a nineteen-year-old homosexual epileptic.

In the opinion of American criminologists, the chief causes of this outbreak were the overcrowding and idleness. When this riot broke out, Jackson Prison was so overcrowded that men were sleeping in cots in cell-house corridors. And conditions almost as bad have recently been reported in more than one English prison. This American prison had industries, a farm, and forestry departments; but nearly 2,000 inmates were completely idle because no work could be found for them.

Sometimes the first sign of the coming emotional storm takes the form of drum-beating of spoons on tin cans; sometimes of prolonged shouting in the cells, and soon mass hysteria ensues. Similar manifestations occurred in the Middle Ages in nunneries, of which the most famous example is that of the mewing nuns.

In England and in America there are prisons a hundred years out of date and, in addition, badly overcrowded, of which one might say that no more useful employment could be found for their inmates than their demolition.

The modern policy, both here and elsewhere, is to substitute probation for prison whenever possible. This calls for the investigation of the offender after conviction, but before sentence. For without an investigation a judge or magistrate may, lacking knowledge of extenuating circumstances in the social and psychological situation of the offender, give too heavy a sentence or one where none would have been the better choice.

Investigation of the offender may serve other purposes also, since by that means the perpetrator of a minor offence may be recognized as one likely to go on to more serious crime, including crimes of violence, as, for example, in the case of Ronald True, discussed in Chapter Sixteen.

One American criminologist, Will C. Turnbladh, quotes a

prison warden as estimating that between 25 and 40 per cent of men sentenced to imprisonment would have been suitable for probation. And he sums up:

" At least two conclusions are inescapable: first, that the use of probation can be substantially increased if a sufficient number of qualified probation officers are available to the criminal courts, and, secondly, such an increase will provide at least as much protection to the public as will a low use of probation and a high rate of imprisonment."

Since the Criminal Justice Act 1948 our courts have greater freedom to discharge with conditions or without, to fine, or make probation orders, including direction for medical treatment.

" To send a socially sick man to prison," wrote Sir Norwood East, " for, say, five years, is not very much more sensible than it would be to send a physically sick man to hospital for a period of time. In both cases the term should end when cure, or believed cure, has been achieved. This would mean, in the case of the criminal, that stage of his rehabilitation that gave promise of future good behaviour."

But when an accused pleads guilty he acts, as it were, as his own physician. If his plea is accepted, all that remains for the court to do is to hear his record and pass sentence. This procedure is analogous to a medical treatment prescribed without diagnosis. For guilt is a condition of mind, and not dependent on some admitted act of a criminal kind.

In England there is a tendency to prefer a trial, even where the accused suggests a plea of guilty, for in the process of trial all relevant, or most relevant, circumstances may be brought to light, and so assist magistrate or judge in assessing appropriate punishment.

Not every man is competent to judge of his own guilt; though he may know that he has committed an offence, he may still be wondering how and why he committed it. Thus, a plea of guilty reduces to a mechanistic judicial process punishment assessment, and consequently the process is unrelated either to justice or science.

In the United States, however, over 80 per cent of prison

sentences result from pleas of guilty in major offences. Thus, in that percentage of cases offenders are sent to prison with sentences arbitrarily arrived at. In some States in the Union, however, the law provides for the pre-sentence investigation of the prisoner by a probation officer. For example, under the California laws of 1947 this pre-sentence investigation is required in all cases of felony.

CHAPTER FOURTEEN

East and Hubert: A Prison Experiment

HYPOTHESIS: That the criminal may need psychological
help

I

IN March 1934 an official investigation began in Wormwood Scrubs "to ascertain the value of psychological
treatment in the prevention and cure of crime."

It was decided to limit treatment to male prisoners over
seventeen years of age, so that youths from Borstal were transferred to Wormwood Scrubs together with selected cases of
adult prisoners from various prisons throughout the country,
these prisoners being chosen as likely subjects for psychiatric
treatment while serving sentence.

At Wormwood Scrubs men sent in as likely subjects were
investigated by the senior medical officer, Dr H. T. P.
Young, and those chosen for treatment were then passed to
Dr W. H. de B. Hubert, who carried out the actual psychiatric
work.

Four hundred and six cases were investigated and 214 selected
for treatment. Of this total, 169 concluded treatment, 56 of
these lapsing later with reconvictions.

Sir W. Norwood East, sometime HM Commissioner of
Prisons, was also actively associated in the experiment, both
with Dr Hubert and the prison medical officer.

This experiment in prison psychiatry has a significance far
greater than that suggested by its limited measure of success,
for it reflects an open-minded official approach to the value of
psychiatry applied to the prison population. It also raises the
question of whether, for such an experiment, prison is the
appropriate place, and the investigation made too late in the
criminal's career.

II

For the period of the psychiatric treatment the prisoner becomes the patient. He is encouraged to discuss himself and his affairs, to consider just what causes landed him where he is, and whether those causes persist, and how they may best be removed. He is encouraged to consider to what extent past emotional upheavals and difficulties of his daily life in relation to family and work may still be propelling him towards evil courses. In short, he is invited to see himself as in a mirror, so far as he may be capable of doing that.

" Exactly the form treatment takes will depend largely upon the type of case," write Drs East and Hubert, " for example, ordinary criminality, personality abnormalities and mild psychoses may be helped by means of the re-educative kind."

The authors, in their *Psychological Treatment of Crime*, give examples of a wide range of psychological types; but they include also a number of cases where criminality is present without discoverable psychological cause, such as the cases now to be briefly described.

III

1. He is a man of twenty-five and is serving a sentence for theft. His parents are people in humble circumstances, but he held himself out as the son of an officer in the Guards who had been killed in an accident. Befriended by an elderly lady, he robbed her house in her absence. Before his first trial he was examined medically and found to be sane. He protested his innocence and talked of a breakdown in health; but he was in good health. He was ingratiating and plausible and a cunning liar, and he attempted " to enmesh the psychotherapist in the same sort of situation in which he had collected his other victims."

2. He is a man of twenty-six years of age, serving a sentence of eighteen months for housebreaking and larceny. No family history of insanity. His father deserted his mother, whom he disliked. He had no home life, stole and lied from an early age. Went to sea, abandoning it at twenty-two, after a severe

motor accident. Lived with a married woman older than himself. She incited him to steal to procure for her luxuries she craved. This is his first conviction, but eleven other charges were taken into account.

He is found to be healthy, intelligent, and straightforward. As a child he stammered, still does so, and is distressed about it. It is worst under emotional excitement. No evidence of psychosis. Treatment cured the stutter and changed his outlook. Seen after discharge he appeared to have made an excellent adjustment.

3. He is a man aged twenty-three, convicted of an attempt to break and enter: four months, second division. No bad family history. Father killed in Great War. Matriculated. Worked for business diploma while employed as clerk. Headache, mental depression, lack of concentration. Set up with girl of lower social status, got her with child; his family opposed marriage to her. Left her and attempted suicide. Snatched a handbag from a woman in circumstances making arrest inevitable. Sent to mental hospital as suspected case of schizophrenia. Joined the Services, was quickly discharged on medical grounds. Attended at out-patients' department of a psychiatric clinic, later admitted to another mental hospital. Improved, was discharged and got employment as a salesman. Stole property of fellow lodgers; attempted suicide, gave himself up. Was bound over. Next drank disinfectant and nearly died. Had several more jobs, but never for long. Five convictions—for theft, attempting suicide. Had sporadic homosexual experiences.

He was intelligent and co-operated with Dr Hubert.

" He was not anti-social and was anxious to rehabilitate himself. While never showing a well-developed schizophrenia or definite schizoid personality, he yet showed for many years features which are frequently found in a person who eventually develops a severe attack of the former. Psychotherapy probably helped him a great deal, but was very unlikely to prevent further delinquency. He was an ideal case for special supervision in a suitable colony."

IV

These three cases, which are set out at length in the Home Office Report, represent three widely-differentiated types. The first is the portrait of a rogue, and rogues there will always be, whatever the remote causes of their predatory way of life, for which reason there will always be prisons to protect the community from them.

The other cases are those of men whose offences have some relation to emotional or physical conditions, or both. They prompt, for the layman, two questions: Is prison the appropriate remedy for such offenders; secondly, if so, is it the most promising place for psychological treatment?

Drs East and Hubert do not appear to think so. They advocate " the creation of a special institution for the care, study and treatment of a selected group of criminals " where treatment would include psychotherapy alone, or combined with training, or a general training alone.

V

Criminal courts have now the power to elect for probation in place of imprisonment, so that the offender has a fair chance to mend his ways and escape the stigma of a prison record. Drs East and Hubert would restrict such probationary treatment to first offenders in need of psychological investigation and, where necessary, psychiatric treatment.

Mr Claud Mullins, with a very wide experience as stipendiary magistrate, is not of that view.

Dr Young, the chief medical officer of Wormwood Scrubs, writing an appendix to the Report, takes the view that the atmosphere of suspicion of a prison is detrimental to psychological treatment, but also sees its advantages, on the other hand, in cases involving drug addiction, including, it may be presumed, alcoholism and " certain types of abnormal personalities who fail to attain stability except under a discipline which they cannot escape."

VI

Nevertheless, so far as the writer can judge, the general opinion among those competent to express a view is that treatment at an earlier stage, and outside either an ordinary prison or a " prison without bars," both of which involve restraint and limitation on liberty and activity, offers the best chances of cure, since any form of prison militates against a desirable relationship between psychotherapist and patient.

There are now two important institutions that are acting both as therapeutic centres for the treatment of cases and as research laboratories. They are the Institute of Medical Psychology—the Tavistock Clinic—and the Institute for the Study and Treatment of Delinquency, and between them and the magistrates' and the juvenile courts there is close liaison.

Psychology has as yet no place in legal education, as one hopes it will one day have, and consequently only those magistrates and judges who acquire it of their own choice have any knowledge of the subject. Yet many of the problems that come before them involve psychological factors.

But the influence of such institutions as those named, and the value of Home Office Reports of experimental work in prisons, are trends which show how psychology is steadily making headway, despite, here and there, considerable resistance on the part of those administering the criminal law.

The judge or magistrate who knows nothing of psychology has a considerable handicap. He will not recognize abnormality, but see it as turpitude, and so proceed to punish what should be the subject of treatment.

In this connection, Mr Claud Mullins tells in his book *Crime and Psychology* of a case in point.

The accused was an elderly man who firmly refused to pay his fare on the London Transport buses, but always readily gave his name and address.

His defence was that the London Passenger Transport Board, as it then was, ought to issue omnibus season tickets, and that by refusing to do so they were persecuting him.

There are still courts where an accused making a defence

of that kind would run the risk of being sentenced to imprisonment. But not in a court where the magistrate had any
knowledge of the curious twists that are so often taken by
persecution mania.

In this case the accused was referred for a medical report
and was found insane and duly certified.

VII

Since the early days of this century the formerly exaggerated
estimate of the role of the mental defective in swelling the ranks
of the criminal population had undergone revision. The
defective is a social liability. He cannot pull his weight
economically, and, in female form, reproduces with a
formidable fecundity. But the type is not now considered
to be the principal reservoir of recruits to the criminal
population.

The criminal elements of the population, it is now accepted
(excluding the psychopathological elements), are composed
mainly of individuals with minor mental diseases of emotional
origin, conditions that have their roots in painful emotional
experiences of childhood or at the dangerous adolescent period
of development.

" The study of minor mental disorders," wrote Sir Norwood
East, " as well as the introduction of new methods of treatment
in later years, have opened up new possibilities in the scientific
attack on crime. . . . Perhaps the most outstanding feature of
the association of the modern psychologist and the criminal is
the recognition of the importance of the emotional rather than
the intellectual genesis of crime."

SUMMARY

All subsequent progress in criminology and penology stems
from propositions first enunciated by Beccaria. Bentham,
who knew Beccaria's theory, failed to apply it in his project
for " the perfect prison." The Panopticon scheme would
have resulted in such a prison as would have made bad men
worse, and weak men weaker. Bentham had little knowledge

of the world or of human nature. He was a " closet philosopher." Romilly, a great man, derived his power from his moral qualities even more than from his intellect, which was a powerful one. He saw unreasoning veneration of legal tradition—" the wisdom of ancestors "—as an impediment to freedom of thought, thus blocking reform. In particular, the reform of the atrocious criminal laws, for which he would have had moderate laws, stipulating for moderate punishments, but absolute law enforcement as more effective to deter from crime than uncertain legalized atrocities. The value of the work done by Howard and Elizabeth Fry represents the moral contribution of the good heart rather than the clever head. Neither was a thinker or theorist. Both were exponents of the virtues of benevolence and compassion. The tremendous influence exerted by both on penal reform was one exerted on the moral level. They exemplify the power of goodness in action. Osborne's experiences in Auburn and Sing Sing reveal deep insight into the basic needs of all men. He argued for self-governing prison populations and for a measure of freedom of choice, particularly in the form of the open prison. His theory postulates the ingredient of goodness dormant in all men; his experience justified that faith. The relative failure of the prison experiment carried out by Drs East and Hubert, with the prison medical officer, should not be read as the failure of psychiatry, but of its employment in the wrong place and under the worst conditions. A man cut off from the world, preoccupied with the plight of his family and what may await him on release, is not likely to co-operate very fully with the well-meaning psychiatrist intent on probing the causes of his criminality.

PART THREE

MURDER AND MADNESS

CHAPTER FIFTEEN

The Trial of Daniel M'Naghten

I

ON January 21, 1843, the following item appeared in *The Times*:

"Yesterday afternoon a most determined attempt was made to assassinate Mr Drummond, the private secretary of Sir Robert Peel, in the open street, and in the broad face of day.

"The motives of the assassin are at present involved in mystery, not the slightest clue being yet obtained to the cause that should have impelled him to the commission of so aggravated a crime.

"But whatever may have been the reasons influencing his mind it will be seen from the subjoint account, that his purpose was carried out with a most cold-blooded determination, though, fortunately, no fatal results are at present expected to result from the wound which he succeeded in inflicting on his intended victim."

It so happened that Mr Drummond was an extremely popular man, rich, handsome, talented and of a charming disposition. His association, as secretary, with the Prime Minister, Sir Robert Peel, made him a public character.

II

The accused man, Daniel M'Naghten, was duly sent to stand his trial at the Old Bailey. But before it took place the charge had to be amended. Mr Drummond died of his wounds; and the charge became one of murder.

Now public indignation and anger rose against M'Naghten, who was seen as a vile assassin. For this violent mass reaction there existed a reason quite unconnected with the case itself.

Not long before, a man named John Ellis had been brought

before the magistrates at Rochester and ordered to find bail
for twelve months for threatening to assassinate the Queen and
Sir Robert Peel. He had failed to find this bail, and so had
been sent to prison.

These two outrages, following closely the one on the other,
produced a profound feeling of disquiet and of apprehension
for the lives of royal and public personages. That Daniel
M'Naghten would be convicted and duly, and very properly,
hanged, was a foregone conclusion.

III

The trial opened at the Old Bailey on March 9, 1843,
before Chief Justice Tindale and Williams and Coleridge *JJ.*
The Solicitor-General prosecuted, and M'Naghten was defended by one of the most brilliant advocates of the time, Sir
Alexander Cockburn, who later became Lord Chief Justice.

The trial caused a tremendous sensation, as the following
extract from *The Times* shows:

" Every avenue leading to the court was at an early hour
thronged to excess by numbers of well-dressed persons of both
sexes, anxious to hear the case, the excitement of which had
not been surpassed by any of the extraordinary events of a
similar character which have taken place during the last
quarter of a century. Several of the desks were removed
from the Bench and their places taken by chairs for the
accommodation of those who had obtained tickets of admission.

" One of the entrances to the court was so blocked up that
benches etc., were placed in the passage in order to accommodate the public. There were ladies on the Bench, Count
D'Aumale, the Belgian, American and Saxon ministers, the
Earl of Jersey, Lord A. Lennox, Lord Paget. . . ."

All this commotion to witness the trial of a madman, a trial
which was to be stopped by the judges after hearing the evidence of the medical experts on insanity. At which point
one should, perhaps, consider what was the law of insanity at
that date.

IV

The law of insanity was at that time based on a number of leading cases, the first of which was R. *v.* Arnold, 1724, in which the trial judge, Mr Justice Tracy, used these words of definition:

" It is not every kind of idle and frantic humour of man, or something unaccountable in his actions which will show him to be such a madman as it is to be exempt from punishment. A man cannot be acquitted on the ground of insanity unless he was totally deprived of understanding and memory, and did not know what he was doing any more than an infant, a brute, or a wild beast."

Next came the case of R. *v.* Bellingham, 1812. The test now applied was whether, *when the act was done*, the prisoner was capable of distinguishing right from wrong, or was under the influence of any delusion which rendered his mind insensible to the act.

This case was followed by the trial of a youth named Oxford, only three years before the M'Naghten case; and here Mr Justice Denman took the definition a step further:

" Persons *prima facie* must be taken to be of sound mind till the contrary is shown. The question is whether the prisoner was labouring under that species of insanity which satisfies you that he was quite unaware of the act he was committing, or, in other words, whether he was under the influence of a diseased mind, and was really unconscious at the time he was committing that act, that it was a crime."

Such, in short, was the law upon insanity when Daniel M'Naghten stood his trial at the Old Bailey in 1843.

V

Cockburn in his defence of M'Naghten referred to the great Erskine's defence in the case of Hatfield, who had gone to the theatre and fired a pistol point-blank at George III.

" Insanity," said Erskine, " may prevail upon a particular point. Monomania exculpates the individual from the guilt of crime committed under its influence. . . . Reason is not driven from her seat, but distraction sits down upon it along with her."

Erskine had then illustrated his point from personal experience.

" I was defending in a case where a man brought an action against his own brother and the keeper of a mad-house for false imprisonment. During a long examination of him I was unable to extract any but the most rational answers, so that his complete sanity became apparent to all in court.

" I was about to resume my seat when a gentleman plucked at my gown and said, ' Sir, I am a medical man. This man *is* mad. He believes himself to be Jesus Christ.'

" I thereupon changed my mien, adopted an attitude of reverential deference, apologized for my previous lack of respect, and asked, ' You are, I believe, the Christ? ' To which he replied, ' Thou hast said it. I am the Christ.'

" Thus was his monomania made apparent to all in court."

VI

Cockburn called as witnesses for the defence the leading specialists in this branch of medicine, including Dr Forbes Winslow, whose reputation stood very high. They all testified to the same effect—namely, that M'Naghten was completely mad, and that the form of his madness was persecution mania.

In face of such evidence the judges conferred, and, having done so, stopped the case.

Daniel M'Naghten, victim of delusions of persecution, left the Old Bailey to pass into the shadowy world of the mad-house for the remainder of his days.

But the rest was not silence. Far from it. The British public did not by any means endorse the action of the learned judges, or accept the finding of the equally learned medical witnesses.

There followed a nation-wide outburst of misdirected indignation. The Press fulminated against the judges, as recently it fulminated against a psychologist's broadcast in which the speaker questioned the dogmas of Christianity.

There were street demonstrations in London that came near to being riots, and in both the House of Commons and the House of Lords the matter was hotly debated.

In the House of Lords, for example, Lord Broughton demanded new legislation on the subject of insanity, and in the debate that ensued one thing became clear—the universal opinion that M'Naghten was not mad at all, and that he ought to have been hanged.

VII

There exists a constitutional right whereby the peers may summon the judges and have their opinion on matters of law; and this procedure the Lord Chancellor invoked.

Now, the judges did not like to have put upon them the responsibility of defining the law outside their courts, and without the advantage of a threshing out of the issues by counsel; and they stated their objection in a very clear manner.

Nevertheless, they were obliged to comply, and did so, and made answer to a number of specific questions put to them in this extra-judicial way.

Their answers did not constitute law, but opinion only, expressed outside their own domain—the courts. But in the course of time, and through usage, the answers then made have acquired the full force of law and are known as the Rules in the M'Naghten Case.

Thus to this day our criminal courts apply criteria of insanity, or what we now prefer to designate mental disease, which were drawn up by men unversed in psychopathology so long ago as 1843.

VIII

Briefly, the Rules in M'Naghten's Case are as follows:

To establish a defence on the grounds of insanity, it must clearly be proved that at the time of committing the act the party accused was labouring under such a defect of reason from disease of the mind as not to know the nature and quality of the act he was doing, or, if he did know it, that he did not know he was doing what was wrong.

M'Naghten laboured under the delusion that he was being persecuted by the Tories, whose agents followed him from town to town—from his native Glasgow, where he worked as a mechanic, so far afield as the French ports.

To rid himself of this persecution, he conceived the plan of shooting the chief enemy, the Prime Minister.

Quite plainly, M'Naghten knew what he did, but not that what he did was wrong. Thus the answers made by the judges to the peers endorsed the action of the judges in stopping the trial.

Criticism of the Rules has been sustained and sometimes bitter. It has come not only from the medical profession, but from judges, too.

For example, in 1885, a man named Ware, an inmate of an asylum, got hold of an iron bar and killed another patient with it. He was brought to trial for murder. The depositions made it clear that the accused was perfectly aware of the nature of his act at the time he committed it, and that he knew that it was wrong.

Ware's case did not get so far as the jury, for he had before then been removed to Broadmoor Criminal Lunatic Asylum. But the judge, Mr Justice Hawkins, had this to say of the law of insanity, as applied by the yardstick of the M'Naghten Rules:

" It would be impossible to say that Ware did not know that he had killed a man, because he said himself that he had. And it would be impossible for anybody to urge that he did not know it was wrong, for he wanted a promise that he should not be punished. But unless one put a totally different construction on the law, *that* would have to be proved, although no man in his senses would suppose that any jury would find Ware responsible for what he had done."

IX

The M'Naghten Rules are unsatisfactory because they proceed from the fundamental proposition that all acts are volitional; none impulsive.

Cockburn, who defended Daniel M'Naghten, when he had risen to become Lord Chief Justice gave evidence before a

Select Committee of the House of Lords on the vexed question of the legal definition of insanity.   He then said this:

" I have always been strongly of opinion that, as the pathology of insanity abundantly establishes, there are forms of mental disease in which, though the patient is quite aware that he is about to do wrong, the will becomes overpowered by the force of irresistible impulse; the power of self-control when destroyed or suspended by mental disease becomes, I think, an essential element of irresponsibility.

" When in a criminal trial the issue is that of insanity, then the duty of determining moral responsibility rests on society. It rests upon society as represented by the law and by psychological medicine, and, unfortunately, the two do not see eye to eye."

A given offence can be defined in precise words; but not so insanity.   For insanity is protean, takes many forms, adopts disguises, sleeps to awake, and then sleeps again.

There are no clearly indicated boundaries to this dark realm of aberration, and the psychologist who enters it does so as an explorer in a land of ghosts.

The truth is, no definition of insanity has yet been formulated which can be applied to a particular individual, to determine insanity and moral responsibility.   It had even been put forward by an officially appointed committee, under the chairmanship of a celebrated judge, Lord Justice Atkin, that insanity and moral responsibility can coexist.   But the ancient Rule was not endorsed in its entirety, since the committee recognized the existence of irresistible impulse by reason of disease of the mind.

In practice the mental condition of an accused is interpreted in cases of alleged insanity by medical psychologists.   The task of such a witness for the defence is to describe and interpret to the court, who have never visited it, the country of the insane, which he himself knows only as a vague and shadowy realm.

There is a lack of precision in terminology, resulting in hesitancy, involved and obscure answers to questions, and often a lack of self-confidence in the witness, so that the general effect produced upon judge and jury is one of incredulity.

Thus, such witnesses are often subjected to rough treatment at the hands of prosecuting counsel, and sometimes to gibes from the Bench.

It is, of course, easy to ridicule or pour contempt upon a man who has to offer, in explanation of an accused's actions, mental and emotional states arising from hidden causes the very nature of which appear improbable, far-fetched, or absurd.

Freud's theory of the sexuality of children, now generally accepted both by the numerous schools of psychology and by those versed in child-welfare work, met with bitter opposition. It was reasoned that a sexualized child could no longer be deemed as being " innocent," and a sentimentalized picture of childhood was thus marred.

How simple is the task of the pathologist in the witness-box. He deals in concrete facts, can point to material exhibits, expound universally accepted facts of chemistry, anatomy, and so forth.

But the psychiatrist in the witness-box faces the lawyer under an initial handicap, for he is himself psychologically conditioned by the knowledge that what he has to put forward will make him appear in the eyes of the jury as a peculiar sort of crank, remote in his approach from the business in hand, and lacking in all " common sense."

A good example of this effect upon a sensitive type of expert witness occurred during the trial of Neville Heath when the late Dr Hubert, Sir Norwood East's collaborator in a Report dealt with in an earlier part of this book, suggested in Heath some degree of insanity.

The general effect produced on judge and jury by the hesitancy and nervousness of this witness, his obvious inability to meet the rain of " common-sensical " questions poured upon him, could not but have produced on the jury a sorry effect.

The difficulty of placing clearly before the court the psychological facts has tended to increase with the advance of psychological medicine. There is only one criminal law, but there are numerous psychologies, each with its own terminology. One consequence of this is the appearance of psy-

chiatrists on both sides, thus providing a spectacle scarcely
warranted to impress judge and jury with the value of their
contribution to justice.

X

Today a jury can find an accused unfit to plead by reason of
insanity; they can also bring in a special verdict of Guilty but
insane.

This curious special verdict, as absurd as anything in
Alice in Wonderland, is due to an incident that took place in 1883,
when a lunatic fired at Queen Victoria. Shortly after that
event, and as a result of it, an Act was passed—the Trial of
Lunatics Act 1883—providing for this special though illogical
verdict; illogical, since guilt implies moral responsibility,
which is absent in the insane.

Equally illogical is the law touching moral responsibility in
cases of infanticide.

Before the passing of the Infanticide Act a woman who took
the life of her baby shortly after its birth was deemed morally
responsible and guilty of murder.

Under that Act she was deemed to be without moral responsibility if when she committed the act the balance of her mind
was disturbed by reason of not having fully recovered from the
effects of child-bed, or by reason of the effect of nursing.

But this Act, which thus exonerates the mother thus placed,
exacts penalties, since it provides for a life sentence even though
the purpose of the prosecution is to prove the fact of
irresponsibility.

The writer recalls a case at the Maidstone Assizes that left
a deep impression on him.

A middle-aged working-class woman was charged with
having killed her new-born infant by winding the caul about
its neck, thereafter concealing the body in a cupboard. She
had been confined alone and had had no medical help or
attention.

A widow with two small children, she had supported herself and them, according to police evidence, by the hard work
of a washer-woman. A workman had come courting her, had

got her with child under promise of marriage, and then deserted her on becoming aware of the pregnancy for which he was responsible.

When the jury found her guilty, as they were bound to do, the poor woman wept in the dock and cried: " Oh, what will become of my children? "

" What does she say? " inquired the judge.

" She says, my lord," said a barrister sitting immediately in front of the dock, " ' What will become of my children? ' "

" You will go to prison for six months," snapped the judge.

That may well appear to the reader as a reflection on the criminal law and upon its administration.

It is, incidentally, reminiscent of the case which so moved the heart of Voltaire—which has been described in an earlier chapter of this book.

CHAPTER SIXTEEN

Madness and Murder (I)

HYPOTHESIS: That the legal definition of insanity is out
of date

I

NOT every madman has straw in his hair or a wild eye.
That man passed in the street or observed in a
public vehicle or restaurant, who talks to himself,
gesticulates, is, the long chances are, a psychotic who is contriving to exist in a world of reality which has become for him a
shadow world, beside that vital and so real world, the creation
of his disordered mind.

Such a one may remain harmless to the end of his days,
or he may commit some crime of violence. He is an inhabitant
of Sinister Street, and in the purlieus of that dark place he
may come upon the spectre that beckons him on to the
commission of some horrible crime.

But it is not always like that. Many individuals destined
to end as murderers display no such visible symptoms of their
mental disease, but pass, at worst, as somewhat tiresome
eccentrics, as braggarts, persistent liars, spendthrifts, passers of
bad cheques, and incorrigible idlers.

Such a man became suddenly notorious in the year 1922.
He was tall and handsome and, when he wished to be, charming. He dressed well, moved among decent people, talked of
his war record in the Royal Flying Corps with affected modesty,
spent freely, charmed such women as cared to give him their
company. In short, was well known as one of that curious
species, a man-about-town.

Nobody who knew Ronald True thought him mad.
Eccentric, yes, and all those things just enumerated: but that
does not add up to insanity.

Friends and acquaintances tolerated him, despite his

propensity to brag and the repeated disclosure of his lying.

But as time went on stories concerning Ronald True multiplied, and certain changes in his manner were noticed. He had talked freely of his exploits in the RFC. But the truth leaked out. He had been an appallingly inefficient flying officer who crashed his machine and injured his leg.

He had come into the Mess on getting his wings with a specially designed pair three times regulation size.

Then it was whispered that he was carrying a revolver in the pocket of his well-cut lounge suit.

One day a woman who had at first found pleasure in his company, but did so no longer, wished to break with him. He threatened her, producing the weapon as a threat.

Next, True began to talk rather a lot about murder. He was forming a Murder Club. The subject seemed to be uppermost in his mind. Friends sheered off, acquaintances, with few exceptions, cooled. And even the little prostitute with whom he had gone on several occasions began to fear and to devise ways and means of putting him off with a view to being finally rid of him.

One day Gertrude Yates, this unfortunate victim, was found battered to death in her bed in her Fulham basement flat.

Circumstances pointed to Ronald True as the murderer. He was traced without difficulty, charged with the crime, and put on his trial at the Old Bailey.

If this trial had not involved the issue of sanity it would not be worth recalling. But it did. More: it created a crisis and a public uproar that shook the administration.

II

At the trial the medical evidence of True's insanity was overwhelming. Among the medical witnesses called for the defence was the late Dr Norwood East, later knighted, who had at that time twenty-three years of experience as medical officer of Brixton Prison.

Although subjected to a very searching cross-examination by Sir Richard Muir, a master of that difficult art, Dr East left the witness-box unshaken. One person at least in that court was by then convinced by him of True's insanity—namely, the judge, Mr Justice McCardie, an enlightened, humane, and unconventional judge.

But the judge was tied by the M'Naghten Rules, though these he gallantly attempted to stretch to meet the patent facts of modern psychological knowledge. And he used these words in his summing up:

" Even if the prisoner knew the physical nature of the act and that it was morally wrong and punishable by law, yet was he through mental disease deprived of the power of controlling his actions at the same time? If so, the verdict should be Guilty but insane."

The jury, which inevitably shared the popular repugnance for so brutal and sordid a crime, rejected the medical evidence, disregarded the loophole offered them by the judge in his summing up, and returned a verdict of Guilty. The verdict was a very popular one.

Ronald True had social connections and relatives in a financial position to fight for his life. There was an appeal. The Court of Criminal Appeal was presided over by the Lord Chief Justice, Lord Hewart, who, if not a reactionary, considered as a jurist was certainly a man who disliked changes that moved in the direction of liberal ideas. Thus, for him, the trial judge's direction to the jury, framed in the words quoted above, was not justified, since it went wide of the M'Naghten Rules.

The appeal was dismissed, and thus the death sentence stood.

Why, then, was True not hanged? He was not hanged because of the intervention of the executive in the person of the Home Secretary, Mr Shortt, who fell back on powers conferred on him by an Act of 1884, the Criminal Lunatics Act.

Under that authority he ordered an independent medical investigation of True's mental state, and the three eminent medical experts confirmed the findings of Dr East as given in evidence at the trial.

True was accordingly sent to Broadmoor Criminal Lunatic Asylum, where he remained until his death some thirty years later.

III

Was True what he was because of a handicap put on him even before his birth? Was he one of those cases where the mother fails to supply the growing child with the essential blood and lymph for normal development?

This might well be the case, for True was conceived of a child of fifteen and born of a mother not long turned sixteen years of age.

He had never been a normal child, for in addition to this likely biological handicap, he now came under adverse environmental conditions. He was, it is true, provided for so far as material things were concerned; but he was a natural child, and through the early formative years lacked those conditions generally accepted as essential for the healthy development of character.

He succeeded in nothing he did. He was shipped to the Dominions, but came back. He did nothing for long, nor anything at all well. The crash had left him with an injured thigh, and to this handicap he added the misfortune of contracting syphilis.

Probably beginning in medicinal doses to alleviate pain, True started to take morphia. He soon became an addict. He was sent to a home for treatment, but, with characteristic cunning, obtained the drug by means of false prescriptions.

Only his near relatives knew of this addiction, or that the apparently carefree playboy was, in fact, a confirmed morphomaniac, tolerant to daily doses of that drug as much as a hundred half-grain tablets.

And nobody knew, until it was too late, that the syphilitic morphomaniac had developed into a homicidal maniac who moved towards his crime with a horrible appearance of predestination.

IV

Though the reprieve and certification of True made the Home Secretary very unpopular, a new storm almost at once broke over his head.

Lady White was an old lady of benevolent disposition who lived in a London hotel. Working there as boot-boy was a lad named Jacobi. Lady White took a fancy to him. She befriended him and showed him many kindnesses.

Jacobi rewarded her by battering her to death in her bed.

Jacobi was tried for his crime, convicted, and duly hanged.

It was at this point that the storm broke.

Here were two murders in many ways comparable. But one murderer was saved from the gallows, after being convicted by a jury; while the other was hanged. And it was freely suggested that the fact that True was not hanged, while Jacobi was, merely showed what social position could do for a man in the clutches of the law, and the penalty for the lack of it.

On the face of it, the unfortunate juxtaposition of the two cases supported the suggestion of a favouritism of the well-to-do and socially influential. Yet there was no substance whatsoever for the popular outcry.

Had the defence of Jacobi been that of insanity, as in True's case, it would have been open to the Home Secretary, had the jury rejected that defence, to appoint a medical committee, as in the case of True. But no such defence was set up.

The worst that could have fairly been said against the administration of justice in these two cases was that clemency might perhaps have been shown Jacobi on account of his youth and the strong indications of psychological disorder suggested by so senseless a crime.

In his play *Night Must Fall*, Emlyn Williams uses as raw material the Jacobi case for a brilliant and psychologically convincing portrayal of a pathological murderer.

Shortly after these two cases the Lord Chancellor set up a Committee to review the existing law, practice, and procedure, where the plea of insanity was raised as a defence to a criminal charge.

This Committee made one important forward step to bring the ancient Rules rather more into line with modern psychological knowledge :

" It should be recognized that a person charged criminally with an offence is irresponsible for his act when the act is

M

committed under an impulse which the prisoner may by mental disease be deprived of any power to resist."

V

Who, then, is to demonstrate to judge and jury the reality of an irresistible impulse in the psychological make-up of an accused? Only that man who can claim to have found the key to the hidden truth; that is to say, the psychologist whose branch is psychiatry.

This witness does not claim infallibility for his science. He offers a view, an estimate, based upon it. That is all; nor could it well be more, since no man can enter the mind of another, and all the available psychological data flow from a single source—the mind of the accused.

It is the task of the psychiatrist to sift the statements made to him by the accused, to estimate what is approximately truth, half-truth, distortion, exaggeration, and invention, and thereafter to offer a diagnosis.

How difficult this task is in a criminal court, as now constituted, may be seen from the trial of John George Haigh for the murder of Mrs Durand-Deacon, in 1949.

VI

The circumstances of the case need be referred to only briefly, since the medico-legal aspects of it are dealt with in a later chapter.

Mrs Durand-Deacon was an elderly widow of independent means who lived as a permanent resident in a Kensington hotel. Also resident there was Haigh, a good-looking man of thirty-nine, with pleasant manners and a way calculated to please an elderly woman.

Haigh first won the confidence of this lady and then, under pretext of showing her certain experiments that might be of value to her in a scheme she had for the manufacture of plastic finger-nails, took her to a small workshop in Crawley, Sussex.

There he shot her in the head from behind and destroyed her body in a tank of sulphuric acid. He then sold her possessions, and so relieved his financial embarrassment.

Since Haigh, when arrested, did not deny the charge, that is all that need be said of the actual crime. What is generally the main task of a prosecution—the bringing home to the accused of the act—was consequently disposed of when Haigh entered the dock at Lewes on July 18, 1949. The whole case turned upon responsibility.

Haigh was defended by the present Lord Chancellor, Lord Kilmuir, at that time Sir David Maxwell Fyfe, KC, a man with a vast experience of criminal work, and a brilliant advocate. He opened his defence with these words:

" The disorder of the mind which, I submit, afflicts the reason of the accused is that rare but quite well-known type of mental aberration called in psychological terminology pure paranoia. Paranoia means complete and permanent alteration of the entire personality which overwhelms the mental outlook, the character, and the conduct of the victim.

" Broadly and fundamentally, it was the result of the patient's interests and energies being turned in on himself and withdrawn from the real world around him in an early stage in his existence. . . . The jury will hear in this case how a dream-ridden existence has been pressed on the subject by his mother.

" In the case of paranoia it really amounts to practically self-worship, commonly expressed by a conviction in the mind of the patient, that he was in some mystic way under the control of a guiding spirit meaning more to him, and having a greater authority than human laws or rules of society. His secret life of fantasy has got to be lived alongside the ordinary life of the world. The paranoiac is, therefore, lucid and shrewd when acting under the influence of his fantasy, and in such cases takes steps to avoid trouble."

VII

Haigh's parents belonged to the primitive sect of Plymouth Brothers, a sect more rigid than the Calvinists. In his home not even newspapers were allowed, though books on dreams abounded. Suddenly his parents abandoned the sect and became Anglo-Catholics—a violent transition.

The boy, John, was at that time adolescent. He began to

have dreams of the bleeding Christ which were repetitive. He next began to believe himself under divine guidance. He next acquired the habit of drinking his own urine, claiming divine authority for this, the purpose being to increase the vital force in him.

Next the dreams changed in character. Now he saw in the dream-state forests of crucifixes. One tree changed, became a man who collected from the dripping trees what appeared to be blood. As the dreamer dreamed he felt an overwhelming desire to have blood.

When committing his murders (for he committed a number by his own confession for which he was not tried), Haigh claimed that he was carrying out a divinely indicated course.

To convince the jury that this strange farrago of apparent nonsense was, in fact, a true picture of the mind of a mad murderer, was the onerous task that fell to the expert witness for the defence, the highly qualified and widely experienced psychiatrist, Dr Henry Yellowlees, consulting psychiatrist to the British Expeditionary Force in France during the War.

Was Haigh's account of his fantasies of blood, his dreams, his belief in a divine impulsion to kill, an invention to deceive justice and so escape the death penalty, or a substantially true recital that built up into a true picture of a recognizable disease of the mind?

Dr Yellowlees based his opinion of the mental state of Haigh on two grounds. First, thirty-seven years' experience as a practising psychiatrist; secondly, on three interviews with Haigh in Brixton Prison. His diagnosis was pure paranoia, a rare disease of the mind. He agreed under cross-examination by the Attorney-General that Haigh was a liar and his statements concerning himself open to the gravest doubt; but he did not consider it possible for him to have invented dreams that so closely resembled the practices of primitive peoples, and he considered these to be evidence of atavism.

To achieve the purpose for which he was called by the defence, it would have been necessary to bring out in evidence two incontrovertible facts. First, that in the expert witness's opinion Haigh was suffering from mental disease; secondly, that such disease had rendered him incapable of understanding that in committing murder he did wrong.

Neither proposition was proved; for Dr Yellowlees cited as his authority a treatise on paranoia by the late Professor Tansi, when the following exchange occurred between the witness and the Attorney-General.

A. G.: You would call him a lunatic, in ordinary everyday language?

Dr Y.: Among doctors I would.

A. G.: Professor Tansi says: " The paranoiac is an anomalous being, but he is not a lunatic in the common meaning of the term. Paranoia is to be regarded as a simple developmental anomaly, the production of a passionate temperament and a methodical and pedantic mind." You do not agree with that?

Dr Y.: Yes, I do not agree with any sentence, taken out of its context, applying to anyone thirty years after the writer is dead; but I agree entirely with the views expressed in that chapter, and indeed it was I, as I have told you, who discovered how important it was and brought the book here.

A. G.: What I put to you was the specific statement, three times repeated in the chapter, that this was not a disease but a constitutional anomaly and that a man suffering from it is not a lunatic in the ordinary sense of the term?

Dr Y.: My answer is that that is the terminology of forty years ago and it is written in general, and it has no application whatever to our present conceptions of disease or to this particular case.

Thus the very authority whose treatise had been described earlier by Dr Yellowlees as " a classic," by clear definition, rejected the witness's own view of pure paranoia as a disease of the mind. Somewhat later further questions undermined the defence of irresponsibility arising out of knowledge of turpitude.

A. G.: Why do you think that he procured sulphuric acid in order to destroy this body, and procured it in advance?

Dr Y.: You have answered the question, have you not—in order to destroy the body.

A. G. : Why do you think he thought it necessary to destroy the body?

Dr Y. : Because I presume he wished to escape detection.

A. G. : Why do you think he wished to escape detection?

Dr Y. : Because he did not wish to be punished.

A. G. : Does it not follow from that that he knew that if he were detected he would be punished?

Dr Y. : I certainly think he knew that murder is punishable by law, as a general proposition undoubtedly.

A. G. : Is it your opinion, then, that he was acting in obedience to a higher law?

Dr Y. : Yes, he said so.

A. G. : But he realized the law of this country was binding upon him?

Dr Y. : I am not satisfied about that; I wish I could be. I am not satisfied that he did not know that it was wrong; but the word " know " is so difficult that it is not an expert opinion. (Here the judge suggested the witness accept the word " believe " for " know.")

The Judge: Then would you substitute the word " believe " for " know," and then answer the question: Did this man believe that what he was doing was wrong?

Dr Y. : I think it is very doubtful. I think he believed that he was acting under a guidance of a higher power, but I do not know.

A little later:

A. G. : I am not asking you whether the man decided in obedience to a higher power to do what he realized was wrong. I am asking you to look at the facts and tell the jury whether there is any doubt that he must have known that according to English law he was preparing to do, and subsequently had done, something which was wrong?

Dr Y. : I will say " Yes " to that if you say " punishable by law " instead of wrong.

A. G. : Punishable by law and, therefore, wrong by the law of this country?

Dr Y : Yes, I think he knew that.

VIII

These answers, and others, brought Haigh within the M'Naghten Rules, if they were accepted by the jury. This the judge pointed out in his summing up, saying: " Members of the jury, if I were to say to you that you ought to follow the opinion of Dr Yellowlees, that would be in terms telling you to find a verdict of guilty in this case, because there is no doubt that Dr Yellowlees, although it was very much against his will, was in the end forced to say: ' I cannot doubt that this man did know what he was doing '—he said so in terms—' and that it was wrong; I cannot doubt that.' "

A medical man, long learned in his science, had offered to a criminal court his view of the mental state of an accused. He gave it as his opinion that the prisoner was either a paranoiac or of paranoid constitution. He ascribed this condition to two factors: heredity and home environment.

Unfortunately, as to the first factor, all that came to light in this trial was that Haigh's father was a man of the utmost uprightness of character. Narrow, it is true, by modern standards, but in no wise tainted by the stigmata of degeneracy.

As for the home, there was great affection for the only child, though an impossibly high standard of behaviour was demanded of him.

What may well have been an important consideration in any psychological estimate of Haigh's mental and emotional make-up—obviously that of a great abnormal—were the conditions of the family before and at his birth, and the age of his mother, giving birth for the first time close on the change of life. The father was then, and had been for a long time, out of work. It was a home of want, of semi-starvation.

May it not have been that Haigh's destiny was determined before birth? An endocrinologist might accept that as a feasible theory.

Otherwise, there is nothing whatsoever to explain why this quick-minded, handsome man became, after a normal child-hood and adolescence, the horrible creature he did become. And nowhere but in psychology can an answer be sought.

After the conclusion of the case, another psychiatrist of wide experience, Dr Clifford Allen, wrote a monograph on the medical aspects of the case. It is a remarkably clear and, to the present writer, convincing diagnosis. Dr Allen suggests five possible reasons for Haigh's abnormal behaviour: paranoia, psychopathic personality, sadism, murder for gain without obvious illness, a mixture of any two or more of these.

Thus, had it chanced that Dr Allen had been called for the defence, the science of psychology would have offered a completely different explanation to the judge and jury of the prisoner's psychological make-up.

Here, then, is the crux of the difficulty of lawyer and layman when the psychiatrist offers as science a view of the mental condition of an accused, namely, the protean nature of his science, which has bifurcated into as many schools as Christianity sects.

Dr Yellowlees saw Haigh as a pure paranoiac. Dr Clifford Allen, having perused all available material concerning Haigh, concludes that Haigh was a psychopathic personality with a sadistic component in his emotional make-up.

It is probable that an orthodox Freudian would have come forward with a theory of the sexual etiology of the mental abnormality that developed into criminal behaviour.

It is fairly certain that while psychiatry remains so protean a science it will continue to be looked at somewhat askance by both the Law and the laity.

IX

As in the case of Ronald True, the Home Secretary directed an examination of Haigh's mental condition after his conviction. This was no *pro forma* affair, for every known test was applied before final judgment.

First, four experienced prison doctors examined him for far longer periods than had Dr Yellowlees. They came to a unanimous conclusion: that he was simulating insanity in order to secure certification and admission to Broadmoor.

Next, the defence were permitted to call in three eminent

psychiatrists who came to the same conclusion as the four prison medical officers.

This might well seem to have disposed of the matter, but, no. The Home Secretary appointed a special medical inquiry by three eminent psychiatrists whose duty it was to review the whole case. They were unanimous that Haigh was simulating insanity for his own purposes, namely, to save his skin.

The investigation of the mental state of Haigh was not limited to interrogation and observation, but included a physical test, one that may, and many now think should, always be employed where the issue of sanity is to be determined in criminal proceedings—namely, a recording of the electric discharges of the brain itself by an instrument known as the electro-encephalogram.

CHAPTER SEVENTEEN
Madness and Murder (II)

I

MR CLAUD MULLINS, a former London stipendiary magistrate and one of the most open-minded, quotes with approval in his wise book *Crime and Psychology*, Dr Bernard Hollander as saying: " That the question of insanity in a case of murder should be left for decision to the wisdom of a jury seems to me outrageous."

" There are on record," the author goes on, " cases of grave insanity when the jury refused to accept convincing scientific evidence; the case of Ronald True was one."

It is possible that at some future date a judicial decision in criminal matters that involve the issue of insanity will be based upon the findings of a machine, thus rendering a jury unnecessary and redundant.

Sir Norwood East, in his book *Society and the Criminal*, quotes the American psychologist S. D. Ingham (1938) " that all thought and all behaviour are the results of physical and chemical reaction in living tissues," an opinion, the reader will recall, similar to that of the endocrinologist, Schlapp, described briefly in an earlier chapter.

Results obtained by the electro-encephalogram, commonly known as the E.E.G., by two experimenters, Hill and Watters, quoted by East, showed that there is a similar electronic reaction from the brains of young children as from those of aggressive psychopaths. Another experimenter, D. Silverman, a neurologist, found that in a group of seventy-five criminal psychopaths 80 per cent revealed abnormal or border-line abnormal E.E.G. tracing.

Other experiments have shown the effect on behaviour of hydration (excess of liquid intake, alcohol or otherwise), hyper-ventilation and hypoglycæmia, in bringing about aggressive behaviour.

II

The E.E.G. is a delicate electrical recording apparatus that provides a reading of the electric discharges given off by the brain. The recordings, shown in the form of a graph somewhat similar to that of a barometer, reveal the rhythm of the brain.

There are four lines to this graph, instead of one as in the case of a barometric reading, and each represents the electrical impulses measured between five electrodes clamped across the head.

The brain-pulse frequency is about six and a half cycles per second. This is shown graphically by the top line of equidistant one-second " pips." Four parallel lines show a brain frequency of about ten cycles per second in a normal person.

The standard type E.E.G. is about the size and shape of a refrigerator. It is controlled by the operator by means of twenty-six black knobs. Its seventy-eight valves amplify ten million times the brain's infinitesimal voltage, which is between twenty and sixty micro-volts in adults.

A rubber skeleton headgear is fitted to the patient and seventeen solid silver electrodes are connected by clips. The patient's hair is parted beneath the electrodes and the scalp moistened with a saline jelly to ensure good electrical contact. Sometimes the reclining patient is covered by a metal cage to cut out extraneous interference.

When the motor of the E.E.G. is set in motion, the paper recording tape begins to move, and four self-inking pens record the changing voltages between any preselected five electrodes. Thus, each part of the head is examined in turn.

When the electrical discharges are normal, behaviour is normal. When they are abnormal, the individual may, at certain times and under certain conditions, behave completely out of normal character. The decent man may become murderous; the irritable woman may become savagely aggressive.

The normal electrical discharges of the various divisions of the brains for babies, small children, adolescents, and adults

are now known.   These rhythmic discharges are shown by the
E.E.G. as plainly as a barometer's record of the day's variations
of atmospheric pressure.

At birth the frequencies are slow, but up to the age of sixteen
they increase.   In normal children the E.E.G. record is
variable and unpredictable; but in normal adults it follows a
fairly regular pattern.

A " normal " person's brain rhythm is from eight to fourteen
cycles per second, a basic pattern known as the *alpha rhythm*.
But if a psychopath is tested round the head just above the
ears, the frequency is often found to be from five to seven cycles,
known as the *theta* rhythm.

A very wide range of E.E.G. readings have shown that from
15 to 20 per cent of Britain's population must be rated
abnormal.   In other words, they are potential criminals.

Yet, as we know, nothing like that percentage of the population commits crimes of violence, the majority passing through
life as law-abiding citizens.

This 15 to 20 per cent of the population is liable to break
down under strains greater than their self-control can withstand.   Such a one who commits a murder at that moment
may be deemed insane by the criteria of science, but deemed
sane by the yardstick of the M'Naghten Rules.

III

On the night of December 30, 1942, Derek Lees-Smith, who
shared a comfortable flat and a comfortable income with his
mother, returned home and brutally bludgeoned his mother to
death.   It was one of those senseless and motiveless crimes
that raise at once doubts as to the mental state of the perpetrator
of them.

For rather more than a week before the crime Lees-Smith
had been passing through a bad emotional phase.   He had
been missing his meals and had been drinking rather heavily.

It was decided to test Lees-Smith's brain by E.E.G.   The
result was a clear indication of abnormality.   The brain's
electrical rhythm was shown on the graph as a shaky line that
suddenly flared up to a sharp peak.

When an E.E.G. graph does that, it tells the psychiatrist that he has located a part of the patient's brain where there are possibly epileptic tendencies.

It is at this time, when the brain is "firing off," as it is called, that the man of irreproachable character may become a killer.

In Lees-Smith's case it was found that the firing-off point depended on the sugar content of his blood. When there was no lack of sugar the brain's rhythm was normal; as it sank, the changes were faithfully recorded by the E.E.G.

This argument was put forward by the defence of Lees-Smith at the Old Bailey in March of the following year, when the judge directed the jury that they must accept the verdict of this electronic witness.

Derek Lees-Smith was accordingly found Guilty but insane.

IV

Margaret Allen was one of those women who wear their hair cut short and go about dressed like a man. There was nothing outwardly feminine about her. She was a spinster nearing the change of life who for a considerable period had worked as a bus conductress.

She had never shown signs of being of the aggressive type, though she was regarded, as such women are, as something of an oddity.

One day Margaret Allen found herself out of cigarettes, of which she was a heavy smoker. Not far from her own home at Rawtenstall, lived sixty-eight-year-old Mrs Nancy Chadick, with whom Margaret Allen had been on neighbourly terms.

To the home of this elderly woman she repaired and brutally battered her to death. She then dragged the body across the road without attempt at concealment, with the intention of throwing it into the River Irwell.

Was there ever such a senseless murder!

Why did she do it? What was the motive?

Asked that, Margaret Allen made this curious reply: " If I hadn't been out of fags and irritable, I wouldn't have done it."

She was tried for this murder, convicted, and hanged.

Yet from the personality of the wretched woman, the sense-lessness of the crime, and the complete absence of motive or gain, the suggestion of insanity seems to have been overwhelming. It is therefore fair to consider what might have been the result had Margaret Allen been tested by the E.E.G.

One theory alone plausibly accounts for a crime so purpose-less, namely, that its perpetrator committed it in a state of epileptoid frenzy for which she was not responsible " by reason of disease of the mind."

Since that execution there have been others in which some-times the suspicion, and sometimes the fact, of epilepsy has not saved the accused from conviction and execution.

In the opinion of a leading psychiatrist known to the writer, a number of epileptics whose mental disease should have secured for them the appropriate verdict Guilty but insane, have been hanged. One of the difficulties is that the disease may be masked, and thus not recognized, and so not pleaded as a defence.

The day may come when mass E.E.G. tests for emotional abnormality will be as commonplace in preventive crime as the use of mass radiography to detect early signs of tuberculosis. An X-ray negative is concrete evidence of a pathological material fact, the lesions in the lungs; the E.E.G. graph is concrete evidence of a pathological physiological fact, the abnormal electronic discharge of the brain.

Both require expert interpretation.

If this forecast of future trends in preventive measures seems far-fetched, it should be recalled that when finger-prints were first mooted as evidence of identity, the claims made for their uniqueness by Herschel, Galton, and others were met with scepticism and even ridicule.

V

In his *Emotion and Delinquency*, L. Grimberg expresses the same opinion as Schlapp with regard to the role of defective endocrine function, including the pituitary, thyroid, adrenals, and gonads, the function of each of which conditions in as many ways bodily activity. Grimberg adds another factor, organic inferiority.

But the fate of Lombroso's teaching is a warning to the specialist who succumbs to the monopolistic approach to a complex scientific problem. Everybody knows the type of individual who has a panacea for some ill or other. It may be orange-juice, or wholemeal bread, or deep breathing that is offered as panacea, and such people are generally dismissed as harmless cranks or injudicious enthusiasts. When exaggerated claims come from a scientific quarter, then a quasi-priestly authority, by inhibiting criticism, may mislead with false hopes, divert research into a cul-de-sac by mistaking the part for the whole.

Human nature being what it is, the conquest of crime is a victory never likely to be won, since it presupposes perfection in what is imperfect—that is to say, human nature. But even if one may never hope to arrive at one's destination, it is as well to travel in the right direction.

Crime can never be eliminated from human societies; but the steady development of new and scientifically sound methods of prevention and reformation, of prophylaxis and cure, may achieve over the social disease, crime, triumphs as great as those achieved by medicine over the great plagues of the past.

VI

When a defence of insanity or some such mental state as that known as psychopathic personality is set up in a murder trial, there is likely to be a suspicion in the minds of judge and jury that mental disease has been trumped up for the purposes of the defence.

It is for this reason that it is generally asked: What signs of this alleged insanity did the accused betray *before* the crime?

And when the answer is, None, suspicion of the bogus character of the defence is intensified. Yet the defence may be genuine and scientifically well founded. As East pointed out, there are mental diseases that may culminate in murder without giving any premonitory indication or warning, and he cites a case of cyclothymic insanity. This is a mental disease in which there is an emotional swing between deep, even suicidal depression and states of tremendous elation and intellectual brilliance or activity. The disease has been well described by a victim of it.[1]

A man aged twenty-three killed sadistically a young woman, and shortly thereafter a little girl. He refused to allow a defence of insanity and was duly convicted and sentenced to death.

As the result of the post-trial medical inquiry ordered by the Home Secretary into the mental state of the convicted man, he was diagnosed as a manic depressive whose sadistic impulses were periodic and irresistible. Knowing this, the man had desired his own death, having no faith in his power to control this criminal impulse, the passing of which left him horrified at his own terrible acts.

He was certified insane and sent to Broadmoor Criminal Lunatic Asylum.

" Some writers," commented East, " emphasize the fact that the so-called ' typically insane murder ' shows a pattern in which an innocent victim is killed in a crude ill-planned manner for no rational or intelligible motive. But many murders by insane persons are anything but typical, even if this word is rather loosely used. Often the motive is intelligible if ill founded, and the manner in which it is carried out may be carefully elaborated."

Between appearance and truth in a murder case there may be a sort of iron curtain put up by the murderer himself to deceive. East cites such a case.

Three prostitutes are murdered in quick succession and horribly mutilated in a sadistic manner. On the face of it, these were the crimes of a sex maniac with sadistic urges, and conformed in every way to a well-recognized pattern, as in the crimes of Neville Heath. Yet in each case the real motive was robbery, and the mutilations were inflicted deliberately to mislead the police by their suggestion of sadistic crimes.

A psychiatrist invited to give evidence for the defence of a

---

[1] *Wisdom, Madness and Folly*, by John Custance. Gollancz, 1951.

man on trial for these crimes, and who founded his opinion on the nature of the crime and the criminal's own version of them, might in all good faith completely mislead the court, being himself completely deceived. For the apparent is not necessarily the true; and the picture of his crime made by a predatory criminal may be a forgery of the sadist's crime, much as a Van Meegeren may be forged to pass as a genuine Vermeer.

VII

Mr Frank Dawtry, secretary of the National Probation Officers' Association, in the course of a lecture at the Indian Institute of Culture, when the writer was in the chair, startled his audience by remarking: " Murderers do very well."

He was speaking as a Probation Officer and from personal experience. For the murderer who is reprieved may be released after some years, when he will come under the care of a Probation Officer.

If such a statement as that astonishes, it is because the murderer is regarded as a person remote from the ordinary run of mankind. But a murder may be committed by Mr Everyman, or his wife, if he has the misfortune to be overwhelmed by an intensely emotional situation, and so for a brief moment find himself out of control.

Such murderers, usually reprieved, seldom deviate again from the normal, and are, though long confined, fit to return to the outside world, no longer dangerous, but, as Mr Dawtry attests, likely to do well.

In one case a young man of good character, kind and generous, killed his fiancée, believing that she had behaved treacherously towards him in a sexual sense. He struck her on the head with a hammer and then used the weapon on himself, injuring his head. He then gave himself up to the police.

As " a lifer "—for he was reprieved—this young man was described as affectionate, loyal, kind, thoughtful, upright, and generous. Given no evidence of any sort of mental abnormality, may one not see in such a case the tragedy of a spiritual catastrophe that might befall any one of us?

N

" Some murderers," said Mr Claud Mullins, " could safely be placed on probation; sometimes even the supervision of a Probation Officer would not be necessary to prevent a repetition of the crime."   And elsewhere he says: " In some cases a psycho-therapist would find it easier to cure a murderer than, for example, a sexual pervert."

Psychiatry, as handmaiden of Justice, is really still in its early days.   But the time has surely come when judge and advocate would do well to acquire a working knowledge of the techniques of the psychiatrist; and the psychiatrist, on his side, would be wise to familiarize himself with the legal definition of insanity, and also to acquaint himself with the rules of evidence.

Too often, in the criminal courts, the psychiatrist witness gets himself badly mauled by counsel, leaving a false impression on the court of the value of his science.

On the other side, there is still a tendency to regard all psychiatric evidence as a sort of high-falutin mumbo-jumbo enlisted by the defence to save the allegedly mad murderer from the gallows.

Today, whatever may be advocated by way of reform, nobody reading a verbatim report of a murder trial, or of any other offence, can but be impressed by the civilized way in which the proceedings are conducted.

But it was not always so.   Formerly, criminal law was barbarous, and a criminal trial was disfigured by procedure that imposed on an accused a terrible disadvantage, so as often to deprive him of his rights and to deny him justice.

Against those evils were raised the voices of the criminal law reformers and of the humanitarians.

CHAPTER EIGHTEEN
Judgment of Death

BECCARIA'S HYPOTHESIS: That punishment of death is a war of a whole nation against a citizen whose destruction is considered necessary, or useful for the general good. It is neither useful nor necessary, save, when living, the criminal endangers the security of the State.

THE AUTHOR'S HYPOTHESIS: That doubt always exists as to the guilt or moral responsibility of a convicted person; and that the innocent have in fact been hanged, or judicially murdered.

I

PAUL PFEFFER, a young working man, was convicted of the murder of Edward Bates, a twenty-two-year-old USA naval mechanic, by smashing his skull in a parked car near New York beach.

He was convicted on a signed confession, to which, as extra weight, the police put in evidence of a childhood escapade. The sentence was twenty years to life for second-degree murder.

In 1954 a fourteen-year-old girl was murdered in New York. A man named John F. Roche confessed. He also confessed to the murder of Edward Bates. This second confession, involving the possibility of a miscarriage of justice, was sifted anxiously, and found to be true.

Had Pfeffer's trial been at the Old Bailey and there ended with the same verdict, since we have no second degree murder, he would have been hanged. Thus the subsequent establishment of his innocence would have been of no avail, save to clear his name and wipe out the stigma on his family.

II

On October 30, 1949, a young man named Timothy John Evans walked into the police station at Merthyr Tydfil and gave himself up for " disposing of the body of his wife." He later made a second statement as to the manner of disposal, neither statement being true; and neither statement being a confession of murder.

There was a child, fourteen-month-old Geraldine, but Evans said nothing of her to the Welsh police.

On December 2, 1949, the bodies of Beryl Evans and the child were found, strangled, in an outhouse in the yard of 10 Rillington Place, London, W.11, where the Evans family had occupied the top floor.

Evans then made two further statements to the police in which he confessed that he had strangled both wife and child. As an accused is never tried for more than one murder at a time, and the Crown decided it in that way, Evans was tried only for the murder of his little daughter, the charge of wife murder being shelved.

The chief witnesses for the Crown were Mr and Mrs Christie, who occupied the flat below the Evans. Now, on trial for his life, Evans retracted his confession and accused Christie of both murders.

Evans was duly convicted, his appeal dismissed, and the sentence carried out according to law.

III

Three years pass. Evans is forgotten. Mr and Mrs Christie are still at Rillington Place. Then, on March 24, 1953, three bodies were found in a kitchen cupboard of the Christies' flat. They were the bodies of three gassed and strangled women. Later the body of Mrs Christie, murdered by the same means, was found under the floorboards. Later still, the skeleton remains of two more women were found by the police buried in the back yard.

Christie, who had run away, was caught and put upon his trial, being charged with the murder of his wife, one of four separate indictments.

Christie confessed to all these crimes, and he also confessed that it was he who had murdered Mrs Evans. He told the police that he had warned Evans that, since it was known that he fought with his wife, he would be suspected.

At his trial Christie told in detail how he had killed Mrs Evans; but he denied murdering the child, Geraldine.

These startling revelations led to widespread public misgivings as to the justice of the verdict in the Evans case; and the Home Secretary ordered an Inquiry to be made, appointing an eminent member of the Bar, Mr J. Scott Henderson, QC, and Mr George Blackburn, a high police officer, for that purpose.

While awaiting execution, Christie repeated his confession to Mr Scott Henderson. But the finding of the Inquiry rejected this confession as false; found Evans properly tried and convicted; and, more, that Evans was also guilty of the murder of his wife, for which he was never put on trial and which was consequently never the subject of a judicial investigation.

IV

The summary of findings of this Report leaves untouched aspects of this remarkable case that, it might have been thought, should have been brought into consideration.

There is such a thing as what Edgar Allan Poe called the Calculus of Probabilities, and it is when one considers this case in terms of probabilities that one sees how unsatisfactory is a legal system which includes capital punishment as one of its sanctions.

For what we have to ponder is this:

In an overcrowded island containing over fifty million inhabitants, what are the chances of two murderers occupying a small house at the same time?

What are the probabilities of two murderers both inhabiting the same house, employing, unknown to one another, identical methods of murder?

What are the probabilities of two murderers, present at the same time, in the same house, suffering a criminal perversion, i.e. the strangulation of the sex object, unknown to each other?

It is when the case of Timothy Evans is looked at from this

standpoint that one sees how flimsy are the grounds upon which the findings of the Home Office Inquiry rest.

Timothy Evans *may just possibly*—though one would not put it higher than that—have murdered his baby daughter and have been responsible for the death of his wife, for which crime, be it again noted, he was never tried; but he would not have been convicted on the evidence of Christie had Christie been known to be a multiple strangler when he stood in the witness-box to testify against Evans.

Timothy Evans, then, was wrongly convicted, and his hanging must be included among the long list of death sentences concerning the justice of which grave doubts exist.

V

Far more numerous than the cases of doubt arising as to the actual commission of the murder charged are those where the issue turns upon insanity or qualified responsibility.

Mr Edward Robinson, in his book *Just Murder*, analyses one hundred and nine murder trials, dividing them, as to the psychological and medical factors, into seven groups: epilepsy, heredity, dementia præcox, uncontrollable impulse, delusional insanity, mental defectiveness, absence of motive.

Thirty-six of the above total were executed: five epileptics, seventeen of bad heredity, fourteen who pleaded uncontrollable impulse.

Twenty-nine were found guilty but insane, thirty-six were reprieved after sentence of death, eight were found insane after sentence.

" Of the thirty-six cases," wrote Mr Robinson, " where evidence was submitted of a family history of abnormality, nearly half the accused were executed. The same could be said where the defence was epilepsy. Of the thirty-two cases where the defence could be classified as that of uncontrollable impulse, fourteen were hanged."

" An examination of the nature of the crimes committed by the fifty persons executed during the years 1927–1931," wrote Mr Roy Calvert in *The Law-breaker*, " shows that half were crimes of passion or sex, and that in no less than seventeen cases there was a medical history of abnormality of some sort. . . . Many had near relations who had died in asylums, one had apparently been certified as insane and the certificate never acted upon, and in two cases medical witnesses pronounced the men to be insane in the dock."

Mr Edward Robinson's investigation led him to the conclusion that the legal view of responsibility in law of the insane has changed little from the medieval conception; that modern psychological medicine, though not unanimous, rejects as inadequate the M'Naghten Rules and regards them as responsible for many errors of judgment. Finally, that public opinion, as indicated by juries, is in advance of both legal and medical theory. " For while some juries' verdicts are less than legally just," he wrote, " they have moral justice."

VI

Writing at a time when the criminal law was harsh and horrible, Dr Colquhoun, that great magistrate referred to later in this book, had this to say of capital punishment:

" The Roman Empire never flourished so much as during the era of the Porcian Law, which abrogated the punishment of death for all offences whatsoever. When severe punishments and an incorrect police were afterwards revived, the Empire fell."

If the capital penalty is, in fact, a deterrent, then we should expect least murders in those States that impose it, most murders in those that have abolished it. The precise opposite appears to be the case.

No country within the circle of so-called civilized States has a higher murder rate than the United States; yet capital sentence is passed, and capital punishment is the law of the States of the Union, with the exception of eight of them.

But the American murderer has a better chance of escaping gallows or electric chair than any other murderer in any State imposing that penalty.

It is the exception (save where the accused is a person of colour) for a convicted murderer to be executed in the United States.

Let us consider the matter from another standpoint. If the capital penalty is the essential deterrent, then its removal should, logically, be followed by an upward curve of the murder graph. But it is not.

The following States have abolished the death penalty: Argentina, Belgium, Brazil, Colombia, Costa Rica, Denmark, Ecuador, Finland, Holland, Portugal, Queensland (Australia), Sweden, Switzerland, Uruguay, Venezuela, and New Zealand.

In none of these States has there been any increase in the murder statistics. On the other hand, in Britain, where, save for the experimental period during the Labour Government, the capital sentence is exacted, homicide has increased slightly during the post-war years.

In 1923 there were 151 murders in England and Wales. In the period 1939–45 there were 1,057, an average, for six years, of 176 a year.

Of the total number of murderers, 1,057, returned in the official statistics, only 474 were brought to trial. What is not generally known is the circumstance that many murderers commit suicide.

VII

A Royal Commission on Capital Punishment issued its Report in 1953. It had been set up by the Socialist Government in 1949. The Commission was precluded by its terms of reference from offering any recommendation on the central issue of abolition.

Its findings reflect very clearly the modern view, which is not at all that of the judges, who tend to be, when not reactionary, markedly conservative.

The Commission recommended the scrapping of the old M'Naghten Rules on insanity in the legal sense. It advocated that the trial jury should be allowed to decide whether sentence of death should be changed to life imprisonment.

This would, were it adopted—which is improbable—impose on the jury a judicial function never before asked of them.

Was that recommendation made with a purpose not directly stated? It was included in the Report, one may believe, in the knowledge that were it adopted capital punishment would be thereby indirectly abolished. For what jury, with so fearful a responsibility thrust upon them, would pass sentence of death?

The Commission also suggested the raising of the age to twenty-one for liability to the death penalty. It also suggested alternative methods of execution, including lethal injections.

None of the recommendations made has been, or is likely to be adopted; for such is the way with the findings of Royal Commissions. But the expenditure of £23,000 of public money, and the labours of ten distinguished men and women, should not be written off as wasted. For this Commission served the valuable purpose of indicating the general trend of thought, or what is sometimes termed the climate of opinion of the times.

SUMMARY

That the M'Naghten Rules are now anachronistic measured by modern mental science. The psychiatrist as witness in a criminal court labours under a heavy handicap. He has to interpret a complex science, often in an atmosphere that is slightly hostile, at others sceptical or even contemptuous. Being human, he is conscious of this, and in consequence often makes a poor witness. He may even become infected by the partisanship of the trial, particularly when he appears for the defence in a criminal trial, when he may lapse so far as to " play for his side," falling into the scientific sin of exaggeration. An example of the customary judicial attitude to the terms of modern mental science is well illustrated by an exchange between Bench and counsel in the Court of Criminal Appeal, the subject-matter being an appeal against a conviction for murder in the lower court.

Darling, J.: " Has it ever been recognized in these courts that there are two minds, one conscious and the other sub-conscious? "

Counsel: " The courts are slow to recognize things of that sort. . . . The medical expert said that there were separate chambers of the mind."

Darling, J.: " How do they know? "

Avory, J.: " What is the meaning of ' all that which is below the surface of the water is the sub-conscious ' ? "

Darling, J.: " Would you separate the waters which are below the firmament from the waters which are above the firmament and let the dry land appear " (*laughter*).

Such ridicule and levity make absurd only those who indulge in it. A more tolerant judicial attitude towards the psychiatrist is needed, for his science has a very valuable contribution to make, both to the prevention of crime by early diagnosis of dangerous psychological trends, and to the scientific assessment of moral responsibility when crimes are committed. Too often he is the unrecognized and unhonoured friend of Justice. Finally, as to capital punishment, the weight of the evidence and modern opinion suggest the time has come for its abolition.

PART FOUR

CRIME: PREVENTION AND DETECTION

CHAPTER NINETEEN

Three Great Magistrates : The Idea of Prevention

I

STIPENDIARY magistrates in cities have a closer and more intimate view of a city's people than have red judges. It is among such that are to be found the men who suggested the earliest practical methods for protecting the citizens from those who preyed upon private property and very often threatened citizens' lives and now and then reduced London after dark to a city of terror.

Both judges and magistrates had a good deal to put up with in eighteenth-century England. They had to administer laws often repugnant to them, as Bill after Bill went on the Statute Book, each with fresh evidence of the ineptitude of Parliament when grappling with the problem of crime. Many judges and magistrates strove to soften the acerbities of the new laws with a tincture of common sense and humanity, and so serve as buffers between Parliament and people.

The country magistrates were the exception, for those who enforced the laws with harshness in the counties were those who passed them at Westminster. The county magistrates belonged to the landed class which alone enjoyed the franchise. Thus there were two types of magistrate, the city-enlightened, and the county-benighted, with, of course, exceptions in each case.

II

Before Sir Robert Peel's " First Thousand " appeared, in the nineteenth century, on the streets of London in their tall top hats and blue tail-coats, the policing of London had been unorganized and ineffectual. There were numerous bodies under a large number of municipal authorities—stipendiaries, City officials, the justices of Middlesex, and the seventy parishes that made up the metropolis.

Parish constables were required to serve for a year, unpaid, their sole qualification for the job being residence within the parish. A parish constable had only one incentive to do his duty: he got a " Tyburn ticket " if he effected an arrest. This carried exemption from further police duty and, incidentally, encouraged false charges and false arrests.

Next, there were the watchmen. Theirs was an ancient order manned by ancient men. The pay of a night watchman was from eightpence halfpenny to two shillings a night. There were about 200 of these decrepit custodians of nocturnal law and order in the City.

These ancients were jocularly known as Charlies. The criminal elements scorned them. Roysterers frequently made game of them, overturning both watchman and box, and sometimes carrying both off to some remote part of the town.

Thus the Charlies, if they added little to the security of London by night, did make a considerable contribution to its gaiety, which is about the best that can be said for them.

III

Among the first of the London stipendiary magistrates to bring forward a practical plan for lessening the dangers of the City's streets were Sir Henry Fielding, the novelist, and Sir John Fielding, his blind half-brother, both of whom, in turn, sat at Bow Street as first magistrate in Westminster, that court retaining its seniority to this day.

Sir Henry Fielding organized the parish constables and secured " information " by a system of bribes to informers; and in this way set about breaking up the numerous and dangerous street gangs who infested not only the streets, but also lonely highways leading out of the City.

Later, under Sir John Fielding, these informers emerged as Bow Street runners. They wore distinctive red waistcoats which earned them the nickname in the underworld of Robin Redbreasts.

In the activities of these eighteenth-century sleuths, most of them men of dubious character, may be seen the origin of the CID of today.

In addition, patrol men were organized, infantry and horse, from which evolved the present uniformed branch of the Metropolitan Police Force.

IV

So early as 1751 Sir Henry Fielding published his *Enquiry into the Causes of the late Increase of Robbers*.   The main argument of this pamphlet was the role of poverty as breeder of vice and crime, and the picture there painted of the condition of the London of that day is Hogarthian in starkness.

" If you consider the destruction of all morality," he wrote, " the whoredoms and drunkenness which is eternally carrying on in these houses (the brothels) on the one hand, and the excessive poverty and misery of most of the inhabitants on the other, it seems doubtful whether they are more than objects of detestation or compassion."

And again:

" I have been credibly informed that a single loaf hath supplied a whole family for a week . . . it is almost a miracle that stench, vermin and want should ever suffer them to be well."

And the writer winds up with these words:

" The wonder in fact is, that we have not a thousand more robbers than we have had; indeed, that all these wretches are not thieves, must give us either a very high idea of their honesty, or a very mean one of their capacity and courage."

This powerful pamphlet Sir Henry Fielding followed up two years later with an attack on the Poor Law.   In this he outlined a scheme for the drafting of the workless into industry, reserving for the unemployable the bare subsistence provided by the Poor Law.

" It is questionable," he wrote, " who are the more dissatisfied, the rich who have to raise a million yearly for the support of the poor, or the poor themselves, many of whom are starved, or found begging or pilfering in the streets today, and tomorrow are locked up in gaols and bridewells."

It may be doubted whether Sir Henry Fielding's theory of poverty as the chief cause of crime can be sustained.   And it seems dubious whether his plan was practicable or likely to produce better citizens by adding to the slaves of the mills and factories.   In any case, it was never put to the test.

In 1770 a Parliamentary Inquiry was set up concerning burglaries and robberies, and Sir John Fielding gave evidence before the Committee conducting it.   He then gave it as his opinion that the increase of crime among youths was due to early influences, to privations, and to bad example, with education confined to practice in the arts of pocket-picking and burglary.

Both these wise magistrates were probing the social sore for its core, and coming somewhere near it.   They were among the first to suggest that poverty was not due to crime and vice, but their parent.

Though the gap in time is considerable, there can be little doubt but that the early work of the half-brothers Fielding as reformers played a large part in directing events to the Metro-politan Police Bill of 1775, a measure which provided for the setting up of nine courts similar to that at Bow Street, under police commissioners.

An interesting sidelight is thrown on the self-importance and stupidity of the City Fathers of the time by their attitude towards this Bill, which, they protested, invaded their ancient rights and infringed their legislative jurisdiction.   The Bill, it was protested " overbears the forms established by the wisdom of our ancestors."

In face of this and other opposition, the Bill was dropped and another, incorporating some only of the first Bill's projects, was passed in 1792.   This gave London seven " Bow Streets," each presided over by three stipendiary magistrates.

V

The most remarkable magistrate appointed under this Act was Dr Patrick Colquhoun, a Scot and ex-Virginian colonist, one-time Lord Provost of Glasgow.   He brought to his new office a mind as open and fair as those of the Fieldings.

After studying conditions in the City for six years, Colquhoun published a *Treatise on the Police of the Metropolis.*   In this he pointed to the Poor Law as a breeding ground of crime, and observed how the system created the criminal mentality, since it provided neither work nor hope for its victims. "Hence it is," he wrote, "that poverty, under such circumstances, contributes in no small degree to the multiplication of crimes."

Colquhoun's plans for the prevention of crime differed from that of the Fieldings. They had been preoccupied with *detection*; Colquhoun was more interested in *prevention*. He advocated a central police authority to be known as the Board of Police Revenue. It was to be a preventive organization, clothed with wide powers.

To this general scheme Colquhoun appended a second, for the policing of the river Thames, where thieves annually caused enormous losses to the West Indian merchants and others.

As a result of Colquhoun's treatise a force, financed privately by the merchants chiefly affected, came into being for the policing of the Thames. This was, according to J. F. Moylan, the first force to which the term "Police" was ever applied to denote an organized body of constables.

Colquhoun had come to the conclusion that the prime cause of crime was economic. In London, indigence prevailed among the native population, anyway; but it was greatly aggravated by the large numbers of poor who migrated from the villages of Ireland in search of work.

Many of these poor people, finding nowhere any sort of work, came on the metropolitan parishes in the end, and were there treated without humanity. Some died, but more drifted, the men into crime, the women and girls into prostitution.

VI

Colquhoun's diagnosis of the social disease included the following etiological factors: first, poverty; next, idleness; last, incompetence.

This humane and astute observer of the eighteenth-century London underworld saw what little chance had the children born under vile and disgusting conditions.

"The infants of parents, broken down by misfortune, invariably learn, from the pressure of extreme poverty, to resort

o

to devices which early corrupt their morals and mar their future success and utility in life . . . they too soon become adepts in falsehood and deceit."

Colquhoun estimated that among the nine million people in the country as a whole, there were a million destitute; a clear proof, as he saw it, of the failure of the Poor Law.[1]

The situation was a curious one. On many London parishes were large numbers of paupers, many of them Irish, who remained more or less permanent charges on the Poor Law. They did so because magistrates were reluctant to label them as vagrants, since an Act of 1792 had provided whipping for such unfortunates. Magistrates consequently, out of pity, let the poor wretches escape by the narrow margin between a pauper on relief and a vagabond beyond the Poor Law's cold comforts.

Colquhoun divided the poor into five categories: First, the useful, namely, those who can and will work. These he held to be important people in the community, who should be safeguarded from want by the government.

Then the vagrant poor, those able to find, but unwilling to do, useful work. Next, the unemployables, by reason of bad character; such men and women, Colquhoun proposed, should be drafted into industry and debarred from the " benefits " of the Poor Law.

Finally, two further classes: the incapable—the aged and infirm, and the children of the workhouse. All these, Colquhoun reasoned, should be the care of the State: especially the children.

Colquhoun suggested another potent source of crime— namely, the gin-shops in which London abounded. In 1801 the population of the City was about 641,000, of which 20,000 were adrift in the underworld.

There were 5,000 gin-shops, 50,000 prostitutes, organized gangs of highway robbers who made the heaths perilous after dark, and so many footpads on the streets that citizens always carried cudgels.

---

[1] This was pre-census time; and all figures for that period were estimates. The generally accepted estimate for 1750 (pop. of England) is 6½ million.

Criminal activities, Colquhoun estimated, accounted for £2,000,000 per annum, to which had to be added another £7,000,000 lost in gaming-houses and fake lotteries.

What, then, was the remedy? Replied Colquhoun: a well-organized police force; the amendment of the criminal law; enforcement of all punishments; *work*.

As few had harkened to Romilly in the House of Commons, so few took heed of the wise, constructive programme against crime of this astute and humanitarian magistrate or of those of the great Fieldings.

VII

In 1811, London, pretty well inured to crime, was shocked by a series of murders. The City became a city of dread; people no longer felt safe even in their own homes, and something like panic broke out. One result of this was a run on rattles, then in use to rouse the alarm. They were sold by the tens of thousands. Many householders took to barring their windows by night and adding extra locks to their street doors.

It was on December 7 when Mr Marr, a lace and pelisse merchant, about to close his shop, dispatched his little maid-of-all-work further along the Ratcliffe Highway to buy oysters for his supper.

When she returned, the girl could not get in. The shop door was shut and locked. She listened and then, becoming alarmed, ran for help.

Men came and broke open the door. The merchant, Mrs Marr and their infant child lay on the shop floor. They had been battered to death.

Twelve days later the landlord of the King's Arms, Ratcliffe Highway, his wife, and their servant were all found battered to death in the same way.

All these murders were traced to one criminal, and he was duly apprehended. But a few months later another murder shocked the country, though it was a crime of quite a different order from those in the Ratcliffe Highway.

On the evening of May 11, 1812, the Prime Minister, Mr

Spencer Perceval, was making his way in thoughtful mood through the Lobby of the House of Parliament when he was startled by the sudden appearance from behind a pillar of a wild-looking man.

A moment later the Prime Minister fell, mortally wounded by pistol shots, and John Bellingham, a man suffering from persecution mania, similar to the case of Daniel M'Naghten, was seized and held.

There was a great outcry following these murders and a demand for better protection for the public and for public men; but little was done to better conditions, and eight more years passed and still London had no proper organization for protecting its citizens from crime and disorder.

Then, in 1820, another crisis arose. The unhappy Queen Caroline returned to London. The people of London were sympathetic to this unhappy lady, and they showed their feelings by demonstrations on her behalf.

So menacing did the crowds become that it was deemed necessary to call out the Guards. But the soldiers shared the sentiments of the people, and many of them took little action to disperse the crowds. Even so, there was bloodshed in Oxford Street and in Piccadilly. In the House of Lords the Duke of Wellington boomed, demanding action.

The Army, he objected, was not intended for that sort of duty, but for fighting battles against the enemies of the country: there must be set up an independent force to handle civil disturbances and to deal with civic strife.

This was the precipitating event which hastened the setting up of two committees by Sir Robert Peel, and which bore fruit in the Metropolitan Police Improvement Act of June 1829, a mere nine years in such matters being comparatively fast work.

Under this measure the police force came into being under two commissioners, with headquarters backing on the present site of Scotland Yard. It was a force of 3,000 uniformed constables. On September 29, 1829, Londoners saw a curious sight. Walking the main thoroughfares with stately tread appeared stalwart, top-hatted and blue-coated men, each armed with a useful-looking truncheon. They were the First Thousand. True, they were very rudely received by the population, and soon such nicknames as Peeler, Bluebottle, Raw Lobster, and so forth were shouted after them by vulgar boys. But that attitude quickly changed, and the Bobby, as the policemen ultimately became known, won both the respect and affection of the public.

From this modest beginning has developed our present-day police system, a great and complex machine for the detection of crime and identification of criminals. Into this service the exponents of many sciences are enlisted: the pathologist, the anatomist, the toxicologist, the chemist, the hand-writing expert, the forensic ballistics expert, the scientific photographer, and the finger-print expert.

CHAPTER TWENTY

Herschel: Witness This My Hand

I

ONE day in July 1858 an official of the old East India Company, stationed at Jungipoor, on the turbid Hooghly, had occasion to call for tenders for a supply of *ghooting*, a material used for road construction and repair.

Among tenders received was one from a certain Rājyadhar Kōnāi. The tender was accepted, and Kōnāi himself drew up the contract. He was about to sign in the customary manner, at the top right-hand corner, when the East India Company official, Sir William Herschel, stopped him.

" We will adopt another method of signing today," he said; " you shall sign with the palm-print of your hand."

The notion was not, in fact, quite so novel to Kōnāi, a literate Hindu, for he was well aware of the customary method of signature in the case of the illiterate, namely, with the tip of a finger, known as a *tep-sai* (*tep* = touch; *sai* = token). The Sahib's suggestion for a more extensive print was, consequently, not so remarkable a departure from custom.

Today that palm-print of Kōnāi, and the original contract in his beautiful script, are in the archives of the Royal Society, London. And they are there because when Kōnāi made that palm-print he made also history.

II

The illiterate Indian who made his *tep-sai* did not regard his mark as a substitute for the written word, or even as a means of identification. For him the procedure was ritualistic in character, and derived its value from the magic of physical contact.

We who touch the red wafer (seal) and declare,"This is my act and deed "; who swear an oath and seal it by a sacred kiss, share with primitive man this irrational sense of fear-tinged mystery, of the magic of touch.

The quasi-religious character of these symbolic acts of touching is supported by their association with the idea of divine, or divinely appointed kingship. In ancient Japan it was customary for the Emperor, the descendant of the Sun-goddess Amatseru, to mark State papers with his hand-print done in vermilion ink. " Touching " for the King's Evil is an example from Stuart times.

III

When first the imprint of hand, finger, or nail was in use for purposes of identification or proof, is unknown; but the system is very old.

The Assyrians used the nail-mark, imprinting it upon brick. There is in the British Museum an Assyrian brick which is, in effect, a conveyance, and it is signed by the nail-mark of the vendor. Sir Francis Galton secured a translation of the text from an official of the Museum, which reads as follows:

Nail-mark of Nabu-sum-usur, the seller of the field (used) like his seal.

In China the nail-mark was also used in legal documents. Mr T. Meadows Taylor gives the following example in his monograph *On Land Tenure in China* :[1]

"The Mother and Son, the sellers, have in the presence of all the parties, received the price of the land in full, amounting to sixty-four taels and five mace, in perfect dollars, weighed in the scales. Impression of the finger of the Mother, of the maiden name of Chin."

An anecdote told of the Empress Wen-leh, of the Tang Dynasty, *circa* 618, is amusing, if of no great historical importance in the story of nail- and finger-prints.

Ngeu-yang-siun, Secretary of Censors, moulded in wax a design made by him for a new coin. It was a round coin with a square hole through its centre.

[1] *Trans. China Branch, Royal Asiatic Society,* Pt I, 1847.

The Empress expressed herself as pleased with the design; but in handling it her four-inch nail pierced the wax, leaving a crescent imprint. This imperial clumsiness greatly vexed the Secretary of Censors, but with true courtly aplomb he declared himself delighted, and the royal nail-mark a great improvement on the general design. He accordingly adopted it, having the nail-mark raised in relief.

IV

Kōnāi's first palm-print was followed by a second when a new contract for further work was entered into. It was made in home-made oil-ink (water-ink is of little use for this purpose). But it had not occurred to Herschel that palm- or finger-prints might be recognized as evidence in courts of law, civil or criminal.

" The very possibility of such a sanction," he wrote, " to the use of the finger-print did not dawn upon me till after long experience, and even then it became no more than a personal conviction for many years to come."

A year later, Herschel was transferred to Nuddea, near Calcutta. The district was at that time in a state of disorder, following the Indigo riots. Fraud, perjury, and forgery were rife.

Herschel has put on record the great difficulties that then faced him as magistrate and official in charge of the prison:

" Things were so bad in this and other ways that the administration of Civil Justice had unusual difficulty in preserving its dignity. I was driven to take up finger-prints now with a definite object before me, and for three years continued taking a very large number from all sorts and conditions of men."

In the prison at Nuddea a certain notorious criminal was at that time serving a sentence. An uncorrupted gaoler noticed one day that there was on the floor of the convict's cell some curiously coloured material. The floor was accordingly dug over, with the result that a complete forger's kit was discovered.

This prisoner, with the connivance of certain gaolers, had been conducting from his cell a thriving business in forgery, dealing mainly with the signatures of landlords as they were made to appear on *pottahs* (agreements for rent).

Herschel was convinced that the only way in which this widespread crime of forgery and personation could be put down was by means of the official use of the finger-print system. But it had no official recognition, and Herschel consequently had to employ it in an unofficial way. This he did, meanwhile, from the year 1859 onwards, making a collection of the finger-prints of a great number of people, European and Indian.

Among these finger-prints was that of Mr Edward Henry, district superintendent of police, Nuddea, who was to become some years later Sir Edward Henry, Assistant Commissioner of Metropolitan Police, Scotland Yard.

It is an interesting recollection that the man who was to write the standard police text-book on finger-printing for police purposes was himself twice finger-printed by Herschel: for the first time on April 13, 1862, at a gathering at Kishnagar, when the Maharajah of Nuddea was also finger-printed; and for the second time forty-six years later, by which time the persistency of finger-prints had long been scientifically established.

V

Few today would deny Herschel's scientific attainments, since he is the originator of an identification system which has transformed police practice. Yet Herschel was not an anthropometrist, in the sense that Lombroso and Bertillon were. He was a great administrator who turned to anthropometry in order to cope with practical difficulties arising out of his official duties.

Herschel turned to the technique of the anthropometrist by way of the processes of reminiscence, a statement which calls for explanation.

When Herschel was a boy he was a keen naturalist, in particular a lover of birds. Among the most treasured of his books was a copy of Thomas Bewick's *British Birds*. This classic of natural history was both written and illustrated by Bewick, the most brilliant wood-engraver of his time.

Now, Bewick took to using as his sign manual, or trade mark, or colophon, the imprint of his thumb, with the words, in his usual hand: Thomas Bewick his mark.

How did Bewick engrave a subject so delicate as the bulb of his thumb? Apparently he first made a printer's ink impression in the wood and then engraved from that.

The memory of Bewick's engraved finger-print came back to Herschel when he was studying the subject with the enthusiasm of an inspired amateur. Was it that memory of boyhood's days that had evoked the idea that day when he had invited Kōnāi to make his mark? Herschel has told us that he believed so.

But the memory brought with it a doubt. For if Bewick could engrave so perfectly his own finger-print, *might not the forgery of finger-prints be within the realm of possibility?*

To decide the question, Herschel invited the best artists in Calcutta to attempt such an engraving. None of them succeeded.

VI

In order to prove the value of his idea Herschel had to prove two things of finger-prints: first, their persistence through life; secondly, their uniqueness to the individual.

There existed hundreds of millions of people—nearly 400,000,000 in India alone. Was it possible that Nature could devise for every one of these finger-markings that were unique?

The question could not be answered until a mass of material had been collected; while persistence could be proved only by " repeats " taken after long intervals of time.

This collection, made with such patience by a busy chief administrator in Bengal, was later to pass into the hands of a professional anthropologist, Sir Francis Galton, who was to endorse in the laboratory what Herschel had demonstrated in the field.

In 1877 Herschel returned to India from furlough to complete his full term of twenty-five years' service. He was now Magistrate and Collector, a joint office conferring very wide powers upon its holder. He was now satisfied of the merits of the finger-printing system he advocated, though he had to admit he was not yet in a position to demonstrate its worth— that is, *its infallibility*—for purposes of identification.

The new method was introduced into three departments: the prisons, the department for the registration of deeds, and the pensions office.

VII

" Registration," Herschel wrote, " appealed most strongly to my desires, but the sub-registrar and his clerks had to be trained, and meanwhile the few pensioners enabled me to break the ice myself. I was not a little anxious lest, officially introduced, Hindus might take alarm for their caste. The memory of the greased cartridges of the Mutiny, so near Hooghly, was indelible."

The Indian Mutiny was the culmination of a complex of causes; but the trigger mechanism which exploded the charge was, by Western standards, a trivial matter—namely, the type of ammunition served out to Indian troops.

The Enfield rifle cartridges had heavily greased ends, and these had to be bitten through in order to free the powder for the barrel.

At Dum-dum a high-caste Sepoy of Bengal and a low-caste arsenal worker came into conflict one day. The latter incensed the susceptible Sepoy by reminding him that every time he put pig-grease-tipped cartridges in his mouth he defiled himself and outraged his religion.

Such was the little spark of caste pride and religious prejudice that ignited so terrible an explosion in a land where religious custom colours nearly every aspect of daily life.

". . . The old lesson had been a severe one," Herschel recalled, " and I thought it well, when acting officially, to take every precaution. I was careful, therefore, from the first ostentatiously to employ Hindus to take the impressions wanted; using, as if a matter of course, the pad and the ink made by one of themselves from the very seed-oil and lamp-black which were in constant use for the office seals in the several departments."

Up to that time it was a common occurrence for a pensioner to present himself for his pension, only to be told that it had already been drawn by someone impersonating him.

It is a curious but admitted fact that as between them, the great families of Man cannot perceive the characteristics that mark one individual off from another. To the Western eyes, most Hindus at comparable age levels look much alike; and with the Chinese the difficulty of identification is even greater.

The pensioners welcomed the new system, which became known as the *sahib's hikmat*, since they realized that it was in their interest.

The old law had attempted to circumvent the forger and swindler, but it had not always been effective.

" The signatures," Herschel explained, " whether in full or by caste mark, or by cross, or, in the case of women mostly, by touching the paper with the tip of the finger wetted with ink . . . were made under the eye of the Registrar . . . nevertheless, fraudulent attempts did still come to light. Signatures were still denied; personations in presenting false deeds did take place, either to swindle, or, in one case, to fabricate an alibi."

VIII

The registration technique devised by Herschel and put into use in 1877 provided new safeguards greatly superior to the traditional methods.

The person had first to comply with the legal formalities of registration. The Registrar then made him print two fingers on the deed. Next he had to repeat the process in a book kept for Herschel's personal use in his anthropometrical capacity. (They were later of great service to Sir Francis Galton, to whom they were given by Herschel.)

Wrongful imprisonment was not an uncommon thing at that time in Bengal. It involved the imprisonment of the wrong person, and thus led to miscarriage of justice, though not in the usually accepted sense of that term.

A poor Hindu would serve a prison term for a fee in place of the real culprit, better placed financially than himself. The practice was known to exist, but it was difficult to detect. Herschel introduced a simple procedure which effectively put an end to this abuse.

Immediately a man had been sentenced he was finger-printed, both for the records of the court and on the warrant to the gaoler. Impersonation was no longer possible.

IX

It was during his last tour that Herschel tried to induce the Inspector of Gaols and the Registrar-General to adopt the system. All who had seen it in operation were convinced of its efficiency and enthusiastic for its general use.

Under date August 15, 1877, Herschel wrote (*inter alia*):

" I enclose a paper which looks unusual, but which I hope, has some value. It exhibits a method of identification of persons, which, with ordinary care in execution, and with judicial care in the scrutiny, is, I can now say, for all practical purposes far more infallible than photography. It consists of taking a seal-like impression, in common seal ink, of the markings of the skin of the two forefingers of the right hand.

" Every person who now registers a document at Hooghly has to sign his ' sign-manual.' None has offered the smallest objection, and I believe that the practice, if generally adopted, will put an end to all attempts at personation. . . . I have taken thousands now in the course of the past twenty years, and I am prepared to answer for the identity of every person whose ' sign-manual ' I can now produce if I am confronted with him.

" As an instance of the value of the thing, I might suggest that if Roger Tichborne had given his ' sign manual ' on entering the Army on any register, the whole Orton case would have been knocked on the head in ten minutes by requiring Orton to make his sign-manual alongside it for comparison."

Nothing came of this appeal, though failure to act was not due to incompetence or indifference, but to the curious reason that its official introduction might fan again those fires which burned so fiercely during the Mutiny and the more recent Indigo disturbances.

In 1880 Herschel, then in retirement, published in *Nature* [1] a brief account of his system of finger-printing. Sir Francis Galton, busy in his Anthropometric Laboratory in the galleries of the Science Collection in South Kensington, read that paper.

Herschel was then ageing and in ill health: Galton was at the peak of his powers.

Writing twelve years later his great treatise on finger-prints, and with that title, Galton paid Herschel a just tribute:

" Sir William Herschel must be regarded as the first who devised a feasible method for regular use, and afterwards officially adopted it."

We will now return from Bengal and see what Galton made of the work of which Herschel was pioneer.

[1] *Nature*, November 25, 1880.

CHAPTER TWENTY-ONE
Galton: Master Measurer

I

THE choice of subject for a degree thesis has resulted in many barren expeditions into the by-ways of knowledge. When, in 1823, J. E. Purkinje read before the savants of the University of Breslau a degree thesis dealing with the skin-patterns of the fingers and palm, the candidate for a doctorate may well have astonished his audience, inured to the obscure, by the novelty of his subject.

Purkinje's was the first scientific study of skin-patterns of fingers and palm. He identified nine standard types and, further, advocated a system of classification. The subject aroused great interest in scientific circles, both in Germany and abroad.

Purkinje's thesis, in the customary clumsy Latin, is quite short; and the pamphlet of fifty-eight pages in which it was published is now exceedingly rare.[1] One copy is in the Library of the Royal College of Surgeons, having been pro-cured by the librarian to assist Sir Francis Galton in his research into the same little-known subject.

Galton translated Purkinje's treatise into English, and in his own treatise, *Finger Prints*, includes passages from it.

Purkinje's interest in the skin-patterns of the hand was that of the physiologist. It did not occur to him that in each of the nine standard types of finger-markings classified by him no two specimens would ever be found to be identical.

II

To every thinker who has fallen in love with a pretty theory comes the temptation to tamper with inconvenient facts.

The pretty theory, this beloved child of the brain, is to be

[1] *Commentatio de examine physiologico organi visus et systematis cutanei.*

defended to the end against all assaults upon it.   It is when this conflict exists between the concept and reality that the objective temper proper to pure science is liable to suffer.   Facts are forced to fit theory, rather than theory to accommodate itself to facts.

Lombroso is an example of a man in love with a theory. He was obsessed by the proposition that there exists a being identifiable as *criminal man*.   He did not always resist the perhaps unconscious tendency to press facts unduly into the mould of his preconceived ideas.

Bertillon—in less degree, it is true—tended to defend his anthropometrical system of identification against all comers, resenting and resisting criticisms levelled at its sweeping generalizations.

With Bertillon, as with Lombroso, the preconceived idea fused with the hoped-for, the irresistibly desired proof.

Sir Francis Galton was entirely free of this fault.   He would willingly admit error and, when necessary, recast research in the light of fuller data.

Lombroso and Bertillon were criminologists by design; Galton became a criminologist by chance.   His work on the patterns of the skin of the hand was begun as an inquiry into the anthropological significance, if any, of them.

There is something almost mechanical and robot-like in the processes of the mind of this remarkable man when engaged on research.   Doctor of medicine, scientist, traveller, and sportsman, Galton was all these, but pre-eminently he was splendidly equipped by Nature for the labours of the scientific laboratory, in his case anthropology, and the measurement of man's mental powers.

Galton's first interest in and subsequent investigations into the nature of the patterns of the skin of finger-bulb and hand-palm came about in this way.

During the later decades of the nineteenth century Galton was conducting researches into hereditary genius.

" For this purpose," he wrote, " I required a vast number of exact measurements relating to the faculties and capacities of both body and mind, and covering at least two generations."

In 1865, Galton therefore approached the celebrated Dr Farrar, later Headmaster of Marlborough College and Dean of Canterbury, and immortalized as the author of the pietistic *Eric, Or Little by Little* and other improving moral works.

Galton descended upon Marlborough and measured the astonished boys. But the sample was insufficient for his purpose. As guinea-pigs the boys of Marlborough had brought little to light; the investigator had need of far larger numbers, and the opportunity arose to secure them with the coming of the International Exhibition of 1884.

Galton's idea was one that foreshadowed the methods of Dr Gallup. The Gallup Poll bases findings on large-scale samplings of opinion: Galton similarly collected large-scale samplings of the population's physical characteristics and capacities.

Between 1865 and 1882 Galton was engaged mainly on anthropological work. In the latter year he contributed an article to the *Fortnightly Review* in which he wrote:

" When shall we have anthropometrical laboratories where a man may from time to time get himself and his children weighed, measured and rightly photographed, and have each of their bodily faculties tested by the best-known methods of science ?"

There, in embryo, was an idea that took concrete shape, to some extent, in the Peckham Health Centre, described by the present writer in the same journal in 1934.

III

It was a good and a clever idea to square a scientific purpose with a popular Exhibition novelty side-show; to extract from people bent only on pleasure and diversion data of scientific value.

Galton has left on record how he implemented his scheme.

" I arranged," he wrote, " a long narrow enclosure with trellis work in front and at its ends. A table ran alongside the trellis work on which the instruments were placed and where the applicants were tested. A doorkeeper stationed at one end

P

admitted a single applicant at a time, who had to pay three-pence. The measurements dealt with keenness of sight and of hearing; colour sense; judgment of eye; breathing power; reaction time; strength of pull and of squeeze; force of blow; span of arms; height standing and sitting; and weight."

This " side show " proved to be very popular. It was fun to emerge from the trellis-work enclosure with a large and important-looking chart recording one's physical characteristics and powers. It was psychologically adroit, too, for nothing gives more pleasure than to be the object of scientific curiosity.

When the International Exhibition closed in 1885 Galton was so encouraged by the results that he asked for and secured accommodation in the South Kensington Museum for a permanent Anthropometrical Laboratory.

IV

Galton's laboratory soon became famous, and many celebrities visited it, among them the philosopher Herbert Spencer, whose measurements Galton recorded, including, of course, his finger-prints.

" It is a curious thing," Galton remarked to Herbert Spencer, " that we do not know the origin of these patterns. Even the fingers of unborn children have been dissected to ascertain their earliest stage."

" That is beginning in the wrong way," objected Spencer. " You should consider the *purpose* the ridges have to fulfil, and then work backwards. It is obvious to me," he continued, " that the delicate mouths of the sudorific glands require the protection given to them by the ridges on either side of them."

" Your arguments are beautiful, my dear Spencer," Galton replied, " and they deserve to be true. But it happens that the mouths of the ducts do not run in the valley between the crests, but along the crests of the ridges themselves! "

At this Spencer laughed heartily, caught out in the act of fitting facts to theory. This he admitted freely, and went on to tell an anecdote in point.

" One evening at the Athenæum," he said, " during a pause

in the dinner-table talk, I remarked, ' You would think little of it, but I once wrote a tragedy'."

Huxley was dining.

" I know the catastrophe," he announced.

" But that is quite impossible," protested Spencer; " I never told a soul about it! "

" Oh, but it is possible," Huxley persisted.

" Then what was it? " challenged Spencer.

" It was a beautiful theory murdered by a nasty, ugly little fact! " Huxley replied.

V

Upon the palms of every man's hands, and upon the soles of his feet, Nature has inscribed a unique signature. There are thousands of millions of human beings in the world, yet no two carry signatures identical—not even identical twins from a single ovum.

These unique and unchallengeable signatures, past all forging, are writ for life, nay, even from before birth, and remain, even after death, in the papillary ridges of the skin surface.

These ridges form patterns that are unique. They are there four months after conception on the tiny, crumpled fingers of the babe in the womb. They remain there until old age, constant, unchanged. They may even be seen on the embalmed hands of mummies who lived and loved when Pharaohs ruled in Egypt.

Galton's interest in finger-prints was quite different from Herschel's. He was not in the early stages concerned in any way with criminal investigation and the identification by these means of the criminal. His interest was with those patterns that might hold secrets of the greatest value to the anthropologist; secrets concerning the laws of heredity, of the nature of genera and species.

After examining a large number of finger-prints Galton concluded that there existed an hereditary tendency for some peculiarity of pattern to recur in the same family. But, curiously enough, in the case of twins he found sometimes marked dissimilarities.

VI

If the reader examines the ball of his thumb, he will observe how the general conformation of the ridges resembles somewhat the ridges left upon the sand by the receding tide. Though they are not visible to the naked eye, these ridges are studded, as Galton reminded Spencer, with minute pores: these are the tiny craters, or vents, of the glands.

When your hand is moist with sweat it is made so by the exudations from these minute glandular ducts through the minute mouths or openings upon the skin-ridge system of your hand.

In criminal investigation imprints left by persons handling objects, such as glass or metal, are known as " latent finger-prints," or sweat-prints. It is such prints that are used by the criminal investigator for comparison with prints classified in the forensic laboratory.

Finger-prints were later classified by Galton under three principal heads: the arches, the loops, and the whorls.

In practice, classification is extremely important, since it narrows the big task of the forensic expert, who, handed a given specimen, has to seek in the records for its pair.

VII

Return, for a moment, to your own thumb.

You will observe that there are ridges that sweep across the thumb bulb. These are known as the arches.

Next you may notice how, in some cases, these arches turn and form a loop. And, again, you may find turns that complete the circle. These are known as whorls.

Galton eventually classified a large number of these arches and loops: arches plain, forked, or tented; loops plain, invaded, eyeletted, and so forth.

He studied, too, the minutiæ with indefatigable patience and thoroughness, until, like an explorer surveying a newly-discovered land, he had mapped the skin-markings of the human hand to the last detail: the loop cores, the whorl cores, the envelopes or rods or staples.

Contrary to general belief, it is not the length, breadth, and diameter of the ridges and valleys that are the prime factors in criminal investigation, but these minutiæ.

The reason why this is the case may be explained.

The dimensions of the hand change with growth and age. For example, the distance between ridges may be found to vary over a long period of time. And, again, distortions may appear which modify and change the relations of one feature to another.

But the pattern as a whole preserves its identity.

If you take a piece of patterned fabric and hold it to the light, you will observe both pattern detail and any blemish or other mark, such as some imperfection in the weave or pattern.

Now pull your patterned fabric so as to distort the design, and you will observe that you have changed the distances between given features. You will have done that: but the patterned fabric will remain, as a whole design, unchanged.

It is so with the skin-patterns of the hand and, in somewhat more simplified form, with the soles of the feet.

Thus, length, breadth, and diameter may be variables that are subjected to the changes of growth, changes brought about by occupation and the passage of time. *But the general pattern and its minutiæ persist.*

VIII

In 1888, three years after he had set up his Anthropometrical Laboratory in South Kensington, Galton was invited to give a lecture at the Royal Institute on the Bertillon system. The French system had then recently been introduced in Scotland Yard, and there was much talk of its value for the identification of criminals.

Galton decided to broaden the basis of his subject-matter by including, along with orthodox *Bertillonage* measurements, some account of finger-prints. But he had at that time little knowledge of them. He therefore invited correspondence, by inserting a notice in *Nature*.

It was in this way that Galton learnt, to his surprise, that

Herschel had been using finger-prints for identification purposes in Bengal.

This was the point of departure for Galton's investigation of finger-prints from the viewpoint of their value in criminal investigation. He took the finger-prints of very many people, of many races, of divers characters and temperaments, including those of lunatics.

He had seen at once the great value that finger-prints might have for the purpose of criminal investigation. That is, if, as he believed, it could be established that (*a*) finger-prints are unique to the individual, and (*b*) they persist unchanged through life.

As Galton saw it, three conditions had to be established. First, the constancy throughout life of the finger-skin pattern. Secondly, the proof of an infinite variety of patterns. Last, the practical possibility of classifying finger-prints for ready reference or comparison.

When he delivered his Royal Institute lecture Galton had accumulated a sufficient number of finger-prints to convince him that here the police had an infallible means of establishing identity, and one immeasurably superior to the cumbrous anthropometric system of Bertillon.

" The patterns," he wrote, " grow simultaneously with the finger, and its proportions vary with its fatness, leanness, usage, gouty deformity, or age. But, though the patterns as a whole may become considerably altered in length, or breadth, the number of ridges, their embranchments, and other minutiæ, remain unchanged."

By 1889 Galton was convinced that finger-prints remain constant throughout life and that no two finger-prints are identical.

In short, Galton realized that this discovery transformed the problem of identification, raising it to the level of an exact science. Here, indeed, was a wonderful weapon for the armoury of the criminal investigator.

" The body of Jezebel," Galton observed of his well-founded conclusion, " was devoured by the dogs at Jezreel, so that no man might say ' This is Jezebel.' And the dogs left only her

skull, the palms of her hands, and the soles of her feet.   What
the dogs left was all that a modern criminal investigator would
ask for, and that would be ample for his purpose."[1]

IX

So much for the forging by science of this beautiful weapon
against the criminal.

What of its practical application?

In modern criminal investigation, finger-prints serve two
main purposes.   They provide a certain means of establishing
whether a person under arrest has a criminal record.   Secondly,
they are evidence of the presence of a person at the scene of a
crime (though not necessarily evidence of his presence at the
time of it, or of his complicity in the offence).

When a criminal grasps a smooth-surfaced object, he leaves
a sweat-print, as described earlier.   Make the experiment
yourself—on glass or silver.

Grasp the chosen object and then examine it.   You will
see, quite clearly, the sweat-print pattern made by your hands,
the fingers and some part, perhaps, of the palms as well.

Sweat-prints found in the course of a criminal investigation
are photographed for the purpose of comparison with finger-
print bureau records.

Naturally, the professional criminal (as distinct from the
criminal by mischance or misfortune) is by this time well aware
of the danger of leaving finger-prints at the scene of his crime.
He takes precautions, and wears either ordinary gloves or
rubber gloves.

These devices do not yield the criminal full protection.
An ordinary glove has at the base of the palm an opening
sufficiently large to expose a portion of the palm pattern;
and such partial palm patterns have been sufficient to establish
evidence of identity.

A rubber glove, it might be thought, would prove completely
efficient and provide absolute immunity.   Yet it is not so.

---

[1] Michael QUERIPEL, 18, convicted of the murder of Mrs. E. CURRELL,
on Potter's Bar Golf Course, April, 1955, was traced by a single palm-
print after over 9000 prints had been taken from local residents.

Expertly turned inside out, and subjected to technical photographic treatment, such a glove yields a sweat-pattern of the wearer's hand.

X

The supremacy of the finger-print as an infallible means of identification has long since been demonstrated. The advantages of the method over the anthropometric methods of Bertillon are its relative simplicity of application, and the absolute elimination of the element of risk of mistaken identity.

Professor Hans Gross, whose *Criminal Investigation* is used by our own and many other criminal investigation departments, cites a case, here summarized, that well illustrates the supreme value of the finger-print for the purpose of identification and its superiority over the Bertillon or any other system, including personal recollection—and that not least.

XI

A woman who was giving evidence for the prosecution in a London criminal court had her character attacked by counsel for the defence, who suggested that, having been convicted of stealing from her employer, she could not be regarded as a reliable witness.

A police officer attested that he had arrested the witness and that he had been present throughout her trial for theft. The former employer corroborated the identification.

Yet the witness persisted vehemently in her denial, and perhaps with so unmistakable an accent of truth that the judge directed that her finger-prints should be taken for comparison with those of the convicted thief with whom she had been identified.

The prints were duly taken, and they at once established the witness's innocence. It is an old legal adage that facts, having no motives, do not lie; which may well be the case without detracting from the late G. K. Chesterton's observations about the perversity of inanimate objects.

In this case sheer mischance of circumstance, astonishing coincidence, close physical resemblance, identity of name, combined with something like blind malignance to implicate an innocent person.   Could an actual case demonstrate more clearly how long indeed may be the " arm of coincidence "?

The tragic case of Adolf Beck, twice wrongfully identified, convicted, and imprisoned, could never have occurred had the finger-print system been in use at that time.

In 1891, Bertillon, who had shown a somewhat unreceptive attitude towards finger-prints, modified his view and included them in the routine of his physical recordings.   This change of front ensued upon meetings between the French anthropometrist and Galton, in London and in Paris.

XII

Certitude is a word out of favour with the scientific mind, which knows well that no scientific truth is an absolute.

Nevertheless, even by 1880, by which time much work had been done without the detection either of identical prints or of prints approximating to identity, the Uniqueness Theory was generally accepted by both anthropometrists and criminal investigators.

There was Galton's final estimate of the chance of two identical prints, calculated by him as *one in 64,000 million*, which is about on a level of probability with Huxley's typewriting monkey, calculated ultimately to produce out of his machine's keyboard the sonnets of Shakespeare after some billions of years of purposeless activity.

All that granted, there remained certain residual doubts to be disposed of.   For example, the effect of wound-scars, of accidents to the corrugated skin pattern, of sickness, and of burns.

In 1880 Dr Henry Faulds, who had become an enthusiast for the new system, made a number of experiments in order to dispose of these doubtful points.   He proceeded in the following manner.

First he took an impression of the finger-prints of the subject. He then erased the corrugations by friction until the skin surface was worn down to complete smoothness.   He then permitted the skin to grow and repair by natural processes the damage artificially done, when he again took prints.   The first and second prints were then found to be identical, and the point thus established that a destroyed skin pattern reappears after repair as it was before destruction.

Dr Faulds repeated his experiment with skin-burn subjects, and with subjects whose skin-patterns had been effaced by peeling, following fever. The results were the same.

XIII

The forensic application of finger-printing is not limited to the identification of persons. It is equally valuable in the identification of documents. The reader will recall that Herschel first applied the method for the latter purpose in his dealings with the Indian road contractor, Kōnāi.

It is remarkable that having, each one of us, a permanent, indestructible, unforgeable, and unique signature upon the tips of our fingers, we make so little use of this perfect safeguard against fraud.

Disputes in the courts, civil and criminal, as to the authenticity of documents would be fewer were most signed both by the print of the hand and by the writing of the hand.

If Herschel may fairly be said to have " discovered " finger-prints, Galton, and, to a rather more limited extent, Dr Henry Faulds, may be said to have made their great value widely known.

It remained for a police officer to implement the work done by these scientists.

CHAPTER TWENTY-TWO

Bertillon: Inspired Police Official

I

WE can only guess why Alphonse Bertillon chose the Criminal Investigation Department of the Paris Prefecture as a career, for he was not at all the usual type to be met with there. In the first place, he was a scholar, with leanings towards his father's department of learning—namely, anthropology.

Dr Adolphe Bertillon was a scientist very well known in his day, if now forgotten, and remembered only as the father of the inventor of *Bertillonage*. But scientists are not commonly wealthy men, and the necessity to become self-supporting in any capacity that offered reasonable pay was probably the commonplace factor which took this grave-faced young man into the ethically murky atmosphere of the Paris Sûreté headquarters. Bertillon junior was quiet and unobtrusive and modest; but, as is often the case with men of that type, with natural reserve went strength of character and steadfastness of purpose.

II

During his period of army service Bertillon had secured a medical course and was for a considerable time engaged in recording the measurements of drafted conscripts.

While thus employed he observed the fact, at once of interest to him, that each individual differed and that in every case the main bone structure had a correlation peculiar to the individual.

Now entering the Sûreté's identification bureau, this experience was recalled by him.

In 1873 the method of photographing criminals had been instituted for the purpose of establishing identity. Bertillon found at his disposal a collection of such photographs.

" How many are here? " he inquired.

" We have a hundred thousand," he was proudly informed.

" And upon what system are they classified? " he asked.

" System?   Why, here they are.   One searches until one finds—or does not find—the face sought for."

That was how it was.   One hundred thousand photographic records of criminals; one hundred thousand completely useless items.   For it is obvious that it would not be possible for this collection to be rummaged every time a suspect was brought in for interrogation or upon a criminal charge.

The unpleasant truth, as Bertillon was to discover, was that police headquarters were neither scientific in their methods of identification, nor always above corruption.

The old system of identification was based on the cupidity of a somewhat underpaid police service, and with consequences that may be imagined.

The old procedure was as follows.   Agents were offered a reward of five francs for every identification.   As batches of arrested men were herded in, agents gathered about in the hope of earning the five francs reward.

Now, such a system clearly invited corruption, since it supplied a pecuniary motive, and when Bertillon entered the department corruption was rife.

One method was to deceive the examining magistrate.

Accused criminals with long records were by these means able to appear as first offenders or as the victims of mistaken identity.

" Has the accused, Durant, a criminal record? " the examining magistrate would ask.

" There is no photographic record of it, Monsieur."

" A first offence, then? "

" It would seem so, Monsieur."

How much had passed between the old criminal and the corrupt agent?   Perhaps as much as a hundred francs, at that period a considerable sum.

Or again, it might go like this:

" What is your name? "

" Marcel Marchant."

" You assert that you are not Albert Homais? "

" Emphatically! "

" You identified him? "   This to the police agent.

" That is so.   But I am not now so sure.   One may make an honest mistake.   I fear I have done so."

III

In such conditions as these Bertillon recalled his army experience in the measurement of recruits and the interesting discovery he had made at that time.   And it occurred to him that there might be here the solution of this problem of identification on lines so scientifically sound that both error and corruption would be eliminated.

He decided that a pilot experiment must be his first step, and since in the course of his routine duties he had to fill up the particulars of the general physical appearance of prisoners, he began to make exact measurements of them, as he had done in the army, and with the end-object of establishing his theory of the uniqueness of every man subjected to scientific measurement of his appropriate parts.

Now, the main bones of the body remain constant in size from late adolescence to old age.   And Bertillon decided to keep his anthropological survey within that age bracket— namely, twenty to sixty years of age.

At the end of eight months, with a mass of statistical material before him, Bertillon found that no two individuals subjected to his measuring tests were identical as to the large bones of their bodies.

This was an important discovery.   For it meant that no disguise, adopted to change the criminal's appearance, could offset the evidence of anatomical fact, for the evasive criminal would be betrayed by the very legs he stood on and by the very arms with which he gesticulated his protested innocence.   Thus, Bertillon contended, the element of doubt in cases of dubious identity would be excluded and all corruption finally countered.

IV

So far Bertillon had been considering the problem of the scientific identification of criminals *after* arrest.   He now turned his attention to the problem of identification of the wanted man by the searching detective. What he sought for was a method absolutely scientific, whereby a trained detective would be enabled to penetrate any disguise. And he contrived a clever system, using his knowledge of the anatomy of the skull for his purpose.

A man " on the run " may affect a disguise by two devices. He may change his appearance *after* the commission of the offence, or he may commit the offence disguised and then at once abandon it.

The first method has many disadvantages and is used generally only by amateurs in crime—for example, by persons in positions of trust absconding. The second method has everything to recommend it, and is used by the experienced professional criminal.

For example, a bank robber will use a mask or other facial disguise and become his natural self as he makes his getaway.

" Can you describe the bandit? " asks the investigating detective.

" I think so," says the cashier. " He has a full red beard."

Thus, even if the police lay their hands on the bank robber, he is not handicapped by the suspicious circumstance that he has just recently shaved off his beard, or dyed his hair, or affected a limp, or used cosmetics to change the general character of his face.

Bertillon hit upon the idea of making photographic records of all criminals apprehended, photographs in profile and full-face, from clear-cut negatives. This type of photograph he named *portrait parlé*. It was devised for the assistance of the detective seeking a wanted man, and it was to arm him with exact anatomical data by which he would, after due training, be able to spot the wanted man, however well disguised he might be.

V

The *portrait parlé* system dealt with each facial particular in great anatomical detail. The *portrait parlé* involved the use of the photograph; but it dispensed with it at the same time.

That is to say, the detective engaged in the search no longer sought for a man resembling the official photographs. He sought for a man with certain peculiarities which had been scientifically indicated in Bertillon's system, about which now a further few words.

Bertillon classified every feature of the face and compiled a Table of Descriptive Marks.   The detective was to ignore the actual face: he was to search for *peculiarities*.

Here is the section of the Bertillon Table dealing with the nose, as quoted by Professor Gross.[1]

The Nose. Depth of the root : small, medium, large.

    Profile :   concave,   rectilinear,   convex,   arched, irregular, sinuous.

    Base : raised, horizontal, depressed.

    Height: ⎫
    Projection: ⎬ small, medium, large.
    Size: ⎭

Particularities.—The root of the nose may be very narrow; or very large; high or low ; the root may be broken.

The profile may be the shape of an S; it may be flat, or broad; or the nose may be broken; it may be curved to the right or left.

The tip may be tapering, or thick, or bi-lobar, or flat; twisted to right or left; blotched and pimpled.

The partition (*septum*) may be stiff or mobile, recurved, dilated, pinched up.

The time was to come when Bertillon was to lecture to detectives on the technique of his *portrait parlé* in a large lecture room in the Sûreté whose walls were lined with life-size photographs of heads that demonstrated the points made in the lecture.

But that time was not yet.   Before it came, Bertillon was to be subjected to several forms of humiliation and injustice, both by his Chief and by his colleagues of the Prefecture.

[1] *Criminal Investigation*, by Dr Hans Gross.

VI

When, after eight months of hard work, Bertillon had convinced himself of the scientific value of his method of identification, he went to his Chief, Monsieur Andrieux, the Prefect. It must have seemed to Bertillon that it was necessary only to set forth the scientific facts for them to be accepted. But he was to be disappointed. M. Andrieux was an official of the old school, a man without the easily aroused inquisitiveness of the scientific temper. He proved to be allergic to Bertillon's idea, and saw little in it that appealed to him.

Bertillon shrugged and returned to his bureau. There were few friendly faces to be met in the Sûreté, few colleagues who greeted him with a smile. For Bertillon's investigations were regarded with mistrust and suspicion as a danger to the comfortable, easygoing established order.

When other officials came late, or went early, nothing was said. But it was notable that the mild little official who chose to poke his nose into matters unconnected with his official duties seldom escaped an official reprimand for these offences.

But some progress had been made, and when, three years later, Monsieur Andrieux was succeeded by Monsieur Camescasse, Bertillon returned to his new Chief's office carrying the evidence of his years of work. The new Prefect was sympathetic. Yes, he agreed, he would make available the convict population of La Santé prison for anthropometrical survey. But the period would be limited to three months, during which time he would expect results and, failing them, would drop the project for introducing *Bertillonage* into the Paris criminal investigation system.

VII

One day, shortly before the end of the test period, a suspect was " brought in." His face aroused in Bertillon a vague memory.

" Your name? " he asked.

" Dupont."

" You are sure? "

" But, yes—Dupont.   One knows one's own name."

Bertillon was not satisfied.   He turned to his files, armed with the measurements of the suspect.   Soon he found what he wanted.

" You are not Dupont," he challenged, holding a photograph up for inspection.   " Your name is Martin! "

There was no disputing it.

A man may grow a beard, or remove it from his face, or dye it.   He may crop his hair, or grow it, or change its colour. He may do much to change his appearance, but without surgical intervention he cannot change the character or measurements of his nose, the angle of the back of his head, the contour of his profile.

Bertillon had succeeded in convincing his Chief, and his system was adopted by the Paris Sûreté, and shortly thereafter was made obligatory for all French police forces.

During the first year Bertillon compiled anthropometrical records of no fewer than 7,336 criminals, and by means of this register identified forty-nine old offenders.   In the following year the figures rose, and as they did so, Bertillon's fame grew. A new word had been added to the language—*Bertillonage*.

Bertillon's system was introduced in 1883.   By 1887 60,000 sets of measures had been made and registered.   The Bertillon Bureau was now an accepted part of the police system, and every man arrested was passed at once to that department and there subjected to measurement and photography by clerks trained by the inventor of the system.

Bertillon had decided on four principal measurements: head-length, head-breadth, middle-finger length, foot-length— these being structural constants throughout adult life (among many others).

These four main measurements he subdivided into three groups: small, medium, large, the total of groupings being eighty-one.   These headings he again subdivided into three classes according to height, span, cubit, length and breadth of ear, height, and bust.

Finally, he classified eye colour under seven heads.

Thus, in all, twelve main measurements were made, eleven

Q

of which were split up into three divisions and one—the eye—
into seven.

This arrangement works out as follows:

$$3^{11} \times 7 = 1,240,029$$

More than one million possible combinations!

VIII

When a new scientific advance is made there is always a
swing of the pendulum of faith, with hope as the prime mover.
This has been universal experience throughout the ages, which
are marked, generation by generation, with the graves of high
hopes.

Koch had discovered the cure for tuberculosis, or so it
seemed to him when, for the first time, he saw the rod-like
tubercles under his microscope. True, he had found the
cause, but the cure is not known, even yet.

And, to come nearer to our own time, the ultra-microscope
revealed the cancer virus—the infinitely minute filter-passing
organism responsible for that disease. Yes, at first high hopes,
high promise of a great medical conquest. And then?
Doubts as to the reality of the virus itself: a scientific argument
in place of salvation.

Bertillonage, as a scientific system for the identification of
criminals, was a tremendous advance upon mere description.
But—and this was the crux—was it virtually *infallible*?

From his chair in his Anthropometrical Bureau, Bertillon
answered with assurance: Yes! And with each success the
brilliance of it all delighted everybody concerned. Vienna
adopted the system, and soon thereafter Holland, Germany,
Hungary, Switzerland, and Italy.

Now, as we have seen, at that time another master measurer,
Sir Francis Galton, was very much preoccupied with the
classification of types on anthropometrical lines.

Galton's notion had been to secure valuable anthropometrical data with a hook baited with amusement. And he
was very successful. When the International Exhibition closed,

Galton continued his work, shifting his laboratory to new quarters in South Kensington.

Bertillon's much-talked-of system for identification of criminals naturally interested the English scientist, and he went to Paris to see the actual work of the Bertillon Bureau at Sûreté headquarters.

" I had the pleasure," he wrote, " of seeing the system in operation in Paris . . . and was greatly impressed by the deftness of the measuring, and with the swiftness and success with which the assistants searched for the cards containing entries similar to the measure of the prisoner then under examination."

But it is one thing to be impressed, another to be convinced. And Galton was not quite sure about the scientific value of *Bertillonage* when he returned to his London laboratory.

" The success," he subsequently wrote, " is considered by many experts to be fully proved, notwithstanding many apparent objections."

One of these objections, as Galton saw it, was the probability or possibility of correlation—the mutual relations of two or more parts or things—producing, on some Bertillon cards, a disproportionately large number of entries. He decided to experiment, and took for his purpose 500 measures made at his own laboratory, selecting, as had Bertillon, four primary features: head-length, head-breadth, middle-finger-length, and foot-length.

The results of his experiment convinced Galton of the value of the method, but without the unqualified enthusiasm that it had evoked throughout most countries in Europe.

The method, he saw, had certain drawbacks and limitations, particularly in its application to police investigations. The search of a Bertillon index, he pointed out, became a very difficult proceeding when the number of the cards to be combed exceeded the 20,000 mark.

Then there was always the element of possible error in measurement. And finally there was the notable omission of the teeth.

It seems curious that the value of the teeth for the purpose

of identification should have been overlooked by Bertillon.
For even allowing for the loss of a tooth or teeth between a
first and subsequent Bertillon measure, the conformation of
both upper- and lower-jaw teeth and empty sockets might be
deemed to be unique to the individual. (Indeed, as will be
demonstrated in a later chapter, the evidence of the teeth may
be the clinching item of evidence in the evidential chain in a
murder trial.)

The Bertillon system was adopted by Scotland Yard in
1903, though it was known that the system, after being given a
trial, had been rejected in 1891 by the American Army
authorities, by whom it had been employed for the
identification of deserters.

IX

Though the Army had found against it, the Bertillon
system continued to be used in most American penitentiaries,
and was so up to the year 1913. In that year a most curious
incident shook the confidence of the authorities in its scientific
values.

One day a prisoner was received into the great Leavenworth
Penitentiary in the State of Texas. He was duly subjected to
the Bertillon measures.

The prisoner's name was Will West, and he was in prison for
fraud.

The staff clerk thought the face familiar, and he turned up
the appropriate cards in the Bertillon Register. There he came
on one relating to one *William* West.

The photographs of William West showed the face of Will
West. The two faces—that before him, and that of the
photograph—appeared to the clerk to be those of the same
person, exact in every particular.

And not that alone: the Bertillon measurements of the
William West of the Register and of Will West in the flesh,
allowing for the margin of possible error which had been noted
by Galton and acted upon by the American Army authorities,
might be described as *almost* identical.

So far, then, on the evidence of *Bertillonage*, William West in his locked cell, awaiting trial for murder, and Will West, convicted of fraud and now in the Bureau office, were one and the same person!

But that, as the clerk realized, was impossible.

This astonishing, but by no means unique trick of Nature, who now and then breaks her own law and produces individuals so alike as to be indistinguishable, exposed the limitations of Bertillon's system, and the danger, even if remote, of depending completely upon it.

What, the Warden of Leavenworth must that day have asked himself, confronted by William West and Will West, would have been the consequences for Will had William not already been in custody?

The possibility of error had clearly been demonstrated, and in the most dramatic fashion imaginable. Two men, unrelated, unknown to one another, each unaware of the other's existence, had been proved to be as like as two peas in a pod.

It was a report of this strange case which finally convinced Bertillon of the necessity for an additional measure for his system, that measure which he had, so curiously, declined to use—finger-prints. He then revised his cards, added fingerprints and evolved the elaborate so-called *Parisian fiche*.

CHAPTER TWENTY-THREE

Forensic Science: Silent Witnesses

I

"THE criminal," wrote Dr Edmond Locard, " is traced by the clues left by him. These, the dumb witnesses, are the only witnesses who never lie, *so long as what they have to tell is understood.*" In illustration, Dr Locard offers a hypothetical case.

A crime has been committed. Neighbours heard shouting, and the thud of a body falling. Nobody saw the perpetrator of the crime. The police find the victim lying amid the disorder of the flat. Investigations lead to a dead end. Nobody questioned has been able to throw any light on the affair.

What data are at hand at the scene of the crime?

On the floor of the room traces of a fierce struggle are visible—the footprints of the murderer and his victim. The door of the flat has been forced, tool-marks are visible on the door-jamb woodwork.

On one piece of furniture there are bloodmarks: they give a clear impression of a hand. In the fireplace there is burnt paper. Under a finger-nail of the dead man is found a single hair. On one of his hands are the marks of teeth. In the dust of a chest of drawers there is the imprint of fabric, as though an elbow had been rested there.

These are the dumb witnesses that neither lie nor make mistakes. All may depend upon the correct interpretation of them. They remain silent, however, until given voice by the magic trumpets of an orchestra of scientific techniques.

Thus, the medico-legal expert becomes the mouthpiece of the dead. He offers technical proof for each assertion made by him, interprets the nature of the wounds, their degree of gravity, and the physical consequences that may ensue from them. He fixes the approximate time of death; states what the dead man ate last, and at what hour.

In turn, the forensic photographer, the finger-print expert, the toxicologist, the pathologist, the serologist, interpret the data within the limits of their science.

Now the silent witnesses begin to speak.

The enlarged photographs reveal the precise type of material whose imprint was left in the dust by the elbow of the murderer.

The serological analysis establishes the presence of human blood, and the name of its group. A single hair is identified as coming from the head of a male—and from no other part of the body.

A burnt paper, subjected to infra-red photographic examination, reveals traces of handwriting.

II

The medico-legal expert, as Dr Locard reminds us, is not by any means a modern product, for he existed already in Roman times, estimating the legal significance of wounds, abortions, simulated illnesses.

The foundations of modern legal medicine were laid in the sixteenth century by Ambroise Paré. He was succeeded in the following century by Devaux and de Blequy and Zacchias. But science at that time was very imperfect, and for that reason, when applied to criminal investigation, a source of possible error and consequent injustice. Even nineteenth-century science faltered at times when called in to determine matters involving accused persons.

The trial of the Stauntons, in 1877, provides an outstanding example of the dangers that arise when a science, still rudimentary, is given too high an evidential value in a criminal court.

Harriet Staunton was said to have been starved to death by her husband, his brother, and that brother's mistress. The dead woman was an heiress in a small way; but she was also physically unattractive and mentally weak. She had been kept locked up by her brother-in-law while her husband lived nearby with his mistress, who was, at the time of Harriet's death, expecting a child.

The motive, then, was clear. The issue: was death due to such criminal neglect by starvation as to amount to murder, or was it due to natural causes?

The trial lasted seven days and ended in verdicts against all three prisoners.

Over the years, it is not easy to appreciate the intensity of the controversy which arose following this verdict. With the verdict, the public interest in a criminal trial usually abates. But in the case of Harriet Staunton it was only then that the trial took the form of a nation-wide protest on behalf of the condemned Stauntons. Charles Reade, the novelist, published a pamphlet arguing that the verdict was wrong. The Press was almost unanimous in the same sense.

Such indications of popular disapproval would, no doubt, have left the Home Secretary unmoved but for a memorial addressed to him signed by no fewer than seven hundred medical men, headed by the celebrated Sir William Jenner.

This document set forth the grounds that supported the medical view of Harriet Staunton's death; namely, that it was due to natural disease.

" We are convinced," ran this document, " that the morbid conditions observed in the post-mortem examination of Harriet Staunton's body were such as indicate death from cerebral disease."

The outcome of this conflict of scientific evidence was the reprieve of the convicted Stauntons; and a widespread feeling of dissatisfaction with the current contribution of science to justice.

Today the medico-legal expert makes two important contributions to justice. First, he makes a contribution to technical proof—and a modern murder trial often turns upon the medical evidence, as it did in the case of Dr Crippen. Then the medico-legal expert will be consulted, before judicial proceedings are begun, as to whether there is a *prima facie* case, giving his opinion of murder, suicide, or natural causes, as the case may be.

Advances in all branches of forensic medicine have gone far

to eliminate such elements of error, or doubt, as arose during and after the trial of Harriet Staunton, though even now medical experts frequently express conflicting views in criminal proceedings, and these conflicting views seem, too often, to be conditioned by the partisanship of a criminal trial.

Finally, the medical witness may be called upon to decide the degree of responsibility of an accused, as to whether he is sane, a psychopathic personality, paranoiac, or schizophrenic. Here the medico-legal witness who comes into court as an expert in psychological medicine stands where the pathologist stood a century ago with regard to his science. For psychology is the most protean of all sciences, a house of many mansions, as the trial of John George Haigh demonstrated very clearly.

III

When a crime under investigation involves the physical sciences, which is always the case where murder is involved, the work is done in one of the Forensic Laboratories of the Home Office. These are under the direction of a scientist, and are staffed by scientists and technically trained police officers.

" It should be borne in mind," wrote Gross, " that in addition to the expert knowledge resulting from scientific training and research, the knowledge derived from training and experience in countless industrial crafts, such as engineering, boat-building, printing, paper-making, furniture-making and weaving, to name only a few, may provide specialized knowledge which is otherwise unobtainable."

The truth of this is demonstrated by many criminal trials.

The trial of Dr H. H. Crippen has an interest that goes far beyond its sensational aspects, for his arrest and conviction were made possible entirely by the forensic application of several sciences, and had these not been available to the police, the crime could never have been brought home to the criminal, and would probably never have been discovered at all.

The scientific evidence that convicted Crippen was provided

by wireless telegraphy, toxicology, pathology, and anatomy with, in addition, and, as evidence, as important, textile technology.

Without the wireless message sent to the master of the S.S. *Montrose* as she approached Rimouski, Crippen and Miss Le Neve would have escaped into the New World. Without toxicology the method of murder—poisoning by the little-known drug, hyoscine, could not have been proved. Without anatomy the small portion of abdominal tissue dug up could never have been identified. Without pathology the character of the abdominal operational scar would not have been recognized. Without the textile expert the portion of material in which the fragmentary remains were wrapped could not have been identified as part of a pair of pyjamas belonging to Crippen, or traced, via the shop that sold them, to the actual loom off which the material was woven.

IV

In 1907 a woman was found with her throat cut in the bedroom of a house in a mean street in the King's Cross area. She had obviously been murdered while asleep.

Suspicion fell upon a young commercial artist named Wood. There was very little evidence to connect him with the crime, but sufficient to justify the investigating police in making very careful inquiries.

The evidence upon which the police had to work consisted of a fragment of charred paper which was found in the grate of the murdered woman's bedroom. The words discernible upon it were few, but sufficient to identify the style of handwriting.

These words had been written in copying-ink pencil.

On the strength of the resemblance between the writing on this charred fragment of paper and that found on a postcard upon which the writer had also drawn a sketch of a rising sun (the name of a public-house rendezvous), Robert Wood was arrested for the murder of Emily Dimmock, a woman of the town with whom, it was not disputed, he had been associating.

In this case it was sought to identify the actual pencil used in the writing of the " Rising Sun " postcard, and the charred paper found at the scene of the crime.

Robert Wood possessed a copying-ink pencil among many others used by him in his capacity as a commercial artist.

It was beyond scientific possibility to prove that the pencil which was used to write the " Rising Sun " postcard was that which was used to write the message partially visible on the charred paper referred to. But identification of the inks of the pencil with that of the paper writing, Wood admitting the authorship of the postcard, had a plain evidential significance.

The material was passed to a chemist versed in forensic work, and the procedure adopted by him may be briefly described.

The ink of the charred-paper writing and the ink of Wood's own pencil were subjected to the action of five reagents. The results of these tests were then tabulated and compared for chemical composition.

Not only was the ink of the one proved to be identical with that of the other, but the ink was actually identified as to its maker.

Though Wood's trial ended, no doubt rightly, in his acquittal, the scientific evidence offered by the forensic chemist is an impressive example of what an exact science can accomplish.

V

At three o'clock in the morning of September 26, 1927, P.-c. Gutteridge, of the Essex Constabulary, met P.-c. Taylor by arrangement on the lonely Romford–Ongar road. They parted half an hour later.

About six o'clock P.-c. Gutteridge was found dead in the road. He had been killed by four bullets, two fired at close range into his eyes. Beside him lay his note-book and pencil.

In this remarkable case, from the finding of the body of the murdered constable to the conviction of the two men involved, the whole investigation was scientific in character.

In the Forensic Laboratory the bloodstains found on a stolen and abandoned car were proved to be human. An empty cartridge case found in the car was identified by the

Home Office forensic ballistics expert as of a type not used by the Army since 1914.

Chemical analysis of the black powder taken from the wounds of the victim revealed it as of a type not used by the Army since 1894.

The question put to the ballistics expert by the police was: Were these four recovered bullets fired from the actual Webley found on Brown's premises?

When the answer came, it was " Yes." How, then, could the expert identify bullets to barrel when the weapon was one of mass production?

The *modus operandi* may be briefly described.

The ballistics expert first fired a bullet from the Webley into a block of soft wood, from which he then recovered it. Next, this control bullet was compared with those taken from the murdered man, this being done by means of the dual eye-piece of the comparison microscope. In the left field of vision lies the control bullet, in the right field lies another, one of those extracted from the murdered man's head.

By means of a delicate mechanism, both bullets are rotated until their surface scratches and markings match (or do not match). Thus, greatly magnified, the bullets are seen to have characteristic markings—a network of very fine lines, or scratches. These are the markings caused by the rifling of the barrel as the bullets are expelled from it, and so are, as it were, the firing weapon's unforgeable " signature."

Microscopic examination shows that of any given standardized, mass-produced weapon no two barrels are scored identically, since the machine tools that are used in the boring wear a microscopic degree with each job done.

There remained the cartridge-case to clinch the matter. Now, a striker pin of any standard, factory-made revolver is imperfect; consequently it leaves on the cartridge case a dent which may be matched with its own slightly imperfect shape.

In the Gutteridge case, greatly enlarged photographs were brought into court so that the judge and jury could see for themselves the result of the ballistical investigation.

Such was the scientific evidence which, along with the circumstantial evidence, resulted in the conviction of the two murderers, Kennedy and Brown.

VI

But the expert who offers himself as a witness in a criminal court does so at his own peril, unless he be a master of his subject; for faulty science, like wrongly interpreted psychological data, is a stick with two ends. Many criminal trials illustrate this danger when the scientific witness appears for the defence, and few more dramatically than in that of Alfred Arthur Rouse, who, in order to fake his own death, murdered and burnt to death a stranger to whom he had given a lift in his car for that purpose.

For the defence it was suggested that the fire was accidental and was caused by a leaking brass union nut while the tank was being filled up. This brass nut was found to be loose, and it was suggested by the Crown that it had been loosened deliberately before the fire, with the object of causing it.

A witness, claiming expert knowledge as a metallurgist, was called by the defence. He gave it as his opinion that the expansion of the metal by the high temperature of the burning car, followed by cooling, loosened the nut.

Well, where lay the truth? Had the loose brass nut caused the fire; or had fire caused the loose nut?

The issue was vital to the defence, and the value of the evidence was enhanced by the circumstance that the expert had come forward and volunteered his evidence in the capacity of a good citizen.

Sir Norman Birkett, KC, who appeared for the Crown, then rose to cross-examine.

"What is the coefficient of the expansion of brass?" he asked. Seeing the witness baffled by the question, one an expert should have been able to answer, he repeated the question: "What is the coefficient of the expansion of brass?"

But, alas for the defence, the witness knew neither the mathematical term nor the well-known fact that the expansion and contraction of metals are constants, and, thus, that a brass nut, cooling after a high temperature, returns to its original condition.

VII

If the role of science in the detection of crime and the administration of justice has an element of danger, it is when it would assume the role of a priesthood, a danger less frequently met with today than formerly, and then mostly where the element of *opinion* enters in; for opinion is a poor substitute for *demonstration*.

When the handwriting experts were first accepted in our criminal courts as exponents of a science, they made exaggerated claims for their " science," and none more recklessly than Neverclift, who, in the mid-Victorian era, was accepted as a scientific oracle with every appearance in the witness-box, complete with large magnifying glass and other impressive paraphernalia.

Neverclift was never in any doubt, and so, in the fullness of time, he met his Waterloo at the hands of that redoubtable advocate, Mr Henry Hawkins, QC, when the following exchange took place:

H. " You say, Mr Neverclift, that your system gives infallible results? "

N. " I do."

H. " And you have taught your son your methods? "

N. " I have."

H. " Then your son, working on your system, is as good as you are? "

N. " Yes."

H. " Well, then, Mr Neverclift, was there ever a case in which you and your son appeared on opposite sides? "

N. (reluctantly).   " There was."

H. " How came it, then, that two infallibles appeared on opposite sides? "

VIII

The modern handwriting expert who gives evidence in the courts does not derive his authority from any *mystique*, such as that claimed by the egregious Neverclift. He is merely a scientific technician, and in support of any proposition he makes, he produces concrete reasons based on experiment. His weapons are micro-photography and chemistry.

The central issue in handwriting identification, as with finger-prints, is that of *uniqueness*. Is every handwriting unique to its owner, as finger-prints are unique?

A. S. Osborn made an investigation, as Galton did with finger-prints, and with a like result. He came to the conclusion that every script is unique to the writer, and that the mathematical probability of two complete scripts being identical is outside the field of probability.

Somewhat earlier, Dr Alfred Binet, the French experimental psychologist, examined the claims of the graphologists that from handwriting the age, sex, intelligence, and character of the writer can be told.

Binet found that sex could be determined in from 63 to 78 per cent of cases; age to within ten years; intelligence fairly easily distinguished from mediocrity. With regard to character, Binet found that handwriting failed entirely to differentiate between the criminal and the ordinary citizen.

IX

The forensic handwriting expert now relies on measurement and comparison. He uses the naked eye and the comparison microscope, photographic enlargements, and chemical analyses of inks and paper fibres. He makes visible and, hence, demonstrable in a criminal court, what was invisible. And, finally, he attempts what is perhaps far more difficult—the identification of a hand deliberately disguised. Here such a master of this art as John George Haigh, perhaps one of the most brilliant forgers who ever employed a great talent for criminal purposes, might fox even the most efficient of experts.

In *Criminal Investigation* Gross shows how slope, height of ascenders and descenders, and other characteristics reveal the genuine from the forged document.

The handwriting expert will also know a good deal about the effect of disease on handwriting, and this is important in forensic applications, for it happens not infrequently that the issue to be determined in court is the genuineness or otherwise of a signature, often that of a testator.

It is in such circumstances that the expert witness has to bring into his calculations the pathological factor. There are a number of nervous disorders that modify or change a script's character; for example, Parkinson's disease, insanity, senility.

The signature of Napoleon at two extreme phases of his career are interesting in this connection. The first is dated 1804, at the time of his coronation. It is firm, sprawling, and full of vigour. The other, dated 1821, and written at St Helena, when the ex-Emperor was a broken and dying man, is a degenerated caricature of the signature at his zenith.

Nevertheless, evidence of handwriting by the method of visual comparison or symbol characteristics can claim no greater authority than that attaching to expert opinion. It has, moreover, a past to live down, as the blunders made by Gurrin show in the trial of Adolf Beck, a case of mistaken identity which twice resulted in a wrongful conviction. Years later, Gurrin deplored his own over-confidence in the witness-box in that tragic case of mistaken identity.

X

On the night of May 15, 1948, Peter Griffiths, a twenty-two-year-old ex-Guardsman, stole a five-year-old child from her cot in the children's ward of Queen's Park Hospital, Blackburn, raped, and killed her.

Officers from the Forensic Laboratory at Preston, with photographic and other apparatus, began an examination of the ward for clues. The footprints of stockinged feet were found, ringed about, and photographed. Doors, walls, and windows, and all objects with appropriate surfaces were examined for finger-prints.

Under the murdered child's cot a Winchester bottle was found. It bore finger-marks, more than twenty finger and palmar impressions, some old, some recent.

Whoever handled that Winchester bottle was possibly the murderer; thus all finger-prints had to be identified. This was done by finger-printing all those who had had access to the bottle. A number of the finger-prints were soon accounted for among members of the staff who had made use of the bottle in the course of their ordinary duties. *But the fresh impressions were none of these.*

Ultimately, seven prints were established as being those of one individual—and that individual the probable murderer.

Then began the most exhaustive investigation on record involving finger-prints in the search for a murderer. Inquiries were made among patients at Queen's Park Hospital, ex-patients, visitors, employees, and tradesmen, and the search among these was extended back two years. By May 18 all these lines of investigation had been completed without the discovery of the sought-for matching finger-prints.

It was next decided to finger-print every male over sixteen years of age in the borough of Blackburn. A public under-taking was given by the Chief Constable that all finger-prints taken for this purpose would be destroyed at the end of the investigation. This was the first mass finger-printing ever undertaken by the police: and it drew a blank.

Next, copies of the " murder prints " were circulated to every police force in Great Britain. That done, the Chief Constable of Blackburn broadcast a request to all police forces in the country asking them to finger-print all drunks, vagrants, persons found dead, and suicides.

Then every man who had been in Blackburn on the night of the murder, but who had since left the town, was traced and finger-printed. Since a number were seamen, this involved international police co-operation. Yet still no success.

In a final effort it was decided to extend the inquiry in another direction, by a check on the cards with the records kept by the local registration officer for the purpose of issuing ration cards.

By August 9 the Food Office check-up having been com-pleted, batches of finger-prints began to trickle in to the Lancashire Constabulary Finger-print Bureau. Each day's supply was checked and returned to Blackburn.

About three o'clock on the afternoon of August 12 another

R

batch of cards arrived.   Shortly thereafter one of the finger-
print experts engaged on the examination exclaimed: " I've got
him!   I've got him!   It's here! . . ."

The search was at an end.

XI

On September 14, 1935, the wife of Dr Buck Ruxton, a
Parsee practising in Lancaster, disappeared. With her
disappeared her maid, Mary Rogerson.

Some weeks later human remains were found in a number of
lonely places near Moffat, in Scotland.   They were taken by
the police to the Forensic Laboratory of Edinburgh University.

There, Professor Glaister, Regius Professor of Forensic
Medicine in the University, assisted by Dr Brash, began the
difficult task of reconstructing two bodies from incomplete and
mutilated anatomical material.

The mutilations had been made with surgical skill, and
plainly with the object of making identification impossible.
For example, lips, teeth, nose, toes, and even the finger-skin
pads had been cut away.

The reconstruction which was made by these two anatomists
of the two bodies, and the establishment of the identity of the
two women as those of Mrs Ruxton and Mary Rogerson, is a
most remarkable example of both patience and skill.

The heads of the two women were matched with the appropriate trunks by the identification of the vertebræ by X-ray
examination.   Photographs of the two skulls were taken, life-
size; and also similar photographs of the heads, as in life.
By superimposing the skulls on positive transparencies, their
agreement with the photographic outlines of the features of
the two women was revealed.

Mrs Ruxton had a bunion: hence the removal of her toes.
She had protruding teeth: hence their extraction by the
murderer.

Dr Brash made a cast in flexible material of the left foot of
each body, and put silk stockings on each cast.   He then fitted to
each foot a shoe belonging to each woman: shoes and casts
coincided.

This was a scientific achievement which drew from the trial judge, Mr Justice Singleton, a tribute to the mastery of anatomy of the investigators and to the scrupulously fair presentation of their evidence.

It is as science plays an ever-increasingly important role in criminal investigation that the odds shorten against even the cleverest of murderers, and so, by making punishment more certain, serves as deterrent.

CHAPTER TWENTY-FOUR

Hans Gross: The Investigator

I

Hans gross, the celebrated author of *Criminal Investigation*, a book that might be described as the Bible of Scotland Yard, had one day to be present at an execution. He was at the time Professor of Criminology in the University of Prague, where, in his lectures, he always stressed the importance to the investigator of direct and accurate observation.

Himself exceedingly observant, he noticed that the executioner, for some unknown reason, wore gloves. Some short time after the execution, the Professor asked four officials who had been present what was the colour of the executioner's gloves?

Three replied, respectively, black, grey, and white, while the fourth stoutly maintained that the executioner had not worn gloves at all.

Though he rates very high the importance of accurate observation in the criminal investigator, Gross demands far more of his ideal detective than that.

" An investigator," he wrote, " should be endowed with all those qualities which every man should desire to possess— indefatigable zeal and application, self-denial and persever- ance, swiftness in reading men, and a thorough knowledge of human nature, education, and an agreeable manner, an iron constitution, and encyclopædic knowledge."

This might, one would think, be high enough standard for an archbishop or a field-marshal, but Gross demands even more for his ideal investigator—a being, one ventures to think, with- out counterpart in any criminal investigation department that is or ever was.

" It is not enough," he continues, " for him to be a clever reckoner, a fine speculator, a careful weigher of facts, and to possess a good business head, he must also be self-denying, unostentatious and perfectly honest, resigning at the outset all thought of magnificent public success."

There is more yet: for this paragon must be absolutely accurate, possess a profound knowledge of men, and be prepared always to waive any claim he may justly have to kudos or the acclamation of the public it is his lot to serve.

The reader may have observed that one quality that might well be deemed of value to the criminal investigator is not among the catalogue of virtues referred to above. That quality is a capacity to imagine oneself into the situation of another: in short, imagination in general.

" Imagination," wrote Dr Edmond Locard, of the Lyons Forensic Laboratory, the equally celebrated criminologist, " imagination, which even in mathematics, plays an essential role, should not be excluded from criminal investigation. . . . Edgar Allan Poe was, perhaps, the greatest of all detectives. The daring of a hypothesis," Locard added, " is the hall-mark of the good detective: though this must be disciplined by the facts. . . . The great detective must have the imagination of a poet."

II

Dr Locard's reference to Poe justifies a short digression. His admiration for the American poet and short-story writer was based on the story *The Mystery of Marie Roget*. The New York police had been baffled by the murder of a pretty cigar-factory girl named Mary Rogers, and rested on a theory of murder by a gang of toughs. The facts of the case fitted this theory. But Poe, in fictional form, and transferring the *locus delicti* to Paris, put forward an alternative theory arrived at by purely logical means from newspaper reports.

It is said that this was the correct solution, but some doubt has been cast upon this claim. But that Poe was a most remarkable natural " detective " there can be no doubt at all.

When Dickens was in the United States these two great writers met. Dickens was then at work on *Barnaby Rudge*, which was appearing serially.

" I will tell you from what is already told, how your story will end," said Poe, and proceeded to do so, greatly to Dickens's astonishment, drawing from him " The devil's in the man ! " in exclamation.

So, too, for Paul Valéry, Poe was " the demon of lucidity, the analytical genius, and the inventor of the most novel and bewitching combinations of logic and imagination, mystery and mathematics, the psychologist of the abnormal." For, as another Frenchman, Baudelaire, said of him : " All the arrows fly towards the same point on the target."

III

The detective, or criminal investigator, has a very humble pedigree, for he may be traced back directly to the Bow Street runner who was merely an alert and ambitious " copper's nark," working for ready cash rewards. Indeed, it was part of Dr Colquhoun's complaint that each of the several " Bow Streets " of his day had only £2,000 a year to cover all expenses, a niggardly grant that left little for the pay, or bribes, of the Robin Redbreasts.

The detective using scientific organizations and scientific techniques came into existence with their application to police work, and so may be said to be a natural growth. The resources that serve him range from finger-printing, photography, micro-photography, chemistry, anatomy, toxicology, metallurgy, and forensic ballistics to an international pool of information and co-operation, and the swift communications made possible by radio, teleprinting, and so forth.

It is the harnessing of these techniques to criminal investigation that tends, now and then, to create in the popular mind an exaggerated idea of the exploits of some detective chosen for glamourization.

But, generally speaking, the popular idea of the detective is derived from fiction, and so there has come to be thrown about the shoulders of a race of men painstaking and efficient, but seldom brilliant, a mantle of rather finer stuff than is their just due.

Nearer to life is the detective of an author who well knew how to observe with imaginative insight, and as the detective of today is the superior in education and intelligence of Dickens's Inspector Bucket; the modern criminal investigator, like that character in *Bleak House*, goes to work from information received.

There are, indeed, many models in fact and fiction of the detective. One of the earliest specimens is Vidocq (1775–1857). He did very well out of crime until he was caught and spent eight years in the galleys.

Vidocq was a man of great resource and cunning, happily unhampered by either scruples or loyalties. Having escaped, he vanished into the underworld of the Paris of the end of the eighteenth century, whence he emerged, an encyclopædia of "information," to offer his services to the newly-formed Detective Corps. There he at once made his mark by betraying those criminals formerly his comrades in crime.

Vidocq throve and became a name in the Paris underworld dreaded as that of Himmler in Nazi Germany. It is pleasant to know that he ended his days discredited, having failed to combine successfully the dual roles of criminal investigator and criminal.

If this sinister character is mentioned here it is because the system he inaugurated in the Paris of 1810, in which year Vidocq became a " detective," still flourishes: it is that same system that served so well Inspector Bucket and still serves criminal investigators the world over: the system of payment by money bribe or promised immunity for " information."

IV

Up to 1839 the Bow Street Runners and the constables of the Police Offices were the only detectives, though a Parliamentary Committee of 1837 preferred to describe them as " private speculators in the detection of crime rather than efficient officers for the ends of justice."

The Bow Street Runner who " got on to a good thing " did not turn his information over until he had struck the best bargain he could get for it. It was, obviously, a bad system, but gradually the Runners began to work in with the new

police. Since they were drawn entirely from the underworld, they were assigned the detection of thieves of all kinds
and of crimes against property generally : the emergent police
force proper dealing with crimes against the person and, in
particular, murder.

An organized detective force was first established in 1869,
and nine years later the Criminal Investigation Department
was set up. Up to the former year constables were never
allowed to discard their uniform, even when off duty or on
holiday. In that year the first " plain-clothes " men began to
mingle with the London crowds as " thief-takers."

The first plain-clothes men were very unpopular with the
citizens of London. They feared the development of a spy
system. If a man was a " copper," they preferred to see him
in uniform. But by the end of 1839 the last of the Redbreasts
had elbowed his way into Bow Street to make his report, and
the Bow Street Runner, so often a figure of romance, had
passed into the City's history.

V

The Criminal Investigation Department of Scotland Yard
was the child of professional dishonour. It came into being
as a direct consequence of the low standards of the detectives
themselves, several of whom were brought to trial for their
part in what has become historically famous as the Trial of the
Detectives.

This scandal in the police force was a major misfortune,
coming as it did at a time when the police were unpopular
with the public. The root of the trouble up to that time was
the method of appointment to posts in the force. These were
generally secured by influence, consequently there was much
inefficiency.

Since that time all promotion in the Metropolitan Police
Force has been from the ranks of the uniformed side, and by
merit only. Thus the best men have risen to the highest
posts by the natural buoyancy of their qualities, and a high
code of professional honour has been generally maintained.

There is no valid ground for demanding of the police a

standard of behaviour or morals superior to that, say, of the Services, or of the public in general. The police are, after all, ordinary people, men and—now—women, too, performing a specialized function in the State. That now and then a rascal is found among them does not detract from the general high standard of decency.

VI

Gross, who stresses so much the qualities mentioned above, was not blind to the importance of some understanding of psychology in the criminal investigator; indeed, he wrote a treatise bearing upon the subject. But psychology has as yet no place in the routine work of our criminal investigation departments, save the rough-and-ready kind all use in daily life.

It is possible for a criminal investigator to think himself into the mind of a criminal only if he is a man of equable temperament and free of psychological quirks, and if the criminal is in the same category. Otherwise, he will assign wrong motives, misinterpret the facts, or draw wrong deductions from them.

Émile Zola describes somewhere the perplexity of a judge confronted by a criminal who was completely without shame for his thefts, but when accused of keeping a stolen object as sexual fetish—a woman's stocking—was at once overwhelmed with shame.

Again, in the same author's *La Bête Humaine* there is another example of the incomprehensibility of motive unless illuminated by psychological understanding.

Roubaid kills his wife's lover: but she had two lovers. Why did he kill only one?

The examining magistrate, M. Denizet, seizes upon this curious discrimination. " Why not both? " he asks. And he proceeds to find an answer in an alternative hypothesis to that of jealousy. That a jealous husband should not kill both lovers is not logical, and so jealousy cannot be accepted as the motive. But human actions are seldom logical and seldom conform to a preconceived pattern of behaviour, but proceed from complex secret mental or emotional states, not fully understood even by the criminal himself.

The wise detective is one who will be surprised at nothing, but doubly wary of the unusual, too. He must recognize the reality of psychological guilt, or its absence, confronted with damning circumstantial evidence.

In *Jocasta and The Famished Cat*, Anatole France deals with this theme of psychological guilt.

In this story the beautiful young wife of the rich old husband becomes guilty of his murder, without murdering him, in that, seeing the valet perpetrating the crime by poison, she does nothing to prevent the inevitable consequences. And thereafter, anguished by remorse, she becomes her own executioner, hanging herself.

Conscience, as we are so often reminded both by precept and by experience, makes cowards of us all: it may also inspire great courage, as in this tale.

" Well," exclaimed the police commissioner, " I have seen many women who have committed suicide, but this is the first I have seen who has hanged herself."

Only the self-condemned woman could know that the Eumenides, whose voices hounded her to death, spoke from the lips of a schoolboy conning a Greek text.

In *The Brothers Karamazov*, Dostoevski presents an unforgettable picture of psychological guilt; and psychological guilt may be the true answer to the riddle, now forever unanswerable, in the case of Timothy Evans, convicted and hanged for the murder of his baby daughter (and wife, though never tried for the latter crime).

Dr Edmond Locard, whose mind is of a more subtle cast than that of Professor Gross, might have applied both mathematics and imagination to this notorious case.

He might, as has been earlier suggested, have considered the probability of two stranglers living in the same house, in the same city, at the same time, with what Poe would have called the Calculus of Probabilities, when the odds against any such coincidence would have come out at some astronomical figure.

He might, also, have considered the two contrasted characters of the principal actors: the curiously subtle and insidious hysteric, the mass murderer Christie, with his established technique of strangulation, and the illiterate, simple-minded Evans.

If the confession subsequently made by Christie be accepted, then all that remains in issue is Evans's guilty knowledge of the deed; his psychological guilt, in short. Many things point to it, and the theory has the attraction of shortening by some millions the mathematical odds against two stranglers being active in the same house at the same time.

In the days of the medieval Republic of St Mark a young baker of Venice was accused of murder, tried, convicted, and hanged, protesting his innocence to the last.

After the execution further facts came to light that entirely cleared the wrongly executed man.

Thereafter it was decreed that whenever a man stood his trial for murder or other offence punishable by death, an ambassador of the Senate should enter the court and make this proclamation: " Remember the poor baker."

Should we, perhaps, do well to do something of the kind, remembering Timothy Evans?

VII

Professor Gross stresses the prime importance in the criminal investigator of objectivity. He must shun *a priori* theory like the devil, and the *post hoc ergo propter hoc* fallacy must be forever in his mind. Even with these solemn warnings ringing in his ears, it is probable that in every criminal investigation there comes a moment when theory demands facts, and when that happens the quest is no longer for truth but for the satisfaction of the demands of the theory formed, which now exists in the investigator's mind, like a jig-saw puzzle lacking one piece to complete the whole.

Theodor Reik, in *The Unknown Murderer*, cites a case that well illustrates the dangerous fascination of the obvious for the criminal investigator.

In October of the year 1886, a farm labourer, returning home, happened to go into a little-used barn on the outskirts of the village of Furkbrunnen, in South Austria. He was shocked to see the body of a woman lying on the straw. From the terrible nature of her head injuries it was clear that she had been brutally murdered.

The police were easily able to identify her as Juliane Sandbrünner, a local character very well known for her loose morals. For some years she had been employed by Gregor Adamsburger, a tanner, and though he already had a wife, he made the servant his mistress and by her had four children.

Gregor Adamsburger also had a bad reputation—that of a hard-drinking man who was apt to be violent in his cups. He was generally disliked in the village.

The evidence went to show that the day before the murder the two had been heard quarrelling violently; and there were plenty of gossips to tell the police how the dead woman, after leaving Adamsburger's service, had gone about accusing him of having incited her to commit arson that he might collect insurance money.

When the investigating officers questioned the tanner, he admitted the quarrel and also that the murdered woman had been in his house within a few hours of her death.

Next, his mother-in-law, interrogated, said that she had heard screams from the tanner's house at about the time when Adamsburger admitted Juliane Sandbrünner had been there quarrelling with him.

" Where did she go when she left you? " he was asked.

" She said she was going to see young Anton Kunz," he told them.

Anton Kunz was a nineteen-year-old baker of meagre physique and shy disposition.

The police checked this statement. Anton Kunz admitted knowing Juliane. He even confided to the police that he had had clandestine meetings with her in a small summer-house behind his father's bakery. But he had not seen her on the day previous to, or upon the day of her death.

On this evidence Gregor Adamsburger was convicted of the murder and sentenced to life imprisonment. And the un-suspected murderer continued to bake bread for the good people of Furkbrunnen, until that day when he found it no

longer possible to remain silent. He then confessed that it was
he who had murdered Juliane Sandbrünner.

He had killed her, he explained, because she had charged
him with responsibility for her condition. On the day of the
murder she had come to him and suggested that they should go
together to the barn to make love, and, pretending to fall in
with this suggestion, he had accompanied her there, where he
had murdered her, leaving her in such a state of disorder as to
suggest a sexual crime.

This classic case illustrates perfectly the dangers that beset
the criminal investigator who reads too glibly the surface
picture of a crime, seizes upon the obvious, taking it for the
truth, and never penetrates below the surface in his search for
the " unknown murderer."

VIII

It is probably true to say that Scotland Yard's Criminal
Investigation Department is the most powerful and efficient
instrument possessed by society for the investigation of major
crime, and that not only in the Metropolitan area is it primarily
concerned to guard, but wherever local police authorities
appeal for a CID detective to assist their own people, which
is quite frequent, particularly in cases of murder. In such
circumstances, Scotland Yard extends its activities throughout
the land.

This famous machine for criminal investigation is modelled
on the French system, the parliamentary committee of 1878
having made that recommendation, i.e. for a united and
separate detective force.

In its early days the system did not work well. The uniformed side looked askance at these new plain-clothes men and
suspected they were being spied upon by them. This defect
was overcome very quickly by transferring to divisional super-
intendents a general supervision over detectives in their area.

The Criminal Investigation Department of Scotland Yard
is now divided into two parts: headquarters staff officers, and
local detectives attached to each of the twenty-three divisions of
the Metropolitan area.

The Department is in charge of an Assistant Commissioner, with deputies for criminal investigation and for what is known as the " special branch," this last the English equivalent of the continental " political " police, its job the protection of royal personages, ministers, and so on.

Ranks range as follows: Chief Constable, Superintendent, Chief Inspector, Inspector, Sergeant, and Constable, the last-named being generally styled " detective" or plain-clothes patrol.

The so-called " Flying Squad " is merely a mobile brigade assigned to special duties. Its value lies in instantaneous communications, speed of movement, secrecy, and ubiquity in the area served by it. . . .

At the end of every criminal trial resulting in a conviction, and before the judge passes sentence, a plain-clothes officer goes into the witness-box. He tells the judge of the prisoner's record, for this will influence the sentence that will follow.

This officer is from Scotland Yard's Criminal Record Office. In this department is the finger-print library, or bureau, a sort of criminal world Who's Who in which criminal techniques are classified by method; and the editorial office that prepares and issues *Information* and the *Police Gazette*.

MO (*modus operandi*), or how was this job done? is one of the first preoccupations of the detective assigned to a case. For every *professional* criminal—and, bear in mind, many criminals are amateurs—has his own technique. Moreover, most professional thieves concentrate on some particular type of crime and tend to repeat themselves. Thus, in a sense, a professional criminal, whether he be burglar or forger or confidence man, nearly always acts in character. This makes it possible from the start for the detective to narrow his field of inquiries.

There has been a sensational safe-blowing job pulled off at a big bank. Chief Inspector Blank is assigned to the case. He consults CRO. There are on file the records of eight " possibles," men operating on highly specialized and skilled lines, and among them there is A. B., recently released from Dartmoor after serving a long sentence for a similar crime.

At once A. B. becomes an object of special interest to Inspector Blank. . . .

But how will Inspector Blank locate the suspected A. B.? He will here be aided again by the organization within which he works. When a convict leaves prison a check is kept on his movements while he is on licence or comes within the scope of the Prevention of Crimes Act. A. B. may be located with surprising speed. He may be able to clear himself at once, in which event the process of elimination of all suspects proceeds along with the actual investigation at the scene of the crime.

Here will be found those " mute witnesses," the material clues, that will presently yield up their secrets to forensic science.

IX

The police officer, whether uniformed or plain-clothes detective, deals always with the harsh realities. Police stations have no ivory towers. So soon as a police officer goes on duty he faces on all sides a challenge to his integrity.

He may have to resist a bribe or risk his life. If he finds himself in a street fracas, the chances are that the public he serves will take sides against him or remain passive. It has truly been said that no sooner does the punishment of the law attach to a criminal than humanity becomes his friend.

The words spoken by Dr Colquhoun, that eighteenth-century magistrate who may fairly be described as the Father of the Force, remain true today as they were in his own time.

" Next to the blessings which a nation derives from excellent Laws, ably administered, are those advantages which result from a well-regulated and energetic police, conducted with purity, activity, vigilance and discretion."

SUMMARY

That the control of the criminal elements of society is dependent on the efficiency and integrity of the police. That the identification of an individual can now be established by scientific techniques that eliminate the possibility of error which formerly sometimes resulted in the conviction of the

wrong person. That the application of the sciences enumerated to criminal investigation reduces the chances of error
to a very narrow margin, but that the possibility of error still
exists. That the skilful interpretation of psychological aspects,
such as motive and behaviour, is as important in criminal
investigation as the discovery of concrete facts.

CONCLUSION

WHAT conclusions, if any, may be drawn from the contributions to criminology described in the foregoing pages? They have been made by men working in widely differing fields, ranging from the social philosopher to the police magistrate; from the anthropologist to the psychiatrist and endocrinologist; they include the humanitarian and the criminal law reformer; the forensic expert and the scientific investigator; the biologist and the biochemist.

We see how the earlier view of punishment as the payment exacted by society of a debt due from the wrongdoer has been replaced by the ideal of his reform, punishment being limited to the furtherance of that purpose.

We find evidence of an increasing consciousness of guilt in society when crime can fairly be attributed to social injustice, to poverty or racial discrimination.

On the other hand there is abundant evidence that crime frequently manifests itself in conditions of social security and well-being; and that, in such cases, the causes are either the biological heritage or defective working of either body or mind.

So the truth would seem to be that the causes of crime are manifold and that to dogmatize involves that sort of danger which befell Lombroso with his rigid theory of " criminal man."

Since Beccaria wrote his celebrated treatise *Dei Delitti* the principles enunciated by him have been generally accepted, and many of the reforms advocated by him have been carried out.

Criminology has now reached the stage of scientific study. Even so, while it remains true that honesty is how we behave when unobserved, the policeman and his complex world-wide organization for crime prevention and detection will remain indispensable.

Crime will always exist in the imperfect societies of imperfect individuals, and nobody but a perfectionist would envisage the possibility of a society perfectly law-abiding and virtuous.

The practical objective is the improvement of all methods which help to reduce the criminal elements of society by prevention and by reform or cure.

As the best study of mankind is man, so is the criminal himself the proper subject for the study of crime. This is the truth that gives unity to the work described in the foregoing pages of this book.

BIBLIOGRAPHY

Adolescent Criminal (The)	MAXWELL, SIR A. 1942
American Prison System	HAYNES, F. E. 1939
Annals of the American Academy of Political and Social Science	May, 1954
Bentham	STOCKS, J. L. 1933
Bentham	ATKINSON, C. M. 1905
Benthamiania	BURTON, J. H. 1843
British Birds	BEWICK, T. 1797–1804
Capital Punishment:	
Report of Commission 1866	
Report of Commission 1929	
Report of Commission 1949	
Case of Jean Calas	MAUGHAM, F. H. 1928
Commentaries	BLACKSTONE, W. 1753
Commentatio	PURKINJE, J. E. 1823
Cries of the Oppressed	FRY, E. 1819
Crime and Psychology	MULLINS, C. 1943
Crime as Destiny	LANGE, J. 1931
Crimes and Punishments (Of)	BECCARIA. 1762
Criminal (The)	ELLIS, H. 1898
Criminal Investigation	GROSS, H. 1930
Criminal Man	LOMBROSO, C. 1896
Criminology	HAYNES, F. E. 1930
Dark Legend (The)	WERTHAM, F. 1947
Dawn of Nineteenth Century in England	ASHTON, J. 1906
Delinquent Woman	LOMBROSO, C. 1898
Dilemma of Penal Reform	MANNHEIM, H. 1939
Distribution, Justice and Mercy	HANWAY, J. I. 1781
English Utilitarians	STEPHENS, L. 1900
Enquiry into the Causes of the Late Increase of Robbers	FIELDING, H. 1751
European Police Systems	FOSDICK, R. B.
Evans Case: H.O. Report on	HENDERSON, J. SCOTT. 1953

Finger Prints   GALTON, F. 1893
Finger Prints, Classification and Uses of   HENRY, E. 1900
Finger Print Identification   FAULDS, F. P. 1905
For the Term of His Natural Life   CLARKE, M. 1874
Forensic Psychiatry   EAST, N. 1927
Foundations of Australia   O'BRIEN, E. 1937

Galton Lecture   EAST, N. 1947

History of Penal Methods   IVES, G. 1914
History of Newgate   HOOPER, E. 1909

Identification   HARRIS, G. E. 1892
Insanity and Crime   H.O. REPORT. 1922
It Is Never Too Late To Mend   READE, C. 1856

Jocasta and the Famished Cat   FRANCE, A. 1879; trans. 1912
Judicial Aspects of Penal Reform   GARDINER and RALEIGH. 1949
Just Murder   ROBINSON, E. 1947

La Bête Humaine   ZOLA, E. 1889
Law and the Criminal   WERTHAM, F. 1938
Le Crimes et les Criminels   LOCARD, E. 1920
Legal Photography   BERTILLON, A. 1890
Lombroso   KURELLA, H. 1911
London in the Eighteenth Century   BESANT, SIR W. 1892

Medical Aspects of Crime   EAST, N. 1927
Memoirs   ROMILLY, S. 1840
Mill on Bentham and Coleridge   Intro. F. R. LEAVIS. 1950

New Criminology (The)   SCHLAPP and SMITH. 1928

Observations on the Criminal Law   ROMILLY, S. 1840
Of Crimes and Punishments   BECCARIA. 1762
Osborne's Place in the History of Criminology   CHAPMAN, J. J. 1927
Outspoken Essays   INGE, R. 1919

Peckham Experiment (The)	GODWIN, G. (*Fortnightly*, 1934)
Peter Kuerten	GODWIN, G. 1945
Photographie Métrique	BERTILLON, A. 1890
Political Crime	LOMBROSO, C. 1892
Portrait Parlé	REISS, R. A. 1890
Principles of Moral and Political Philosophy	PALEY, W. 1785
Probable Influence of the French Revolution	ROMILLY, S. 1790
Psychological Treatment of Crime	EAST and HUBERT. 1939
Psychology of Crime	HAMBLIN SMITH, M. 1927
Psychology of Religion	STARBUCK. 1889
Psychology of the Criminal (The)	HAMBLIN SMITH, M. 1922
Psychology and Criminal Procedure	Institute for the Study and Treatment of Delinquency. 1951
Romilly	COLLINS, SIR W. 1908
Romilly: Speeches	2 vols. 1820
Roots of Crime (The)	EAST, N. 1954
Sadist (The)	BERG, K. Trans. O. ILLNER and G. GODWIN 1945
Scotland Yard	MOYLEN, J. F. 1929
Seduction of the Innocent (The)	WERTHAM, F.
Show of Violence (The)	WERTHAM, F. 1948
Society and Prisons	OSBORNE. 1916
Society and the Criminal	EAST, N. 1949
State of Prisons in England and Wales	HOWARD, J. 1791
Spirit of the Age (The)	HAZLITT, W. 1825
Spirit of Laws (The)	MONTESQUIEU, C. L. 1743
Thoughts on Executive Justice	MADAN, M. 1784
Three Criminal Law Reformers	PHILLIPSON, C. 1923
Treatise on the Police of the Metropolis	COLQUHOUN, P. 1798
Trial of Peter Griffiths	GODWIN, G., Editor N.B.T. Series. 1950
Unknown Murderer (The)	REIK, T. 1936
Vidocq: Memoirs	1828
View of the Evidences of Christianity	PALEY, W. 1794
Wealth of Nations (The)	SMITH, A. 1776

INDEX